Teach Yourself
VISUALLY™
Adobe® Photoshop® CS5

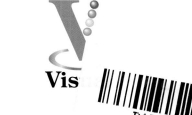

Vis

by Mike V

WILEY
Wiley Publishing, Inc.

Teach Yourself VISUALLY™
Adobe® Photoshop® CS5

Published by
Wiley Publishing, Inc.
10475 Crosspoint Boulevard
Indianapolis, IN 46256

www.wiley.com

Published simultaneously in Canada

Library of Congress Control Number: 2010925692

ISBN: 978-0-470-61263-7

Manufactured in the United States of America

10 9 8 7 6 5 4 3 2 1

Trademark Acknowledgments

Contact Us

For general information on our other products and services please contact our Customer Care Department within the U.S. at 877-762-2974, outside the U.S. at 317-572-3993 or fax 317-572-4002.

For technical support please visit www.wiley.com/techsupport.

Permissions

Brianna Stuart

http://www.stuartphotography.net

Wiley Publishing, Inc.

Sales

Contact Wiley
at (877) 762-2974 or
fax (317) 572-4002.

Credits

About the Author

Mike Wooldridge is a Web developer in the San Francisco Bay area. He has authored more than 20 books for the Visual series.

Author's Acknowledgments

I would like to thank Brianna Stuart for the use of her beautiful photographs in the examples and for her help in preparing the hundreds of screenshots for this book. I would also like to thank Christopher Stolle for his top-notch project editing, Ben Schupak for his knowledgeable technical editing, Kim Heusel for his careful copyediting, and Ronda David-Burroughs, Cheryl Grubbs, and Mark Pinto for all their clever illustrations. This book is dedicated to my wife Linda and my 10-year-old son Griffin.

How to Use This Book

Who This Book Is For

This book is for the reader who has never used this particular technology or software application. It is also for readers who want to expand their knowledge.

The Conventions in This Book

① Steps

This book uses a step-by-step format to guide you easily through each task. **Numbered steps** are actions you must do; **bulleted steps** clarify a point, step, or optional feature; and **indented steps** give you the result.

② Notes

Notes give additional information — special conditions that may occur during an operation, a situation that you want to avoid, or a cross-reference to a related area of the book.

③ Icons and Buttons

Icons and buttons show you exactly what you need to click to perform a step.

④ Tips

Tips offer additional information, including warnings and shortcuts.

⑤ Bold

Bold type shows command names or options that you must click or text or numbers that you must type.

⑥ Italics

Italic type introduces and defines a new term.

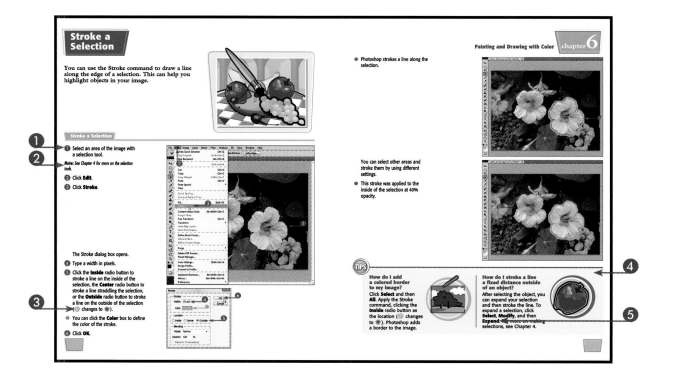

Table of Contents

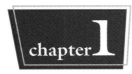

chapter 1 Getting Started

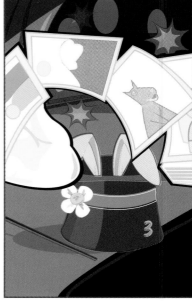

chapter 2 Understanding Photoshop Basics

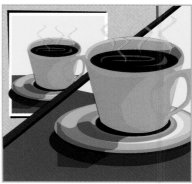

chapter 3 Changing the Size of an Image

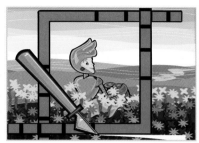

chapter 4 Making Selections

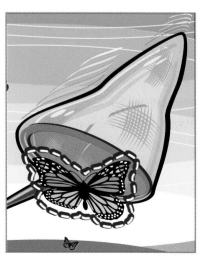

Table of Contents

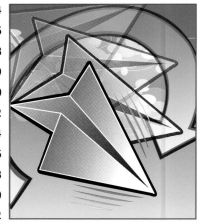

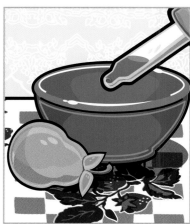

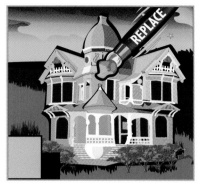

chapter 7 **Adjusting Colors**

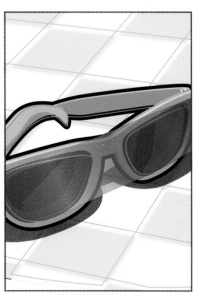

Table of Contents

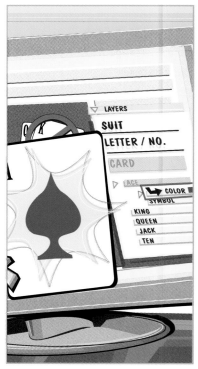

chapter 8 Working with Layers

chapter 9 Applying Layer Styles

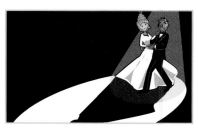

chapter 10 Applying Filters

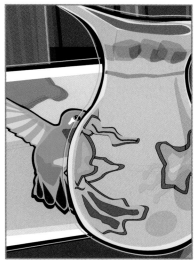

chapter 11 Drawing Shapes

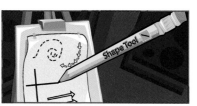

Table of Contents

chapter 12 — Adding and Manipulating Type

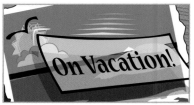

chapter 13 — Automating Your Work

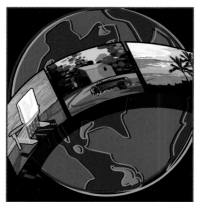

chapter 14 Saving and Printing Images

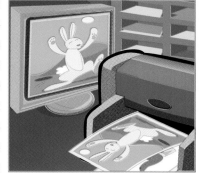

Getting Started

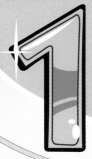

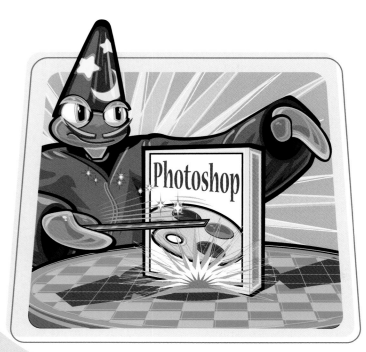

Are you interested in creating, modifying, combining, and/or optimizing digital images on your computer? This chapter introduces you to Adobe Photoshop CS5, a popular software application for working with digital images.

Work with Images

Photoshop enables you to create, modify, combine, and optimize digital images. You can then save the images to print, share via e-mail, publish online, or view on a handheld device, such as an iPod.

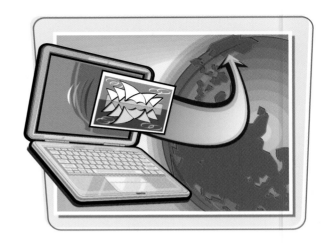

Manipulate Photos

As its name suggests, Photoshop excels at editing digital photographs. You can use the program to make subtle changes, such as adjusting the color in a digital photo or scanned print, or you can use its elaborate filters to make your snapshots look like abstract art. See Chapter 7 for more on adjusting color and Chapter 10 for more on filters.

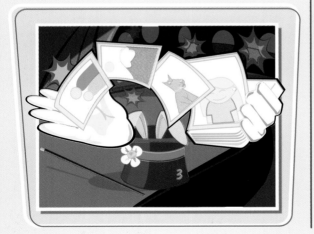

Paint Pictures

Photoshop's painting features make it a formidable illustration tool as well as a photo editor. You can apply colors or patterns to your images with a variety of brush styles. See Chapter 6 for more on applying color. In addition, you can use the program's typographic tools to integrate stylized letters and words into your images. See Chapter 12 for more on type. You can also create geometric shapes, which are covered in Chapter 11.

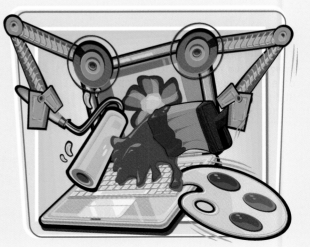

Create a Digital Collage

You can combine different image elements in Photoshop. Your compositions can include photos, scanned art, text, and anything else you can save on your computer as a digital image. By placing elements in Photoshop onto separate layers, you can move, transform, and customize them independently of one another. See Chapter 8 for more on layers.

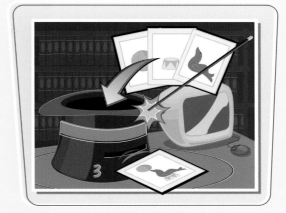

Access, Organize, and Display Photos

Photoshop's Bridge interface offers an easy-to-use tool to access and preview images that are stored on your computer. See the section "Browse for an Image in Bridge." With Bridge, you can easily tag your images with descriptive information, such as where or when they were taken. You can then use that information to sort your photos. Photoshop also offers useful ways to display your images after you edit them. You can display them as a group in a Web photo gallery or combine several sequential images into a single panorama. See Chapter 13 for more.

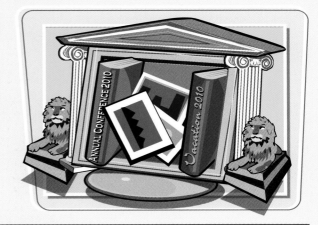

Put Your Images to Work

After you edit your work, you can utilize your images in a variety of ways. Photoshop lets you print your images, save them in a format suitable for placement on a Web page or e-mailing, or prepare them for use in a page-layout program. See Chapter 14 for more on saving images in different formats as well as printing them.

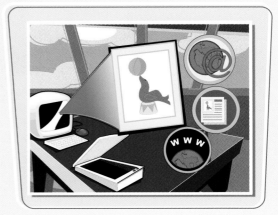

Understanding Photoshop

Photoshop's tools let you move, color, stylize, and add text to your images. You can optimize the contrast and lighting in photographs or turn them into interesting works of art by applying filters.

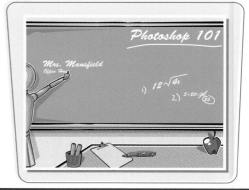

Understanding Pixels

Digital images in Photoshop consist of tiny, solid-color squares called *pixels*. Photoshop works its magic by rearranging and recoloring these squares. If you zoom in close, you can see the pixels that make up your image. For more on the Zoom tool, see Chapter 2.

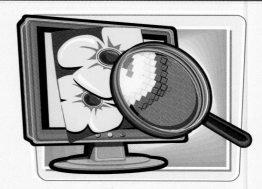

Choose Your Pixels

To edit specific pixels in your image, you must first select them by using one of Photoshop's selection tools. You can make geometric selections by using the marquee tools or free-form selections by using the Lasso tool. See Chapter 4 for more on the selection tools. Photoshop also has a number of commands that help you select specific parts of your image, such as a certain color or range of colors. Special brushes in Photoshop enable you to select objects in your image based on how the colors of those objects contrast with the background.

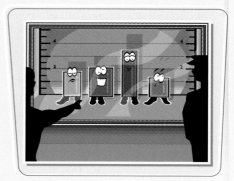

Paint

After selecting your pixels, you can apply color to them by using Photoshop's Brush, Mixer Brush, Paint Bucket, and Pencil tools. You can also fill your selections with solid or semitransparent colors, patterns, or pixels copied from another part of your image. Painting is covered in Chapter 6. Special painting tools help you seamlessly cover up objects in your image or eliminate dust specks, tears, and other imperfections from a scanned picture.

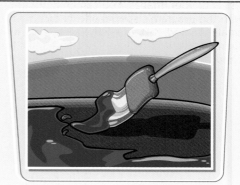

Adjust Color

You can brighten, darken, and change the hue of colors in parts of your image with Photoshop's Dodge, Burn, and similar tools. Other commands display interactive dialog boxes that let you make wholesale color adjustments so you can correct overly dark or light digital photographs. See Chapter 7 for more.

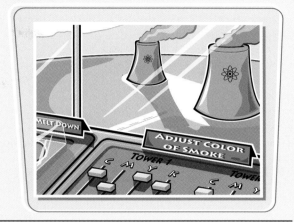

Apply Styles and Filters

Photoshop's layer styles let you easily add drop shadows, frame borders, and other effects to your images. You can also perform complex color manipulations or distortions by using filters. Filters can make your image look like an impressionist painting, sharpen or blur your image, or distort your image in various ways. Chapters 9 and 10 cover styles and filters.

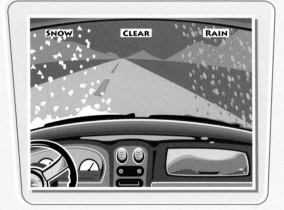

Add Text

Photoshop's type tools make it easy to apply titles and labels to your images. You can combine these tools with the program's special effects commands to create warped, 3-D, or wildly colored words and characters. You can learn more on adding text in Chapter 12.

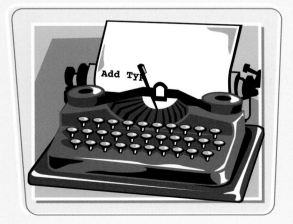

Start Photoshop on a PC

You can start Photoshop on a PC and begin creating and editing digital images.

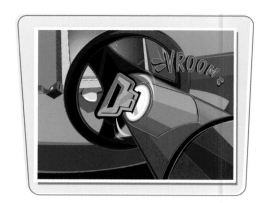

1 Click the **Start** button.

2 Click **All Programs** (All Programs changes to Back).

3 Click **Adobe Photoshop CS5**.

Note: *Your path to the Photoshop program may be different depending on how you installed your software.*

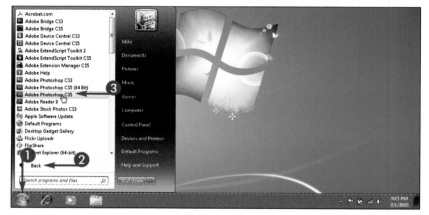

Photoshop starts.

Note: *To learn how to open an image and start working, see the section "Open an Image."*

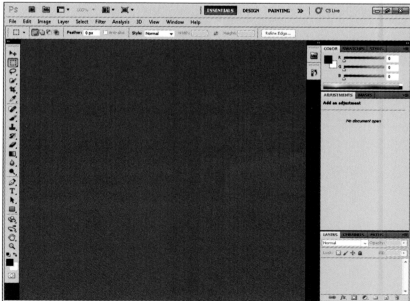

Start Photoshop on a Mac

You can start Photoshop on a Mac and begin creating and editing digital images.

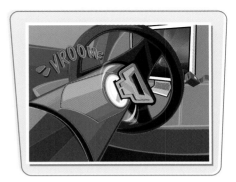

Start Photoshop on a Mac

1 In the Finder, click **Applications**.

2 Click the **Adobe Photoshop CS5** folder.

3 Double-click **Adobe Photoshop CS5**.

Note: The exact location of the Adobe Photoshop icon may be different depending on how you installed your software.

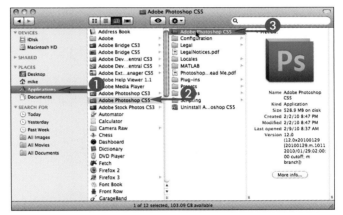

Photoshop starts.

Note: To learn how to open an image and start working, see the section "Open an Image."

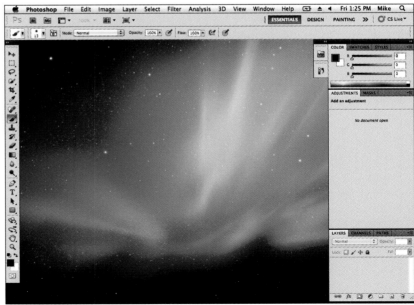

The Photoshop Workspace

In Photoshop, you open your digital images in a main image window and then use a combination of tools, menu commands, and panel-based features to edit the images.

Application Bar

Displays menus that contain most of Photoshop's commands and functions. Special icon-based menus allow you to change the layout of the program. The application bar becomes a single row on wider monitor settings.

Options Bar

Displays controls that let you customize the selected tool in the Toolbox.

Title Tab

Displays the name, magnification, and color mode of an open image. You can switch between images by clicking their respective tabs.

Image Window

Displays the images you open in Photoshop.

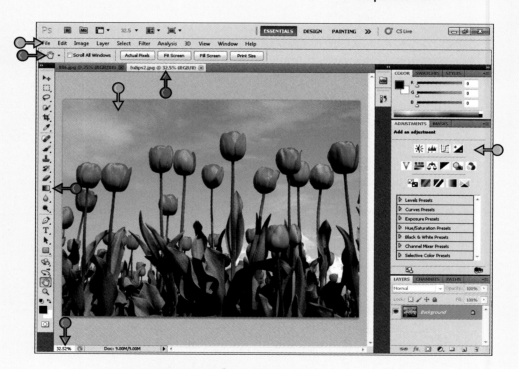

Toolbox

Displays a variety of icons, each one representing an image-editing tool. You click and drag inside your image to apply most of the tools. Also displays the current foreground and background colors.

Status Bar

Displays the magnification of the current image and the amount of computer memory that image is using.

Panels

Small windows that give you access to common commands and resources. You can click the tabs and icons to display and hide panels.

You can get raw material to work with in Photoshop from a variety of sources.

Start from Scratch

You can create your Photoshop image from scratch by opening a blank canvas in the image window. Then, you can apply color and patterns with Photoshop's painting tools or cut and paste parts of other images to create a composite. See the section "Create a New Image" for more on opening a blank canvas.

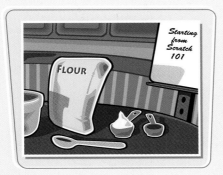

Digital Camera Photos

Digital cameras are a great way to get digital images on your computer. Most digital cameras save their images in JPEG or TIFF format, both of which you can open and edit in Photoshop. The program's color adjustment tools, covered in Chapter 7, are great for correcting color and exposure flaws in digital camera images.

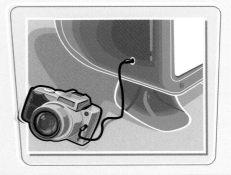

Scanned Photos and Art

A scanner gives you an inexpensive way to convert existing paper- or slide-based content into digital form. You can scan photos and art into your computer, retouch and stylize them in Photoshop, and then output them to a color printer. To automatically separate photos that were scanned together as a single image, see Chapter 3.

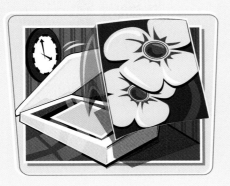

Affordable Online Photos

There are many Web sites that feature images that are in the public domain or are available for noncommercial use. Wikimedia Commons (http://commons.wikimedia.org) is one such site. If you have a little money to spend, you can license images from *microstock* Web sites, which are known for low-cost, downloadable images. iStockPhoto (www.istockphoto.com) is a popular microstock site.

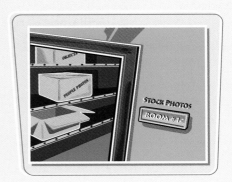

Set Preferences

Photoshop's Preferences dialog boxes let you change default settings and customize how the program looks.

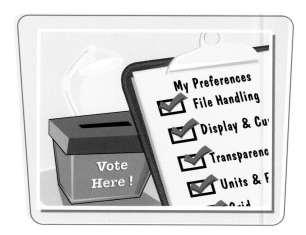

Set Preferences

1. Click **Edit** (**Photoshop** on a Mac).
2. Click **Preferences**.
3. Click **General**.

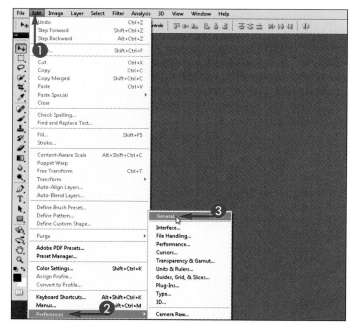

The Preferences dialog box opens and displays General options.

4. Click here (⊟) to select which dialog box opens when you select a color.
5. Select the general options you want to use (☐ changes to ☑).
6. Click **Cursors**.

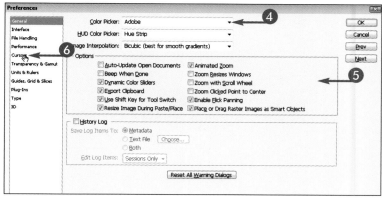

The Cursors Preferences options appear.

⑦ Select a cursor type to use for the painting tools — the Brush, Eraser, and others (◎ changes to ◉).

⑧ Select a cursor type to use for the other tools (◎ changes to ◉).

⑨ Click **Units & Rulers**.

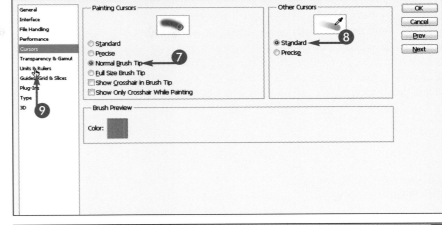

The Units & Rulers Preferences options appear.

⑩ Click here (⊟) to select the units for the window rulers.

These units become the default units selected when you resize an image.

⑪ Click here (⊟) to select the default units for type.

⑫ Click **OK**.

Photoshop sets preferences to your specifications.

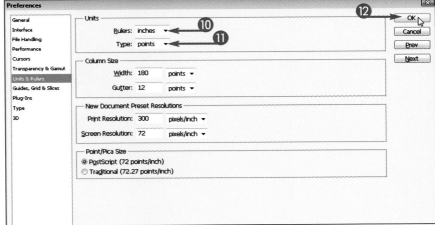

TIPS

What type of measurement units should I use in Photoshop?

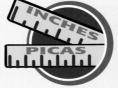

You should use the units most applicable to the type of output you intend to produce. Pixel units are useful for Web imaging because monitor dimensions are measured in pixels. Inches, centimeters, and picas are useful for print because those are standards for working on paper. You can set this under the Units & Rulers preferences.

How can I change the number of operations saved in the History panel?

You can backtrack through your work by using the History panel. To change the number of operations Photoshop remembers, click **Performance** in the Preferences window and then change the History States value. Photoshop can remember as many as 1,000 operations. The default is 20.

Save a Workspace

You can position the different Photoshop panels, define keyboard shortcuts, customize your menus, and then save the arrangement as a workspace. This can be helpful if you work on various types of Photoshop projects that require the use of different tools and commands.

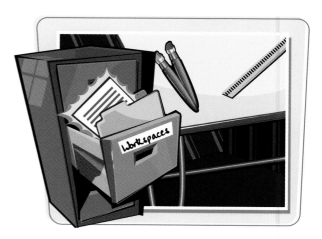

Save a Workspace

Save a Workspace

1 Arrange the Toolbox and panels in the Photoshop interface.

To define keyboard shortcuts or customize menus, click **Edit** and then **Keyboard Shortcuts** or **Menus**.

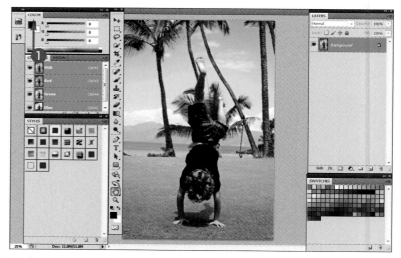

2 Click **Window**.

3 Click **Workspace**.

4 Click **New Workspace**.

● You can also click the **Show More Workspaces and Options** menu (≫) to save a workspace.

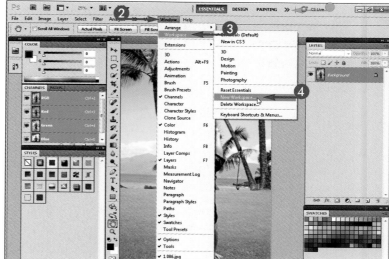

The New Workspace dialog box opens.

⑤ Type a name for your workspace.

⑥ Select the interface elements you want to save (☐ changes to ☑).

⑦ Click **Save**.

Photoshop saves the workspace.

Select a Workspace

① Click **Window**.

② Click **Workspace**.

③ Click a workspace.

You can choose a workspace you have defined previously or one of Photoshop's predefined workspaces.

Photoshop rearranges the workspace.

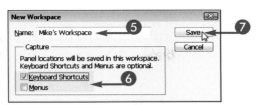

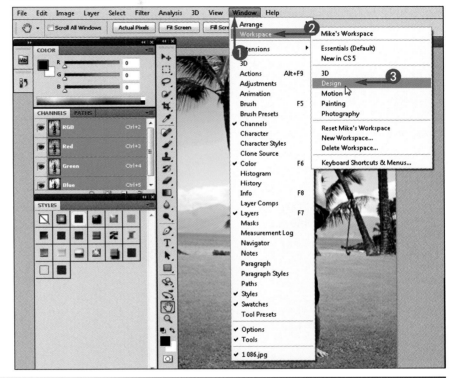

TIP

How do I return to the default workspace?
Follow these steps:

① Click **Window**.

② Click **Workspace**.

③ Click **Essentials (Default)**.

Photoshop returns you to the default setup, with the Toolbox on the left side and panels on the right.

● You can click **Delete Workspace** to get rid of a workspace you have saved.

● You can click the **Reset command** to return the currently selected workspace to its original arrangement.

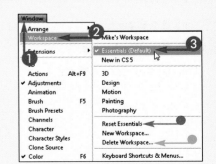

Open an Image

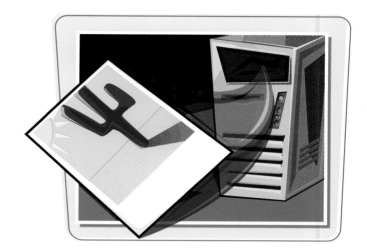

You can open an existing image file in Photoshop to modify it or use it in a project.

Open an Existing Image

1 Click **File**.

2 Click **Open**.

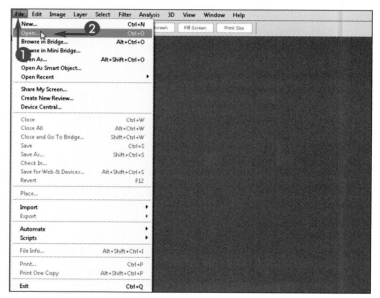

The Open dialog box opens.

3 Click here ( ) to choose the type of files to display in the window.

All Formats is the default and displays all image and nonimage formats.

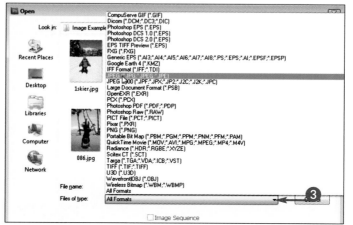

④ Click here (▯) to browse to the folder that contains the image you want to open.

⑤ Click the image you want to open.

⑥ Click **Open**.

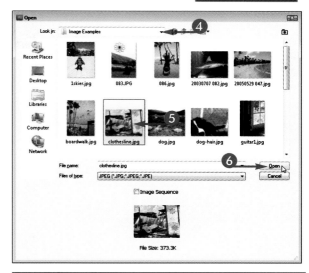

Photoshop opens the image in a window.

● The file name appears in a title tab.

You can specify that images open in floating windows instead of with tabs in the interface preferences.

Note: For more on preferences, see the section "Set Preferences."

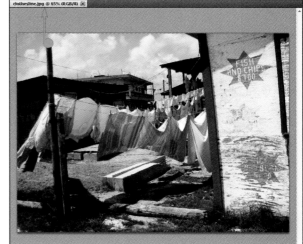

 TIP

How do I open a recently accessed image?

① Click **File**.

② Click **Open Recent**.

A list of recently opened files appears.

③ Click the image's file name.

Photoshop opens the image.

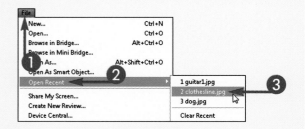

Browse for an Image in Bridge

You can open an existing image file by using the Adobe Bridge file browser. Bridge offers a user-friendly way to find and open your images.

In Bridge, you can also add descriptive information to your images and sort them. See the tasks that follow in this chapter for more information.

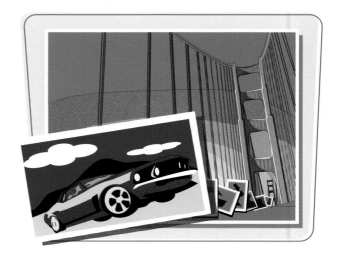

① Click **File**.

② Click **Browse in Bridge**.

● You can also click the **Launch Bridge** button (▣).

The Adobe Bridge file browser opens.

③ Click the **Folders** tab.

④ Click ▶ to open folders on your computer (▶ changes to ▼).

⑤ Click a folder on your computer to browse.

The folders and files inside the folder appear.

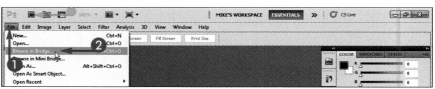

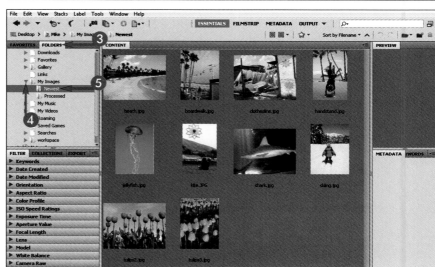

6 Click an image.

● A preview and information about the image appear.

In this example, the right panel has been widened slightly to show more image information.

7 Double-click the image file to open it.

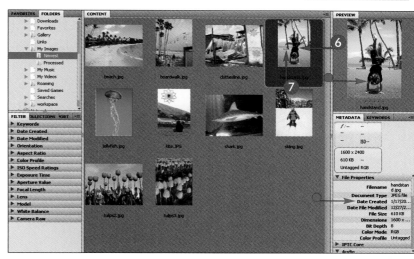

The image opens in Photoshop.

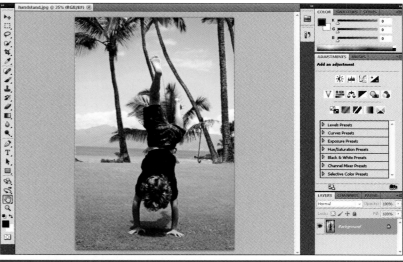

TIPS

How do I add a rating or label to an image in Bridge?

In Bridge, click the image, click **Label**, and then click a star rating or color label. You can apply a rating from one to five stars or a text label such as "approve" or "reject." Applying ratings or labels to your images enables you to sort them by rating or label in the Bridge interface. See the section "Sort and Filter Images in Bridge" for more.

How can I easily access my image folders in Bridge?

You can mark particular folders where you store your images as Favorites in Bridge. To access the Favorites list, click the Favorites tab in the top-left corner of Bridge. To mark a folder as a favorite, click the folder on the right side of the Bridge window and then drag it to the Favorites list. A name and icon for that folder appear. You can remove a favorite by right-clicking on it in the menu and then choosing **Remove from Favorites** from the pop-up menu.

Sort and Filter Images in Bridge

You can sort your images by file name, date, file size, dimensions, and other characteristics in Bridge. This can be helpful when you are dealing with hundreds or thousands of images in a collection and need to find a particular image quickly. You can also filter the information displayed in Bridge, specifying that it show only images with a particular rating or label.

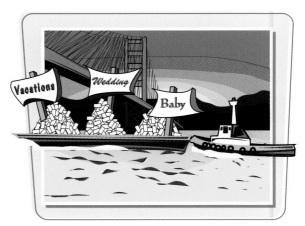

Sort and Filter Images in Bridge

Sort Images

1 Open Adobe Bridge.

2 Click a folder to display its contents.

Note: For more, see the section "Browse for an Image in Bridge."

3 Click **View**.

4 Click **Sort**.

5 Click a category by which to sort.

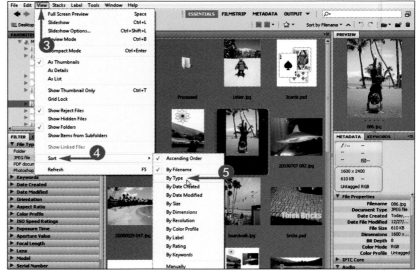

Bridge sorts the images.

● You can also sort images by using the Sort by menu.

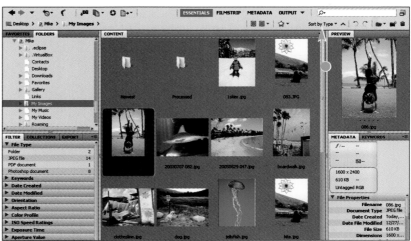

Filter Images

1 Click a category by which to filter your images (▶ changes to ▼).

Photoshop displays filter options for the category.

Note: *For more on applying ratings, labels, and other categories, see the section "Browse for an Image in Bridge."*

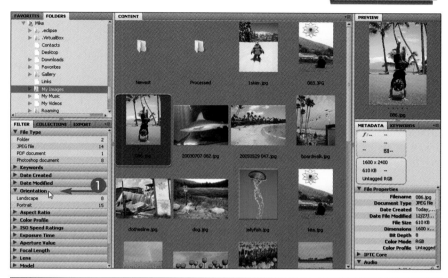

2 Click a filter option.

Bridge filters the images, hiding those that are not relevant.

● A check mark appears next to the clicked filter option.

● You can filter by a rating by clicking **Filter Items by Rating** (☆).

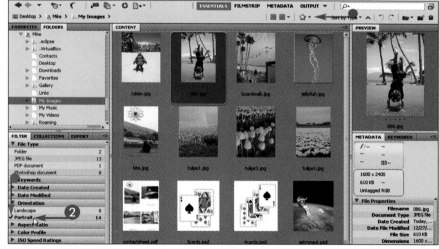

TIPS

How can I hide folders and nonimage files in Bridge so that only images are displayed?

To hide folders, click **View** and then **Show Folders**. The check mark next to the Show Folders menu item disappears, and Bridge hides the folders in the right side of the window. To also hide nonimage files, click **View** and then **Show Graphic Files Only**.

What image-editing functions can I perform in Bridge?

You can rotate images 90 degrees by clicking ↺ (rotate counterclockwise) or ↻ (rotate clockwise). You can delete images by selecting them and clicking 🗑. To perform more-complex editing, you can return to Photoshop by clicking **File** and then **Return to Adobe Photoshop CS5**.

Display a Slide Show in Bridge

You can view a set of images in a folder as a slide show in Adobe Bridge. You can control the cycling of the slide show images by using keyboard commands.

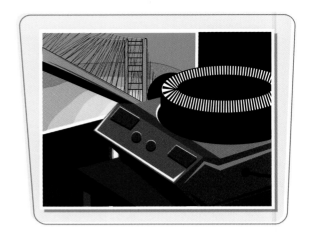

1 Open Adobe Bridge.

2 Click a folder containing the slide show images.

Note: For more, see the section "Browse for an Image in Bridge."

3 Click **View**.

4 Click **Slideshow Options**.

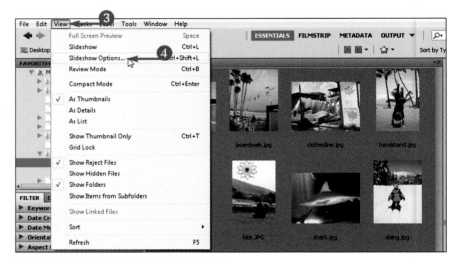

The Slideshow Options dialog box opens.

You can specify the duration between slides, alignment, and other settings.

5 Click **Play** to open the first slide.

Note: On a Mac, the position of the Play and Done buttons is reversed in the Slideshow Options dialog box.

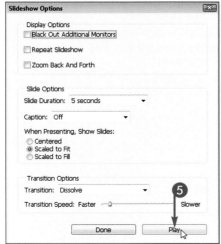

Bridge starts the slide show and cycles through the photos in the selected folder.

● You can press Spacebar to pause and resume the slide show.

The sort order in Bridge determines the order of the photos.

Note: *See the section "Sort and Filter Images in Bridge" for more.*

⑥ Press H.

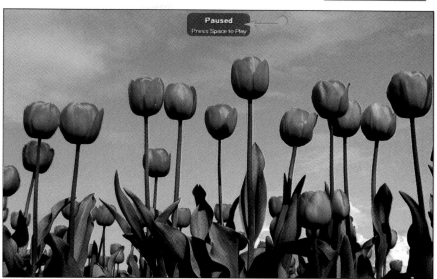

● Bridge displays the slide show keyboard commands.

⑦ Press Esc.

The slide show ends.

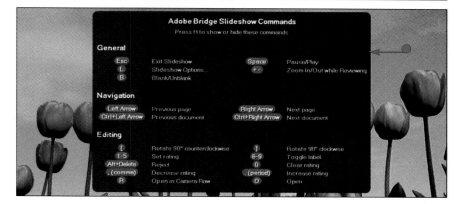

TIP

How can I group similar images in Bridge?

You can group similar images together in Bridge and free up screen space by creating a stack. Follow these steps:

① Ctrl + click to select the images you want to stack.

② Click **Stacks**.

③ Click **Group as Stack**.

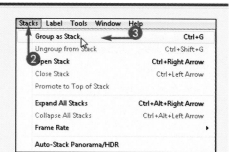

Photoshop creates a single thumbnail for the stack and displays the number of images in the stack.

You can click the number to reveal the stacked images.

You can select the stack, click **Stacks**, and then click **Ungroup from Stack** to ungroup the images.

Manage Images with Mini Bridge

You can access key features of Bridge from within Photoshop by opening the Mini Bridge panel. Mini Bridge allows you to search for and filter images on your computer and then open them in Photoshop without having to open the Bridge application.

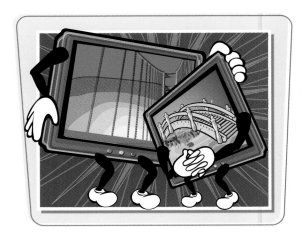

Manage Images with Mini Bridge

View Folders and Images

1 Click the **Launch Mini Bridge** button (⬛).

The Mini Bridge panel opens.

Note: For more on opening and managing panels, see Chapter 2.

2 Click the **Home** button (⬛).

3 Click **Browse Files**.

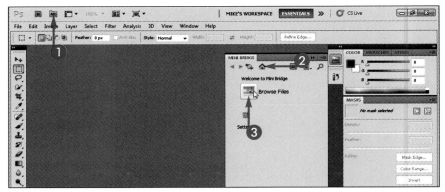

4 Click a category.

5 Click a folder.

● Photoshop displays the folders and images from the selected folder.

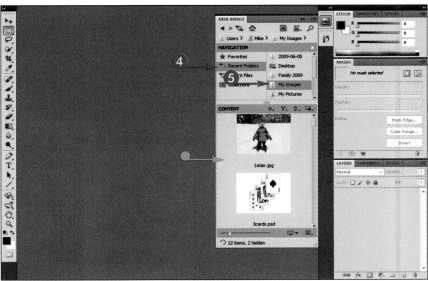

Adjust Thumbnails

6️⃣ Click the **View** button (🖼️) and then click an arrangement to choose how the thumbnail images are displayed.

Photoshop rearranges the images.

● You can click and drag the slider (🔳) to adjust the size of the thumbnail images in Mini Bridge.

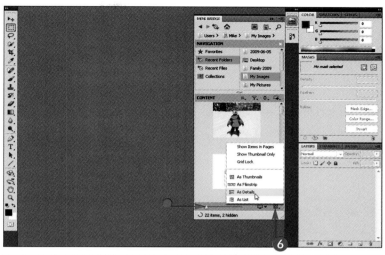

Open an Image

7️⃣ Double-click an image.

● Photoshop opens the image.

You can Ctrl + click multiple images in Mini Bridge and then double-click any one of them to open all of them.

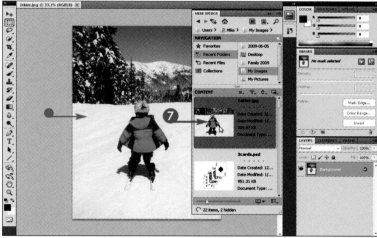

TIP

How do I apply automated commands from the Mini Bridge panel?

1️⃣ Ctrl + click to select the images to which you want to apply a command.

2️⃣ Click the **Tools** button (📋).

3️⃣ Click **Photoshop**.

4️⃣ Click a command.

Note: For more on automation in Photoshop, see Chapter 13.

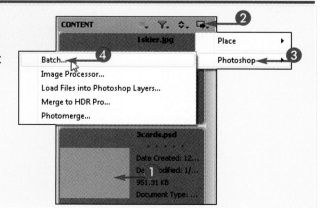

Create a New Image

You can start a Photoshop project by creating a blank image.

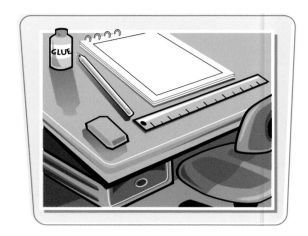

① Click **File**.

② Click **New**.

The New dialog box opens.

③ Type a name for the new image.

● You can click here (⊟) to choose a preset image size.

④ Type the dimensions and resolution you want.

Note: For more on dimensions and resolution, see Chapter 3.

⑤ Click **OK**.

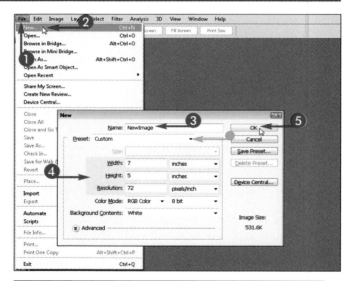

Photoshop creates a new image window at the specified dimensions.

● The image name appears in the title tab.

⑥ Use Photoshop's tools and commands to create your image.

Note: To learn how to save your image, see Chapter 14.

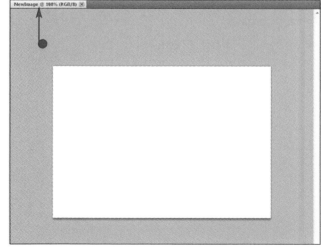

Exit Photoshop

You can exit Photoshop after you finish using the application.

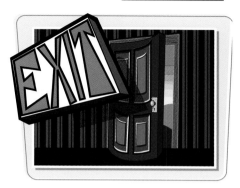

Exit Photoshop

Exit Photoshop on a PC

1 Click **File**.

2 Click **Exit**.

Photoshop closes.

Before exiting, Photoshop alerts you to any open images that have unsaved changes so you can save them.

Note: *See Chapter 14 to learn how to save image files.*

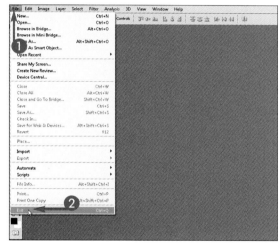

Exit Photoshop on a Mac

1 Click **Photoshop**.

2 Click **Quit Photoshop**.

Photoshop closes.

Before exiting, Photoshop alerts you to any open images that have unsaved changes so you can save them.

Note: *See Chapter 14 to learn how to save image files.*

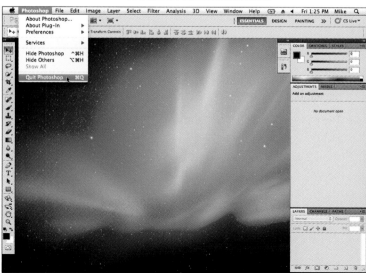

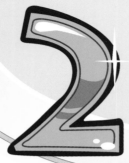

CHAPTER 2

Understanding Photoshop Basics

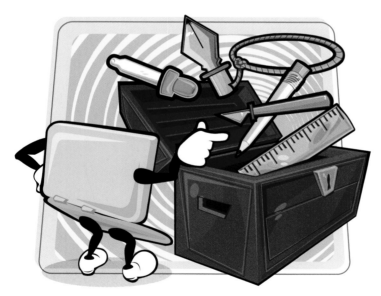

Are you ready to start working with images? This chapter shows you how to select tools and fine-tune your workspace.

Introducing the Photoshop Toolbox

Photoshop offers a variety of specialized tools that let you edit your image. Take some time to familiarize yourself with the Toolbox tools.

You can select tools by clicking buttons in the Toolbox or by typing a keyboard shortcut key. Keyboard shortcut keys are shown in parentheses.

Move (V)
Moves selected areas of an image.

Marquee (M)
Selects pixels by drawing a box or circle around the area you want to edit.

Lasso (L)
Selects pixels by drawing a free-form shape around the area you want to edit.

Quick Selection Brush (W)
Selects pixels with brush shapes.

Crop (C)
Trims an image to create a new size.

Eyedropper (I)
Samples color from an area of an image.

Spot Healing Brush (J)
Quickly fixes slight imperfections by cloning nearby pixels.

Brush (B)
Paints strokes of color.

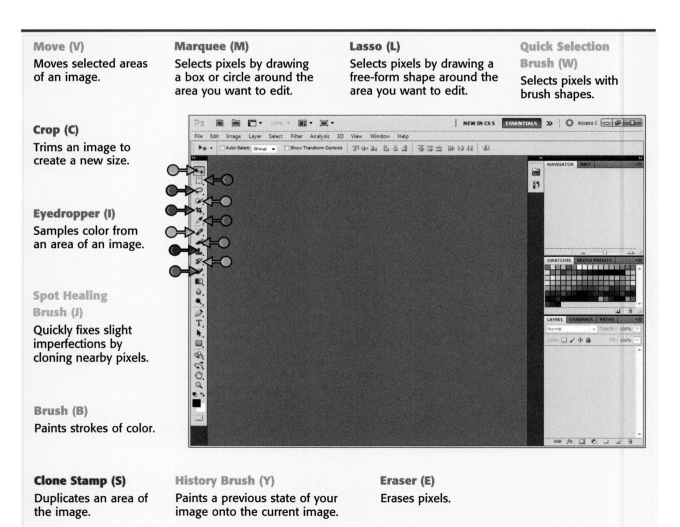

Clone Stamp (S)
Duplicates an area of the image.

History Brush (Y)
Paints a previous state of your image onto the current image.

Eraser (E)
Erases pixels.

Gradient (G)

Fills selected areas with blended color effects.

Blur

Blurs objects in your image.

Dodge (O)

Brightens specific areas of your image.

Pen (P)

Creates custom shapes by drawing and connecting lines or paths.

Type (T)

Adds type to an image or selects type that you have added.

Path Selection (A)

Selects lines that you have drawn with the pen or other tools.

Rectangle (U)

Draws solid, rectangular shapes.

3D Tools

Creates and edits 3-D objects. The tools include the Object Rotate tool (K) and the Camera Rotate tool (N). (These tools are available only in the Extended version of Photoshop and are not covered in this book.)

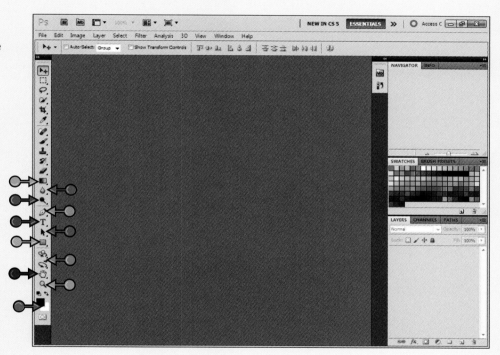

Hand (H)

Shifts an image in the image window to display unseen parts.

Zoom (Z)

Zooms your view of an image in or out.

Foreground and Background Colors

Displays and lets you set foreground and background colors.

Hidden Tools

Tool buttons that include a small triangle (▣) in the corner have hidden tools located beneath them. Click and hold a tool button to access the hidden tools. You can also right-click on a tool to access additional tools. For example, the Lasso has a Polygonal Lasso and a Magnetic Lasso hidden beneath it. You can cycle through hidden tools beneath a tool by typing the shortcut key for that tool repeatedly.

Work with Toolbox Tools

You can use the tools in Photoshop's Toolbox to make changes to an image. Positioning the mouse pointer over a tool displays the tool name. After you click to select a tool, the Options bar displays controls for customizing the tool. Some tools include a small triangle (◢) in the corner to indicate hidden tools.

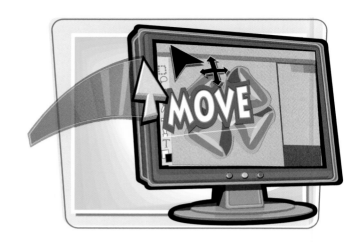

Work with Toolbox Tools

Select a Tool

1 Position the mouse pointer (↖) over a tool.

● A label appears displaying the tool name and the tool's shortcut key, if it has one.

2 Click a tool.

The Options bar displays customizing options for the selected tool.

3 Specify any options you want for the tool.

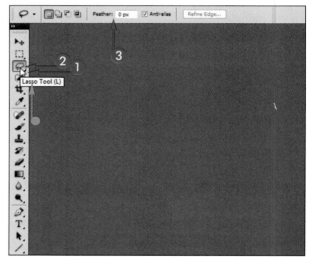

Select a Hidden Tool

1 Click a tool that has a triangle (◢) in its corner.

2 Press and hold the mouse button.

Note: *You can also right-click on the tool.*

A menu of hidden tools appears.

3 Click the tool you want to use.

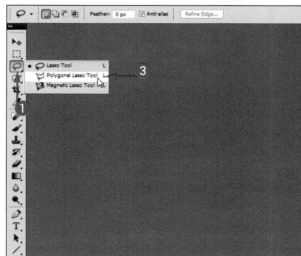

Rearrange the Toolbox

1 Click ⏩.

● Photoshop rearranges the Toolbox tools into two columns.

● You can click ⏪ to switch back to a single column.

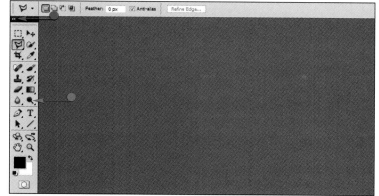

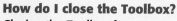

TIPS

How do I float the Toolbox?

You can float the Toolbox to drag it to a more convenient place on the screen. To float the Toolbox, click and drag the title bar of the Toolbox. You can unfloat the Toolbox by dragging it back to near the left edge of the screen. When you release the mouse button, Photoshop snaps the Toolbox to the left edge.

How do I close the Toolbox?

Closing the Toolbox frees up space in the Photoshop interface. To close the Toolbox, click **Window** and then click **Tools**. To reopen the Toolbox, click **Window** and then click **Tools** again. You can also press Tab to open or close the Toolbox as well as all panels. Items that are open in the workspace have check marks next to them in the Windows menu.

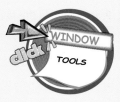

Magnify with the Zoom Tool

You can change the magnification of an image with the Zoom tool. With this tool, you can view small details in an image or view an image at full size.

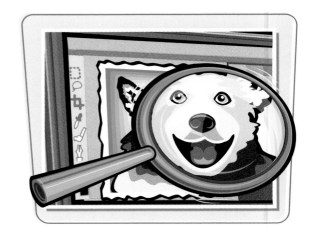

Increase Magnification

1 Click the **Zoom** tool (🔍).

   ▷ changes to 🔍.

2 Click the image.

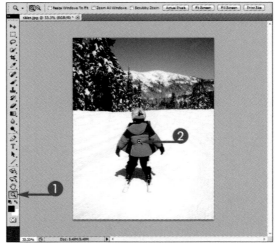

Photoshop increases the magnification of the image.

You can also press Ctrl + = to zoom in (⌘ + = on a Mac).

The point that you click in the image is centered in the window.

● The current magnification shows in the title tab and status bar.

● You can choose an exact magnification by typing a percentage value in the status bar.

● You can also select a magnification in the application bar.

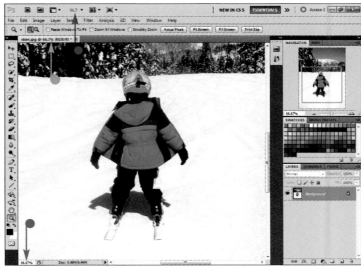

Decrease Magnification

1 Click the **Zoom Out** icon ().

 ⬚ changes to Q.

2 Click the image.

 Photoshop decreases the magnification.

 You can also press Ctrl + - to zoom in (⌘ + - on a Mac).

● The current magnification shows in the title bar and status bar.

 You can also press and hold Alt (Option on a Mac) and then click the image to decrease magnification.

Use Scrubby Zoom

1 Click the Scrubby Zoom check box (⬚ changes to ☑).

 Scrubbing means moving within a multimedia file to find an area of interest.

2 Click and drag with the Zoom tool.

 Photoshop zooms as you drag.

3 Release the mouse button.

 Photoshop magnifies the image.

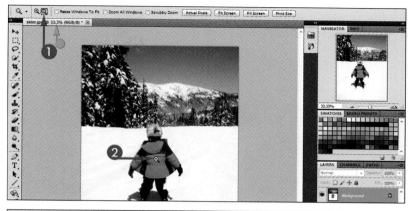

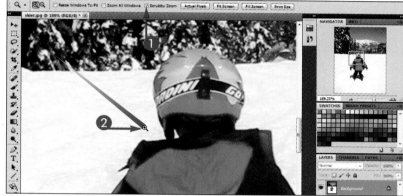

TIP

How do I quickly return an image to 100% magnification?
Here are seven ways to return the image to 100% magnification:

1 Double-click the **Zoom** tool (Q).

2 Click **Actual Pixels** on the Options bar.

3 Click **View** and then click **Actual Pixels** from the menu.

4 Select **100%** from the application bar menu.

5 Type **100%** in the lower-left corner of the image window.

6 Right-click on the image and then choose **Actual Pixels**.

7 Press Ctrl + 1 (⌘ + 1 on a Mac).

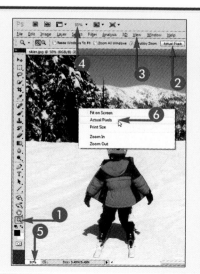

Adjust Views

You can move an image within the window by using the Hand tool or scroll bars. The Hand tool helps you navigate to an exact area.

The Hand tool is a more flexible alternative to using the scroll bars because, unlike the scroll bars, the Hand tool enables you to drag the image freely in two dimensions.

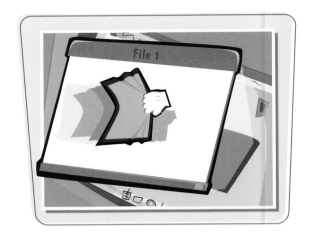

Using the Hand Tool

1 Click the **Hand** tool (🖐).

 changes to 🖐.

Note: For the Hand tool to produce an effect, the image must extend outside the boundary of the image window.

2 Click **Window**.

3 Click **Navigator**.

● The Navigator panel opens to show your current view relative to the entire image.

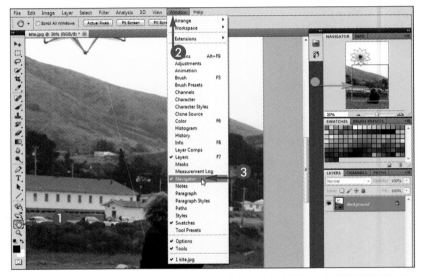

4 Click and drag inside the image window.

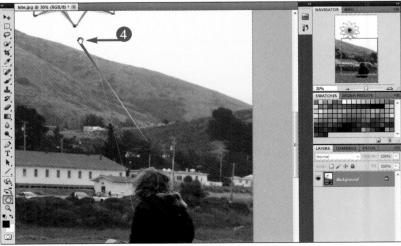

The view of the image shifts inside the window.

● The Navigator panel shows the changed view.

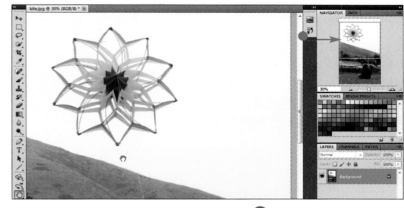

Using the Scroll Bars

① Click and hold one of the window's scroll bar buttons (▲, ▼, ◄, or ►).

The image scrolls.

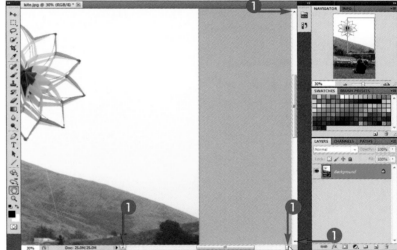

TIP

How can I quickly adjust the image window to see the entire image at its largest possible magnification on-screen?

Here are six ways to magnify the image to its largest possible size:

① Double-click the **Hand** tool (✋).

② Click **Fit Screen** on the Options bar.

③ Click **View** and then click **Fit on Screen** from the menu.

④ Click **Fit on Screen**.

⑤ Right-click on the image and then choose **Fit on Screen**.

⑥ Press Ctrl + 0 (⌘ + 0 on a Mac).

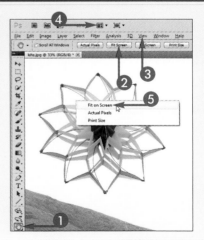

Change Screen Modes

You can switch the screen mode to change the look of your workspace on-screen and give yourself more room to view your current image.

In the Standard Screen Mode, you can view multiple images at the same time, each in a different window. For more on viewing open images, see the section "Manage Image Windows."

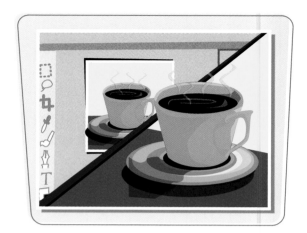

Switch to Full Screen Mode with Menu Bar

① Click the **Screen Mode** icon (▦).

② In the list that appears, click **Full Screen Mode With Menu Bar**.

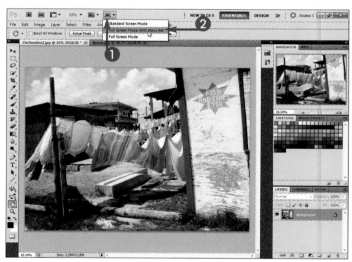

Photoshop hides the title tabs, status bar, and other features to increase the amount of space with which you have to work.

If you have multiple images open, you can switch between them in the Window menu.

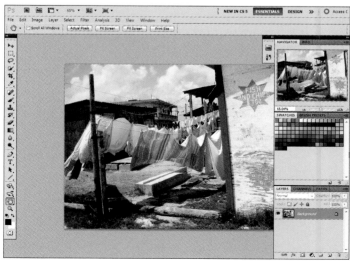

Switch to Full Screen Mode

1 Click the **Screen Mode** icon.

2 In the list that appears, click **Full Screen Mode**.

3 If a dialog box opens explaining Full Screen Mode, click **Full Screen** to close it.

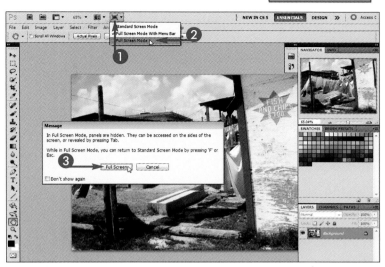

The image appears full screen without the application bar, Options bar, Toolbox, or panels.

You can press **F** or **Esc** to return to Standard Screen Mode.

You can press **Tab** or move your cursor to the sides of the screen to open the Toolbox and panels.

Note: Pressing **Tab** hides the Toolbox and panels in all of Photoshop's screen modes.

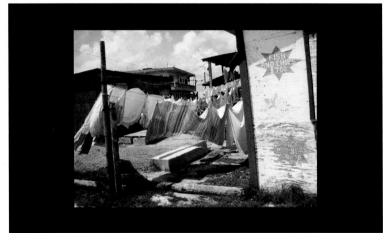

TIPS

Is there a shortcut for changing screen modes?

Press **F** to cycle through the screen modes by using your keyboard. To cycle through in opposite order, press **Shift** + **F**. You can also exit Full Screen Mode by pressing **Esc**.

How do I change tools while in Full Screen Mode?

You can open the Toolbox by pressing **Tab** or you can press a shortcut key. Below are shortcut keys for the more popular tools. For a complete list, see the section "Introducing the Photoshop Toolbox."

Marquee	**M**	Type	**T**
Move	**V**	Zoom	**Z**
Lasso	**L**	Eraser	**E**
Brush	**B**	Quick Selection tool	**W**

Using Rulers and Guides

You can turn on rulers and create guides to help place elements accurately in your image.

Guides help you align elements in your image with one another. These lines do not appear on a printed image.

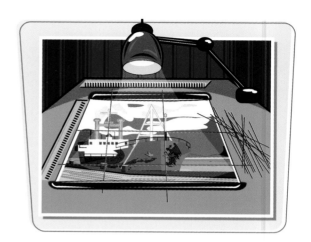

View Rulers and Guides

1 Click **View**.

2 Click **Rulers**.

● You can also click **View Extras** (▦) and then click **View Rulers**.

Note: To change the units of measurement on rulers and make other preference changes, see Chapter 1.

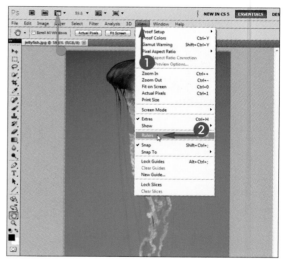

● Photoshop adds rulers to the top and left sides of the image window.

3 Click one of the rulers and then drag the cursor into the window (◊ changes to ↔).

You can drag the top ruler down to create a horizontal guide.

You can drag the left ruler to the right to create a vertical guide.

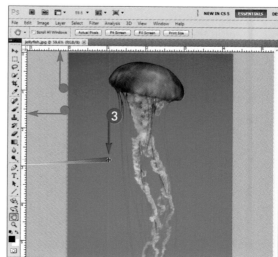

● A thin, colored line called a *guide* appears.

You can also click **View** and then click **New Guide** to add a guide.

To hide and show guides in your image, click **View**, **Show**, and then **Guides**.

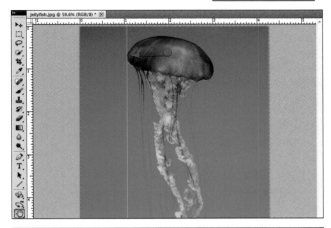

Move a Guide

1 Click the **Move** tool (⊞).

2 Place your cursor over a guide (⌖ changes to +||+).

3 Click the guide and then drag it to a new position.

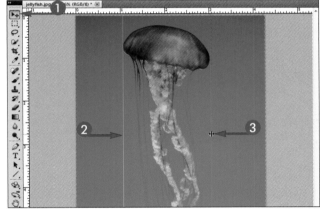

TIP

How do I make objects in my images "snap to" my guides when I move those objects?

You can use the "snap to" feature when you want to align elements in a row horizontally or in a column vertically. To make objects in different layers automatically snap to any nearby guides, follow these steps:

1 Click **View**.

2 Click **Snap To**.

3 Click **Guides**.

Photoshop places a check mark next to Guides.

● When you move an object, Photoshop automatically snaps it to any nearby guides.

Note: For more on layers, see Chapter 8.

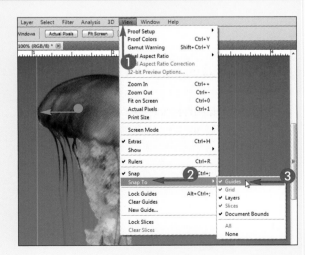

Undo Commands

You can undo multiple commands by using the History panel. This enables you to correct mistakes or change your mind about operations you have performed on your image.

The History panel lists recently executed commands, with the most recent command at the bottom.

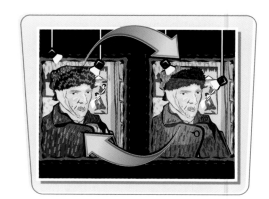

Undo Commands

1 Click **Window**.

2 Click **History**.

The History panel opens.

3 Click the **History** slider (◻)
and drag it upward.

● Alternatively, you can click a
previous command in the
History panel.

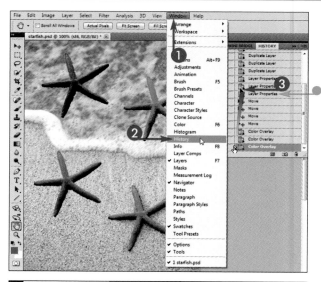

● Photoshop undoes the previous
commands.

● You can click and drag the
History slider (◻) down to
redo the commands.

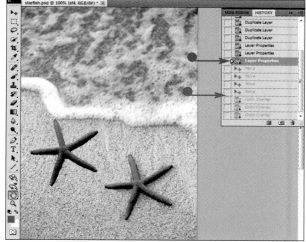

Revert an Image

You can revert an image to the previously saved state and then begin editing your image again.

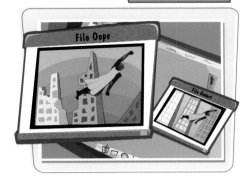

Revert an Image

1 Click **File**.

2 Click **Revert**.

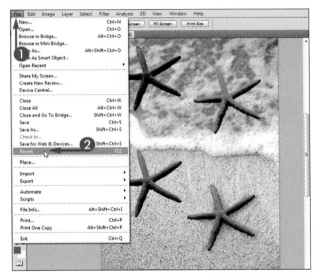

Photoshop reverts the image to its previously saved state.

You can click **Edit** and then click **Undo Revert** to return to the unreverted state.

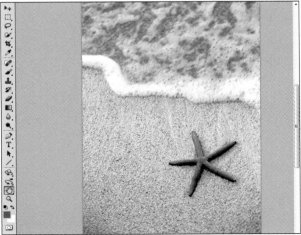

Manage
Image Windows

Each image you open in Photoshop appears in its own window. Windows can take up the entire workspace, and you can select between different ones by clicking tabs. You can also float or tile windows so you can see content from more than one window at once. This can be useful if you are copying content between them.

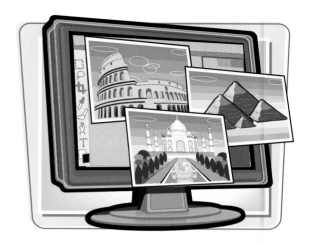

Manage Image Windows

① Open two or more images.

Note: For more on opening images, see Chapter 1.

● The active, or current, image appears here.

By default, the different open images are distinguished by tabs.

② Click the tab for the image you want to view.

You can also select your images from a list at the bottom of the Window menu.

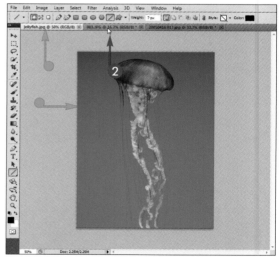

● The image you select appears as the active image.

③ Click **Window**.

④ Click **Arrange**.

⑤ Click **Float in Window**.

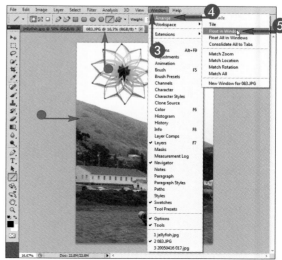

Photoshop displays the active image in a floating window.

● You can click and drag the title bar to move the window.

6 Click **Window**.

7 Click **Arrange**.

8 Click **Tile**

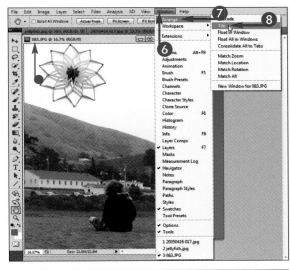

Photoshop tiles the windows so that all images are visible.

● You can click and drag here to resize the window.

Note: *To copy content between two open windows, see Chapter 5.*

You can click **Window** and then click **Consolidate All to Tabs** to return the windows to tabs.

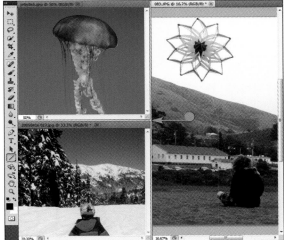

TIPS

How can I make the views consistent between different open images?
You can click **Window**, **Arrange**, and then **Match Zoom** to set the zoom levels of all the open images to that of the active image. You can click **Window**, **Arrange**, and then **Match Location** to make the viewing location consistent across all open images. To match both zoom and location, click **Window**, **Arrange**, and then **Match All**.

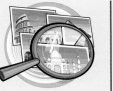

Are there shortcuts for managing tabbed windows?
Yes. You can right-click on a window's tab to access a menu of commands. The commands include Close for closing that tab's image, Close All for closing all the currently open images, and Open Document for opening a new image.

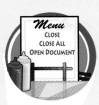

3

Changing the
Size of an Image

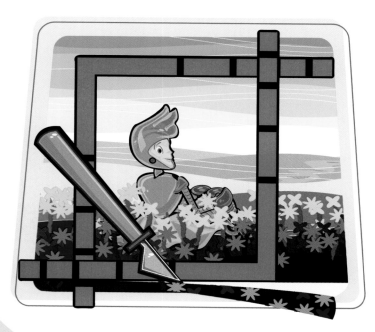

You can change the size of your image to make it fit on a Web page or in a printed document. This chapter shows you how to change the on-screen or print size and print resolution as well as how to crop an image.

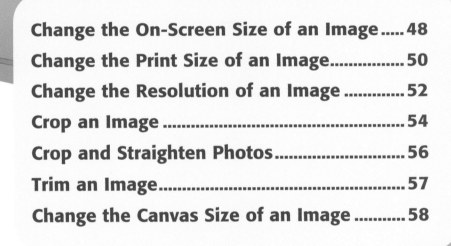

Change the On-Screen Size of an Image

You can change the size at which an image displays on your computer monitor so viewers can see the entire image. To change the on-screen size, Photoshop adjusts the number of pixels that make up the image.

Because you lose less sharpness when you decrease an image's size than when you increase it, consider starting with an image that is too big rather than one that is too small.

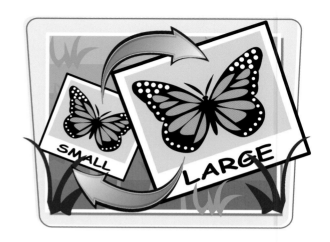

① Click **Image**.

② Click **Image Size**.

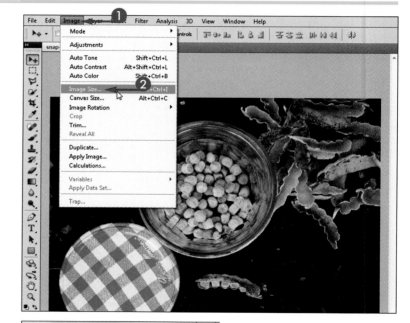

● The Image Size dialog box opens, listing the height and width of the image.

③ Make sure **Resample Image** is selected (☐ changes to ☑) to change the number of pixels in the image.

Changing the number of pixels changes the on-screen size.

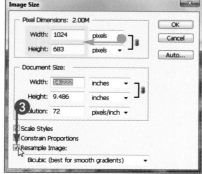

48

④ Type a size for a dimension.

● To resize by a certain percentage, click here (⏷) to change the units to percent. Changing the units of one menu will automatically change the units of the other.

● Click the **Constrain Proportions** check box (☐ changes to ☑), if it is not already selected, to force the other dimension to change proportionally.

● You can restore the original dialog box settings by pressing and holding **Alt** (**Option** on a Mac) and then clicking **Cancel**, which changes to **Reset**.

⑤ Click **OK**.

Photoshop resizes the image.

Note: *Increasing the number of pixels in an image can add blur. To sharpen a resized image, apply the Unsharp Mask filter, as covered in Chapter 10.*

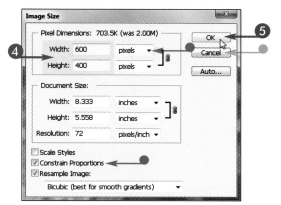

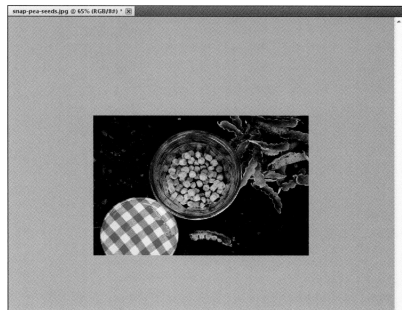

TIP

How do I change the size of an image as I am saving it for the Web?
Follow these steps:

① Click File and then Save for Web & Devices.

The Save for Web & Devices dialog box opens.

② Type a new value in the W or H field to change the dimensions of your image.

③ Click Save to save the resized image.

Note: *For more on saving images for the Web, see Chapter 14.*

Change the Print Size of an Image

You can change the printed size of an image to determine how it appears on paper. The printed size of an image depends on the number of pixels in the image and the resolution, which measures the pixel density on the printed page.

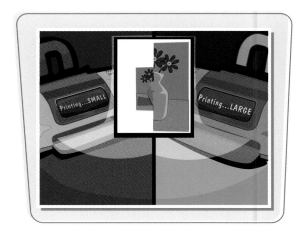

Change the Print Size of an Image

① Click **Image**.

② Click **Image Size**.

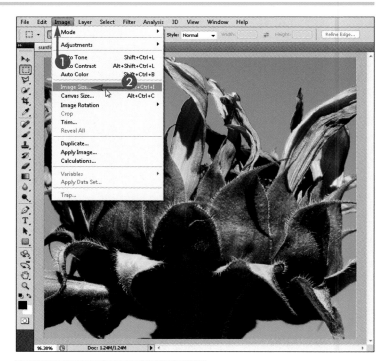

● The Image Size dialog box opens, listing the current height and width of the printed image.

● You can click here (⊡) to change the unit of measurement.

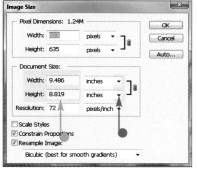

③ Type a size for a dimension.

● You can click the **Constrain Proportions** check box (☐ changes to ☑), if it is not already selected, to force the other dimension to change proportionally.

● You can restore the original dialog box settings by pressing and holding **Alt** (**Option** on a Mac) and then clicking **Cancel**, which changes to **Reset**.

④ Click **OK**.

Photoshop resizes the image.

Note: Changing the number of pixels in an image can add blur. To sharpen a resized image, apply the Unsharp Mask filter, as covered in Chapter 10.

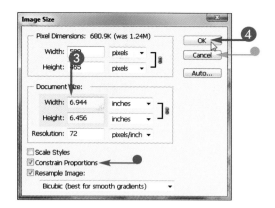

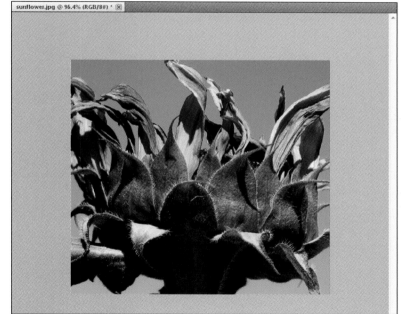

TIP

How do I preview an image's printed size?
Follow these steps:

① Click **File** and then **Print**.

● A dialog box displays how the image will print on the page.

● Other options let you adjust the size and positioning of the image.

Note: For more on printing images, see Chapter 14.

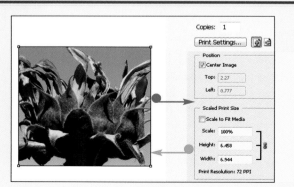

Change the Resolution of an Image

You can change the print resolution of an image to increase or decrease the print quality. The resolution, combined with the number of pixels in the image, determines the size of a printed image. The greater the resolution, the better the image looks on the printed page — up to a limit, which varies with the type of printer and paper quality.

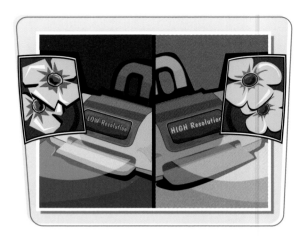

Change the Resolution of an Image

① Click **Image**.

② Click **Image Size**.

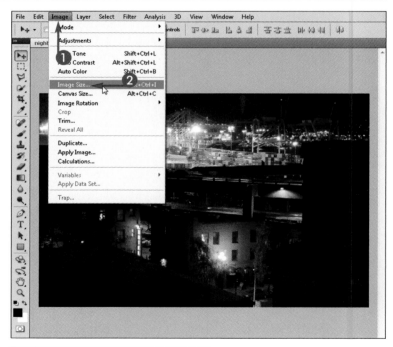

● The Image Size dialog box opens, listing the current resolution of the image.

③ Make sure **Resample Image** is selected (☐ changes to ☑) to change the number of pixels in the image as you adjust the resolution.

● You can click here (⊡) to change the resolution units.

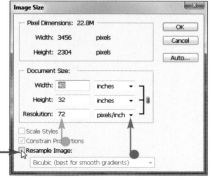

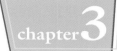
④ Type a new resolution.

● You can restore the original dialog box settings by pressing and holding **Alt** (**Option** on a Mac) and then clicking **Cancel**, which changes to **Reset**.

⑤ Click **OK**.

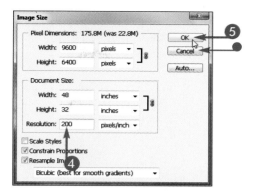

In this example, adjusting the resolution changes the number of pixels in the image. The on-screen image becomes larger or smaller, while the print size stays the same.

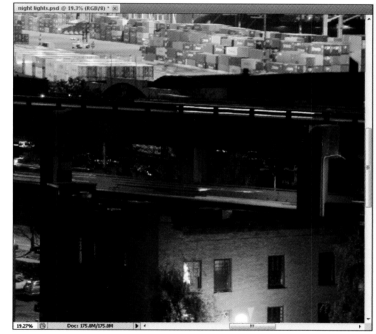

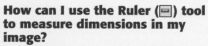

TIPS

What is the relationship between resolution, on-screen size, and print size?

To determine the printed size of a Photoshop image, you can divide the on-screen size by the resolution. If you have an image with an on-screen width of 480 pixels and a resolution of 120 pixels per inch, the printed width is 4 inches.

How can I use the Ruler (▭) tool to measure dimensions in my image?

Click and hold the **Eyedropper** tool (✎) and then click the **Ruler** tool (▭). You can then click and drag inside your image to measure the dimensions of objects. Click **Window** and then **Info** to open the Info panel and see your measurements. You can change the Info panel units in the Units & Rulers preferences. See Chapter 1 for more on changing preferences.

Crop an Image

You can use the Crop tool to change the size of an image by removing unneeded space on the top, bottom, and sides.

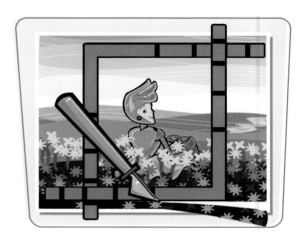

Crop Only

1 Click the **Crop** tool (![crop]).

    ⌖ changes to ⌖.

2 Click and drag ⌖ to select the area of the image you want to keep.

You can also crop an image by changing its canvas size or by selecting with the Rectangular Marquee tool (![marquee]) and then clicking **Image** and then **Crop**.

Note: See the section "Change the Canvas Size of an Image" for more.

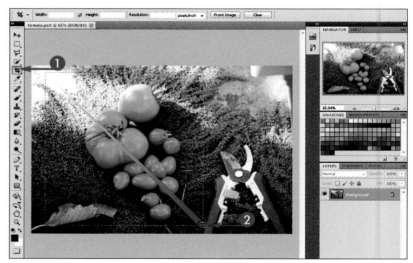

3 Click and drag the side and corner handles (□) to adjust the size of the cropping boundary.

● You can click here (![arrow]) to show or hide guides in the tool. You can choose **Rule of Thirds** to add pairs of horizontal and vertical lines to help line up objects in the image.

● To exit without cropping the image, you can click ![cancel] or press ![Esc] to cancel.

4 To accept the crop, click ![check] or press ![Enter] (⌘ + ![Return] on a Mac).

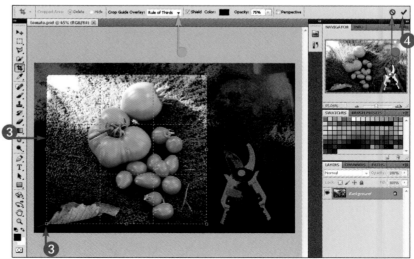

54

Photoshop crops the image, deleting the pixels outside the cropping boundary.

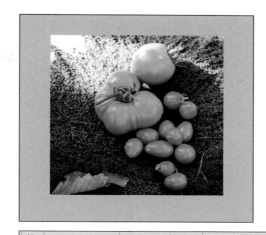

Rotate and Crop

1. Perform steps **1** to **3** on the previous page.

2. Click and drag outside the boundary lines.

3. To accept, click ✓ or press Enter (⌘ + Return on a Mac).

   Photoshop rotates the image and crops it.

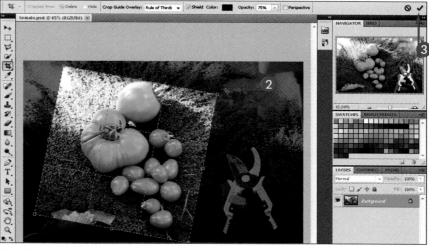

TIP

How can I constrain the dimensions of the Crop tool?

Follow these steps:

1. Type the width and height of the cropping boundary on the Options bar.

   ● You can also specify a resolution on the Options bar.

2. Drag ⌗ to apply the Crop tool.

   Photoshop constrains the rectangle to the specified dimensions.

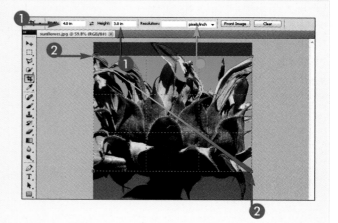

Crop and Straighten Photos

You can automatically crop and straighten one or more photographs in a Photoshop image. After you finish cropping and straightening the images, Photoshop places each image in its own image window. This feature is useful if you digitize several images at the same time on a scanner and want to separate them.

The feature works best when the images to be cropped and straightened contrast with the background.

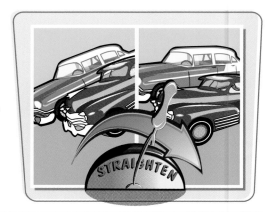

① Click **File**.

② Click **Automate**.

③ Click **Crop and Straighten Photos**.

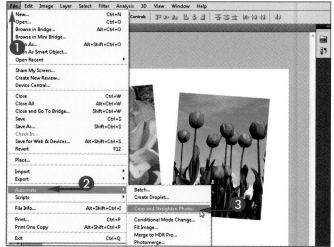

● Photoshop straightens the photos, crops out any blank space, and copies the photos to separate image windows.

Note: *For more on saving newly cropped images, see Chapter 14.*

● The original image remains in its own window.

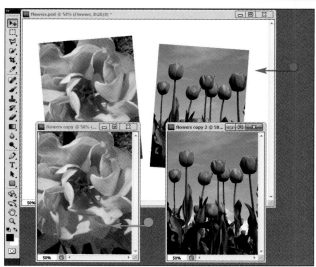

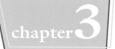

You can use the Trim command to automatically remove any blank space surrounding your image. This can be useful for scanned photos or when you want to minimize the file size of an image. Options let you trim space from all four sides or just some of them.

The feature works best when the image to be trimmed contrasts with the background.

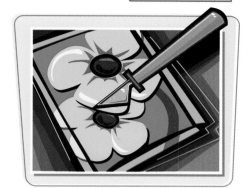

Trim an Image

1 Click **Image**.

2 Click **Trim**.

The Trim dialog box opens.

3 Specify how to select the type of pixels you want to trim (◯ changes to ◉).

4 Select the areas to trim (☐ changes to ☑).

5 Click **OK**.

Photoshop trims the image.

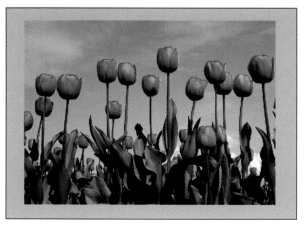

Change the Canvas Size of an Image

You can alter the canvas size of an image in order to change its rectangular shape or to add blank space around its borders. The *canvas* is the area on which an image sits. Changing the canvas size is one way to crop an image.

The Crop tool provides an alternative to changing the canvas size. See the section "Crop an Image" for more.

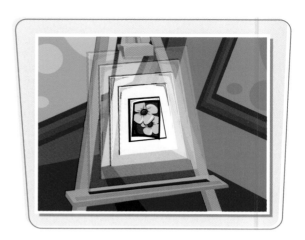

① Click **Image**.

② Click **Canvas Size**.

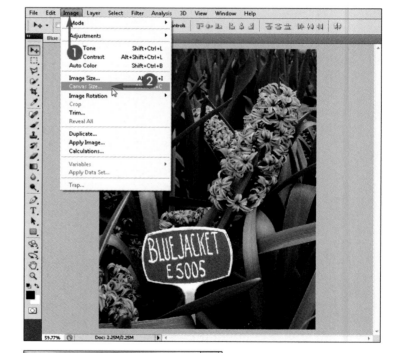

● The Canvas Size dialog box opens, listing the current dimensions of the canvas.

● You can click here (⊟) to change the unit of measurement.

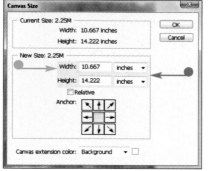

③ Type the new canvas dimensions.

● You can modify in what directions Photoshop changes the canvas size by clicking an anchor point.

● You can specify the color with which Photoshop fills any new canvas area if you enlarge a dimension.

④ Click **OK**.

Note: *If you decrease a dimension, Photoshop displays a dialog box asking whether you want to proceed. Click* ***Proceed***.

Photoshop changes the image's canvas size.

Because the middle anchor point is selected in this example, the canvas size changes equally on opposite sides.

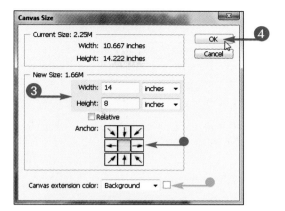

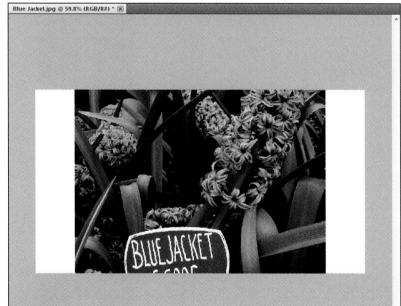

TIPS

How do I increase the area of an image by using the Crop tool?

You can enlarge the image window to add extra space around the image. Then, you can apply the **Crop** tool ( ) so the cropping boundary extends beyond the borders of the image. When you apply cropping, the image canvas enlarges. Photoshop applies the current background color in the new space. For more on selecting colors, see Chapter 6.

How can I crop without making the image canvas smaller?

Use a selection tool, such as the Rectangular Marquee tool ( ), to select a cropping boundary. Click **Select** and then **Inverse** to select the area outside the boundary. Pressing Backspace (Delete on a Mac) crops the image but keeps your canvas dimensions the same. If you are working with a multilayer image, this technique crops content only in the selected layer.

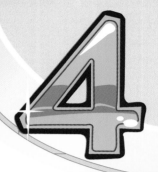

Making Selections

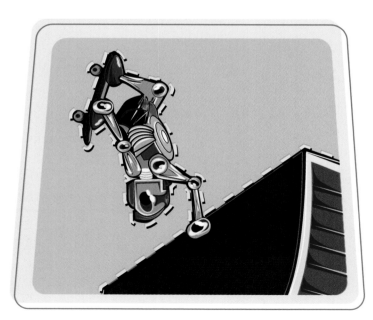

You can move, color, or transform parts of your image independently from the rest of the image. The first step is to make a selection. This chapter shows you how.

Select with the Marquee Tools

You can select a rectangular or elliptical area of your image by using the Marquee tools. Then, you can move, delete, or stylize the selected area by using other Photoshop commands.

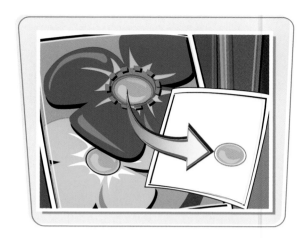

Using the Rectangular Marquee Tool

① Click the **Rectangular Marquee** tool (▣).

   ⬚ changes to +.

② Click and drag diagonally inside the image window.

   You can press and hold **Shift** while you click and drag to create a square selection.

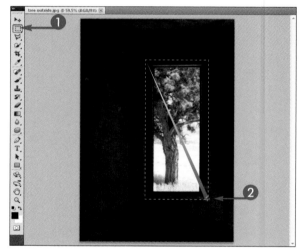

● Photoshop selects a rectangular portion of your image. You can now perform other commands on the selection.

● You can deselect a selection by clicking **Select** and then **Deselect**.

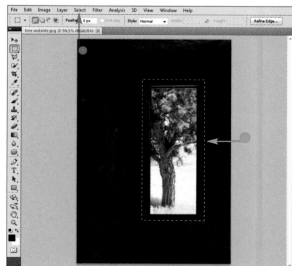

Using the Elliptical Marquee Tool

1. Click and hold the **Rectangular Marquee** tool (▦).

2. In the list that appears, click the **Elliptical Marquee** tool (○).

   ▷ changes to +.

3. Click and drag diagonally inside the image window.

   You can press and hold Shift while you click and drag to create a circular selection and then press Alt (Option on a Mac) to draw the circle directly out from the center.

● Photoshop selects an elliptical portion of your image.

   You can now perform other commands on the selection.

   You can deselect a selection by clicking **Select** and then **Deselect**.

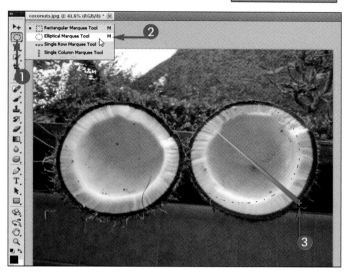

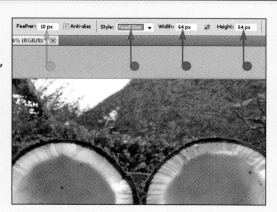

TIP

How do I customize the Marquee tools?
Use the text fields and menus on the Options bar.

● **Feather:** The Feather value softens your selection edge, which means that Photoshop partially selects pixels near the edge.

● **Style:** Define your Marquee tool as a fixed size or fixed aspect ratio.

● **Height and Width:** Add an exact width and height for a fixed-size selection or a ratio for a fixed-aspect-ratio selection by typing values in the Width and Height boxes. These boxes are editable when you select a fixed-size or fixed-aspect-ratio marquee.

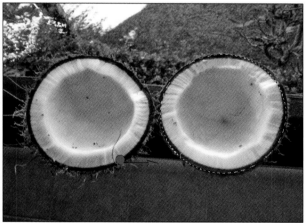

Select with the Lasso Tool

You can create oddly shaped selections with the Lasso tools. Then, you can move, delete, or stylize the selected area by using other Photoshop commands.

You can use the regular Lasso tool to create curved or jagged selections. With the Polygonal Lasso tool, you can easily create a selection composed of many straight lines.

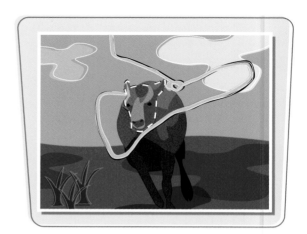

Using the Regular Lasso

1 Click the **Lasso** tool (⬭).

2 Click and drag your cursor (⬭) to make a selection.

● To accurately trace a complicated edge, you can magnify that part of the image with the Zoom tool (🔍).

Note: See Chapter 2 for more on the Zoom tool.

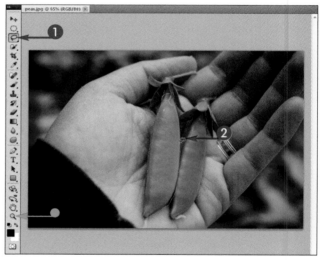

3 Drag to the beginning point and then release the mouse button.

The selection is complete.

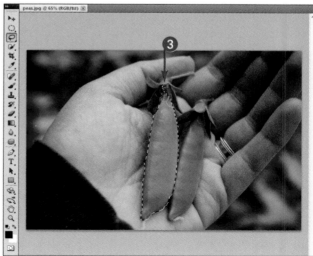

Using the Polygonal Lasso

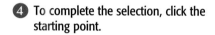

① Click and hold the **Lasso** tool (☺).

② Click the **Polygonal Lasso** tool (♡) in the list that appears.

   ☹ changes to ♡.

③ Click multiple times along the border of the area you want to select.

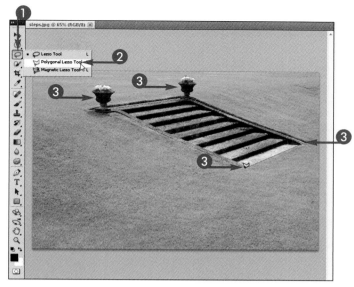

④ To complete the selection, click the starting point.

   You can also double-click anywhere in the image and Photoshop adds a final straight line connected to the starting point.

   The selection is complete.

   You can achieve a polygonal effect with the regular Lasso tool by pressing **Alt** (**Option** on a Mac) and then clicking to make your selection.

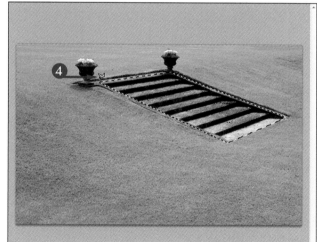

 TIP

What if my lasso selection is not as precise as I want it to be?
Selecting complicated outlines with ☺ can be difficult, even for the steadiest of hands. To fix an imprecise Lasso selection, you can:

● Deselect the selection by clicking **Select** and then **Deselect** and then trying again.

● Try to fix your selection. See the section "Add to or Subtract from a Selection."

● Switch to the Magnetic Lasso tool (♡). See the section "Select with the Magnetic Lasso Tool."

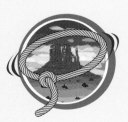

Select with the Magnetic Lasso Tool

You can select elements of your image that have well-defined edges quickly and easily with the Magnetic Lasso tool.

The Magnetic Lasso works best when the element you try to select contrasts sharply with the surrounding content.

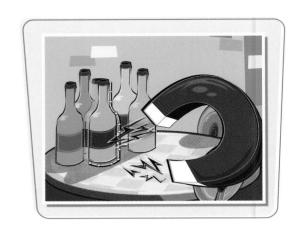

Select with the Magnetic Lasso Tool

1 Click and hold the **Lasso** tool ⬡.

2 Click the **Magnetic Lasso** tool (⬡) in the list that appears.

▷ changes to ⬡.

3 Click the edge of the object you want to select.

This creates a beginning anchor point, which is a fixed point on the lasso path.

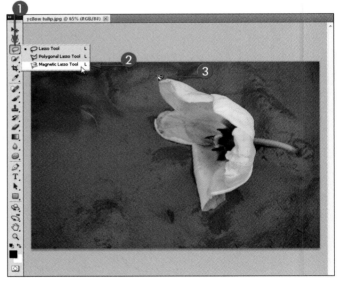

4 Drag your cursor (⬡) along the edge of the object.

The Magnetic Lasso's path snaps to the edge of the element as you drag.

● To help guide the lasso, you can click to add anchor points as you go along the path.

You can press Delete to remove the most recently added anchor point. This allows you to restructure a lasso path that is incorrect.

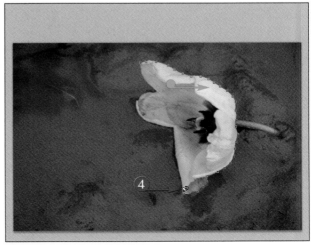

⑤ Click the beginning anchor point to finish your selection.

Alternatively, you can double-click anywhere in the image and Photoshop completes the selection for you.

The path is complete.

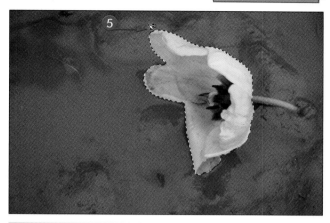

This example shows that the Magnetic Lasso is less useful for selecting areas where you find little contrast between the image and its background.

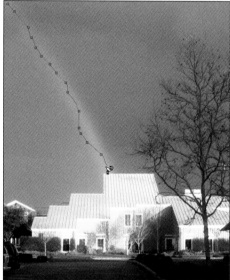

TIP

How can I adjust the precision of the Magnetic Lasso tool?
You can use the Options bar to adjust the Magnetic Lasso tool's precision:

● **Width:** The number of nearby pixels the lasso considers when creating a selection. If you magnify the edge you are selecting, you can typically decrease the width.

● **Contrast:** How much contrast is required for the lasso to consider something an edge. You can decrease the edge contrast to select fuzzier edges.

● **Frequency:** The frequency of the anchor points. You can increase the frequency for better precision when selecting poorly defined edges.

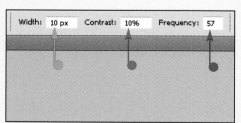

Select with the Quick Selection Tool

You can paint selections onto your images by using the Quick Selection tool. This tool offers a quick way to select objects that have solid colors and well-defined edges.

You can adjust the brush size of the tool to fine-tune your selections.

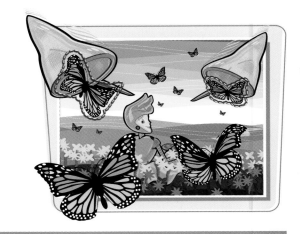

① Click the **Quick Selection** tool (![icon]).

② Click here (⊡) to open the tool's Brush menu.

The Brush menu opens.

In the Brush menu, you can specify the tool's size and other characteristics. Decreasing the tool's hardness causes it to partially select pixels at the perimeter.

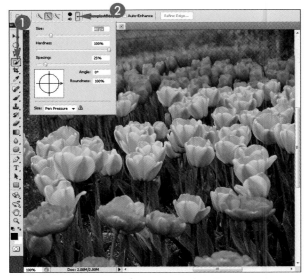

③ Click and drag inside the object you want to select.

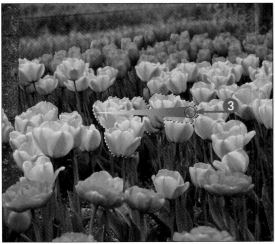

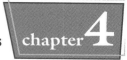

- Photoshop selects parts of the object based on its coloring and the contrast of its edges.

- After you make a selection, the Add to Selection button (⬚) becomes active.

④ Click and drag to select more of the object.

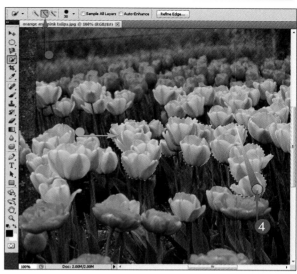

- Photoshop adds to the selection.

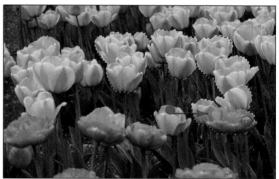

TIP

How can I adjust the selection made with the Quick Selection tool?

① On the Options bar, click **Refine Edge**.

The Refine Edge dialog box opens, and Photoshop turns the unselected part of your image white.

- You can increase Contrast to heighten the sharpness of the selection edges.

- You can increase Feather to make the edges of your selection partially transparent.

- You can use Shift Edge to move the selection in or out slightly.

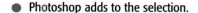
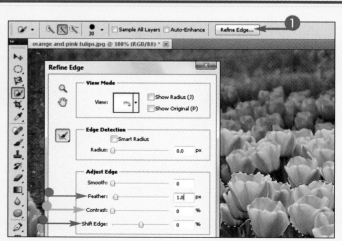

Select with the Magic Wand Tool

You can select groups of similarly colored pixels with the Magic Wand tool. You may find this useful if you want to remove an object from a background.

You can control how precisely the tool makes the selection by choosing a Tolerance value from 0 to 255.

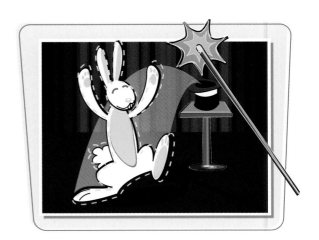

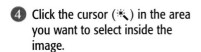

① Click and hold the **Quick Selection** tool (![]).

② Click the **Magic Wand** tool (![]).

   ⬚ changes to ✳.

③ Type a number from 0 to 255 in the Tolerance field.

   To select a narrow range of colors, type a small number; to select a wide range of colors, type a large number.

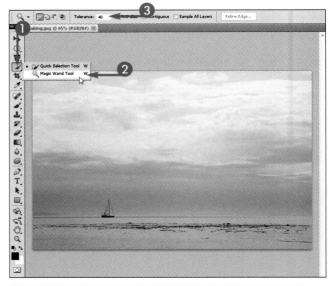

④ Click the cursor (✳) in the area you want to select inside the image.

   Photoshop selects the pixel you clicked plus any similarly colored pixels near it.

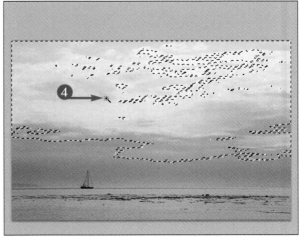

⑤ To add to your selection, press
Shift and then click elsewhere in
the image.

● You can also click the **Add to
Selection** button (□) on the
Options bar.

Photoshop adds to your selection.

● You can click the **Subtract from
Selection** button (□) to
configure the Magic Wand to
remove selected pixels.

Note: *For more, see the section "Add to or
Subtract from a Selection."*

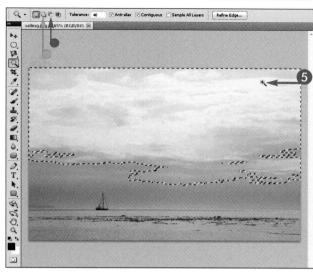

⑥ To delete the selected pixels, press
Delete.

● Photoshop replaces the pixels with
the background color or makes
them transparent if you made the
selection in a layer.

In this example, Photoshop
replaces the pixels with white,
the background color.

Note: *For more on layers, see Chapter 8.*

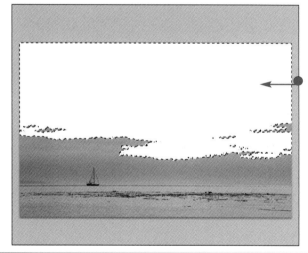

**How can I ensure that the Magic Wand tool selects all the
occurrences of a color in an image?**

You can deselect the **Contiguous** check box (☑ changes to □) on the
Options bar so the Magic Wand tool selects similar colors, even when they are
not contiguous with the pixel you click with the tool. This can be useful when
objects intersect the solid-color areas of your image. You can also click the
Sample All Layers check box (□ changes to ☑) to select similar colors in
all layers in the image, not just the currently selected layer.

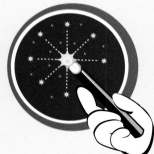

Select with the Color Range Command

You can select a set range of colors within an image with the Color Range command. With this command, you can quickly select a region of relatively solid color, such as a sky or a wall.

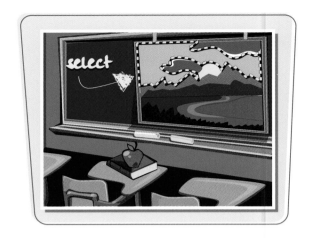

① Click **Select**.

② Click **Color Range**.

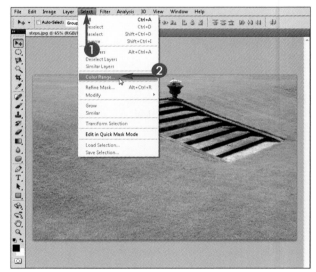

The Color Range dialog box opens.

⌀ changes to ⌀.

③ Click inside the image window.

● Photoshop selects all the pixels in the image that are similar to the pixel you clicked. These areas turn white in the Color Range window.

● The number of pixels that turn white depends on the Fuzziness setting.

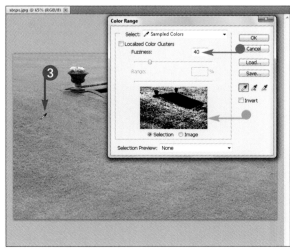

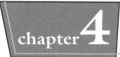

④ To increase the range of color, click and drag the **Fuzziness** slider (◻) to the right.

You can decrease the color range by dragging to the left.

● You can broaden the selected area by clicking the **Add Eyedropper** icon (🖋) and then clicking other parts of the image.

⑤ Click **OK**.

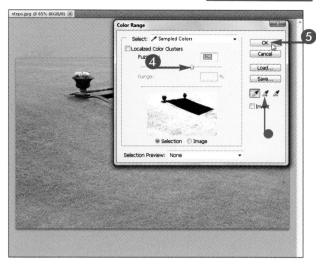

Photoshop makes the selection in the main image window.

Note: Sometimes, the Color Range command selects unwanted areas of the image. To eliminate these areas, see the section "Add to or Subtract from a Selection."

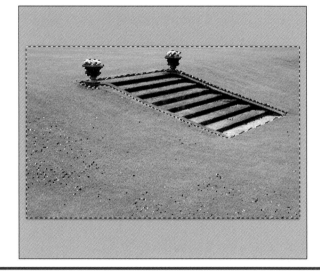

TIP

How do I limit the area of the image that the Color Range command affects?
Select an area of the image — by using the Marquee, Lasso, or another tool — before clicking **Select** and then **Color Range**.

Select All the Pixels in an Image

You can select all the pixels in a single-layer image by using the Select All command. With the entire image window selected, you can easily delete the image or copy and paste it into another window.

For multilayer images, Select All selects all the pixels in the currently selected layer.

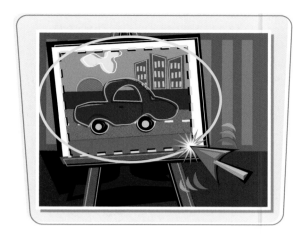

Select All the Pixels in an Image

① Click **Select**.

② Click **All**.

You can also press Ctrl + A (⌘ + A on a Mac) to select all the pixels.

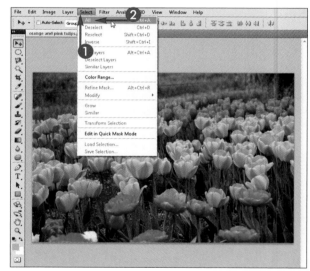

● Photoshop selects the entire image window.

You can delete the currently selected pixels by pressing Delete.

To copy your image, press Ctrl + C (⌘ + C on a Mac).

To paste your image, press Ctrl + V (⌘ + V on a Mac).

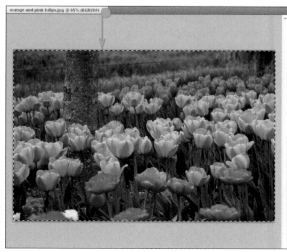

Move a Selection Border

You can move a selection border if your original selection is not in the intended place.

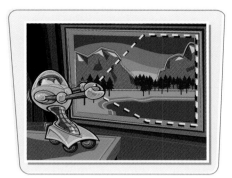

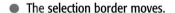

Move a Selection Border

1 Make a selection by using one of Photoshop's selection tools ([⬚], [⌀], or [⬚]).

● Make sure the New Selection button ([⬚]) is highlighted.

2 Click and drag inside the selection.

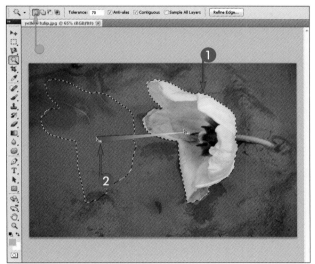

● The selection border moves.

To move your selection one pixel at a time, you can use the arrow keys on your keyboard.

You can hide a selection by clicking **View**, **Show**, and then **Selection Edges**.

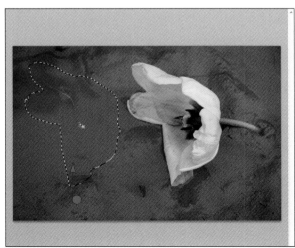

Add to or Subtract from a Selection

You can add to or subtract from your selection by using various selection tools.

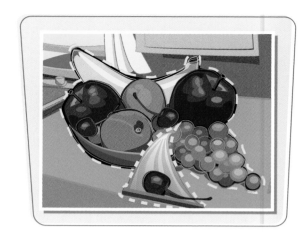

Add to a Selection

1 Make a selection by using one of Photoshop's selection tools (▣, ◯, or ▨).

2 Click a selection tool.

This example uses the Magnetic Lasso tool (▣).

Note: See the previous sections in this chapter to select the appropriate tool for your image.

3 Click the **Add to Selection** button (▣).

4 Select the area you want to add.

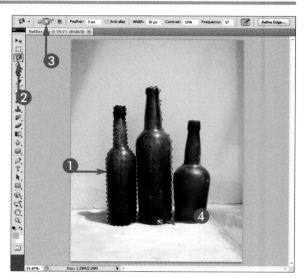

5 Complete the selection.

● Photoshop adds to the selection.

You can enlarge the selection further by repeating steps **2** to **5**.

You can also add to a selection by pressing Shift as you make your selection.

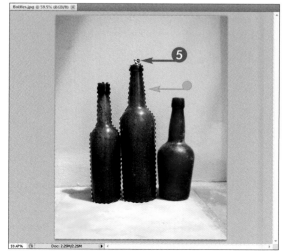

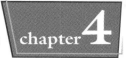

Subtract from a Selection

1 Make a selection by using one of Photoshop's selection tools.

2 Click a selection tool.

This example uses the Rectangular Marquee tool (▣).

3 Click the **Subtract from Selection** button (▣).

4 Select the area you want to subtract.

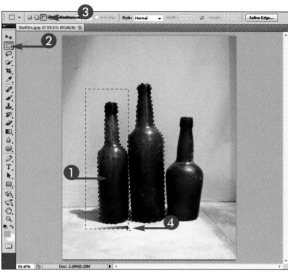

● Photoshop deselects, or subtracts, the selected area.

You can subtract other parts of the selection by repeating steps **2** to **4**.

You can also subtract from a selection by pressing and holding Alt (Option on a Mac) as you make your selection.

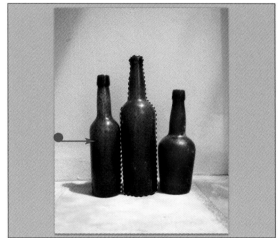

TIPS

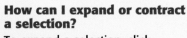

How do I add to or subtract from a selection by using the Quick Selection tool?

The Quick Selection tool features different option buttons for adding to or subtracting from a selection. On the Options bar, you can click ▨ to add to a selection and ▨ to subtract from a selection.

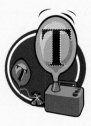

How can I expand or contract a selection?

To expand a selection, click **Select**, **Modify**, and then **Expand**. A dialog box opens, enabling you to specify the amount of expansion in pixels. To contract a selection, click **Select**, **Modify**, and then **Contract**. A dialog box opens, enabling you to specify the amount of contraction in pixels.

Invert a Selection

You can invert a selection to deselect what is currently selected and select everything else. This is useful when you want to select the background around an object.

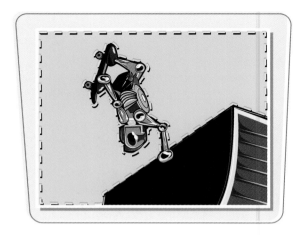

Invert a Selection

1 Make a selection by using one of Photoshop's selection tools (▭, ◯, or ▨).

Note: *For more on the various selection tools, see the previous sections in this chapter.*

2 Click **Select**.

3 Click **Inverse**.

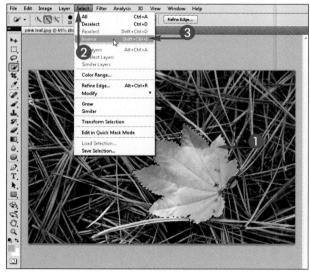

Photoshop inverts the selection.

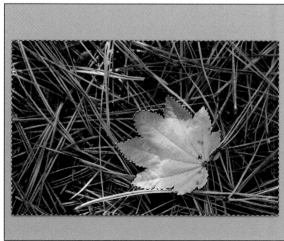

Grow a Selection

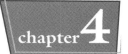

You can increase the size of your selection by using the Grow command, which is useful when you want to include similarly colored, neighboring pixels.

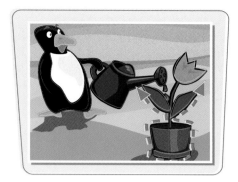

Grow a Selection

1 Make a selection by using one of Photoshop's selection tools (▢, ⬭, or ▨).

Note: *For more on the various selection tools, see the previous sections in this chapter.*

2 Click **Select**.

3 Click **Grow**.

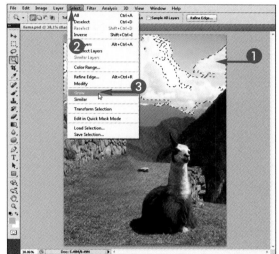

● The selection grows to include similarly colored pixels contiguous with the current selection.

● To also include noncontiguous pixels, you can click **Select** and then **Similar**.

● You can change the number of similarly colored pixels the Grow command selects by changing the Tolerance setting.

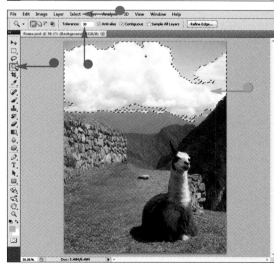

Create Slices

You can divide a large image that you want to display on the Web into smaller rectangular sections called *slices*. The different slices of an image can then be optimized independently of one another for faster download. See Chapter 14 for more.

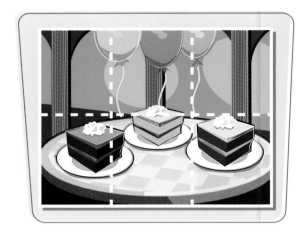

① Click and hold the **Crop** tool (🔲).

② Click the **Slice** tool (🔗) in the list that appears.

  ▷ changes to ✄.

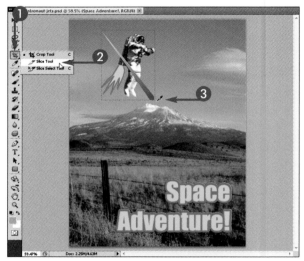

③ Click and drag inside the image to create a slice.

● Photoshop creates a slice where you clicked and dragged.

*Note: Slices you define are called **user slices**.*

  Photoshop fills in the rest of the image with auto slices.

Note: User slices remain fixed when you add more slices to your image, whereas auto slices can change size.

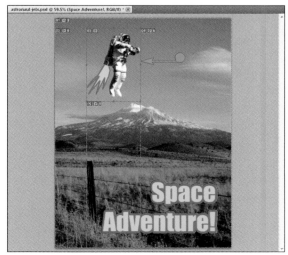

④ Click and drag to define another slice in your image.

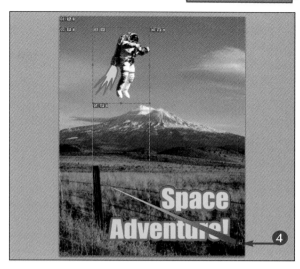

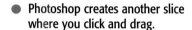

● Photoshop creates another slice where you click and drag.

Photoshop creates or rearranges auto slices to fill in the rest of the image.

Note: For more on how to save the different slices for the Web, see Chapter 14.

Note: To save a sliced image so you can edit the slices later, save the image in the Photoshop format. See Chapter 14 for more.

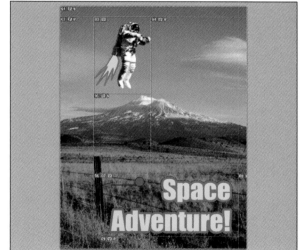

How do I resize or delete slices in my image?
First, click the **Slice Select** tool (⬚), which is accessible by clicking and holding the Slice tool (⬚). To resize a user slice, click inside it and then click and drag a border handle (□). To delete a user slice, click inside it and then press Delete. When you resize or delete slices, Photoshop automatically resizes, creates, and deletes auto slices in the image to account for the change.

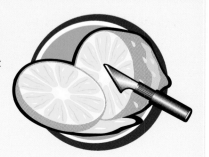

Manipulating Selections

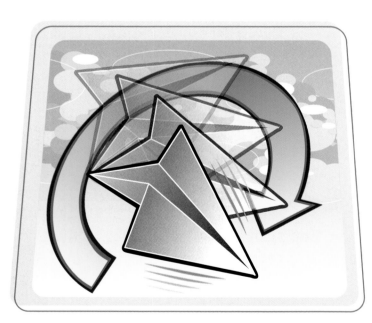

Making a selection defines a specific area of your Photoshop image. This chapter shows you how to move, stretch, erase, and manipulate your selections in a variety of ways.

Move a Selection

You can move a selection by using the Move tool, which enables you to rearrange elements of your image.

You can place elements of your image either in the background or in layers. For more on layers, see Chapter 8.

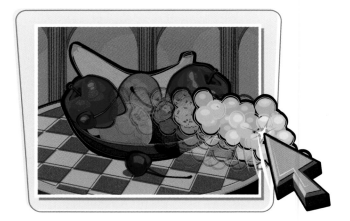

Move a Selection

Move a Selected Object in the Background

1 Click the Background layer in the Layers panel.

If you start with a newly scanned image, Photoshop makes the Background layer the only layer.

2 Make a selection with a selection tool.

Note: See Chapter 4 for more on the selection tools. See Chapter 8 for more on layers.

3 Click the **Move** tool (![icon]).

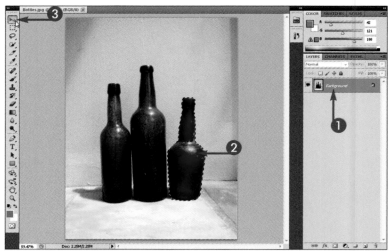

4 Click inside the selection and drag.

● Photoshop fills the original location of the object with the current background color.

● In this example, white is the background color.

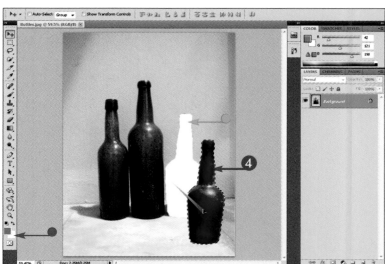

Move a Selected Object in a Layer

① Click a non-Background layer in the Layers panel.

② Make a selection with a selection tool.

Note: See Chapter 4 for more on the selection tools. See Chapter 8 for more on layers.

③ Click the **Move** tool .

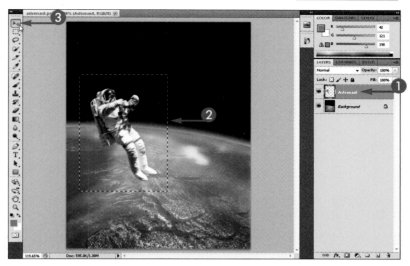

④ Click inside the selection and drag.

Photoshop moves the selection in the layer.

Photoshop fills the original location of the object with transparent pixels.

Note: Unlike the Background — Photoshop's opaque default layer — layers can include transparent pixels.

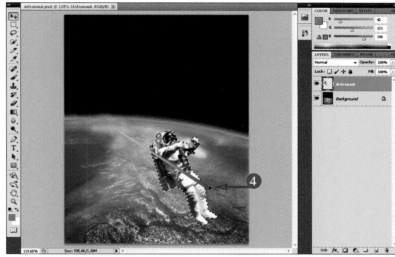

TIPS

How do I move a selection in a straight line?

Press and hold Shift while you drag with the Move tool (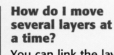). Doing so constrains the movement of your object horizontally, vertically, or diagonally — depending on the direction you drag. You can also use the arrow keys to move a layer horizontally or vertically.

How do I move several layers at a time?

You can link the layers you want to move, select one of the linked layers, and then move them all with the Move tool (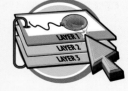). You can also Ctrl + click (⌘ + click on a Mac) to select multiple layers and then move them with the Move tool. For more, see Chapter 8.

Copy and Paste a Selection

You can copy a selection and then make a duplicate of it somewhere else in the image.

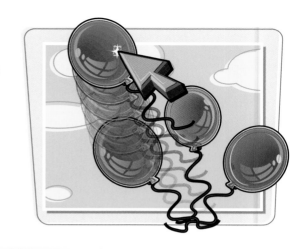

Copy and Paste a Selection

Using the Keyboard and Mouse

① Make a selection with a selection tool.

Note: *See Chapter 4 for more on the selection tools.*

② Click the **Move** tool ⊞.

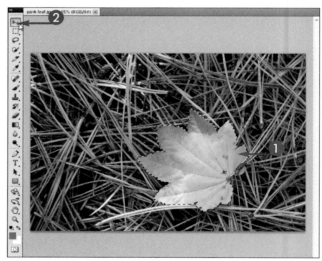

③ Press Alt (Option on a Mac) while you click and drag the object.

④ Release the mouse button to drop the selection.

Photoshop creates a duplicate of the object, which appears in the new location. The duplicate remains in the same layer as the original object.

Note: *See Chapter 8 for more on layers.*

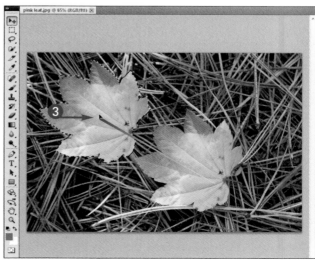

Using the Copy and Paste Commands

1. Make a selection with a selection tool.

Note: *See Chapter 4 for more on the selection tools.*

2. Click **Edit**.

3. Click **Copy**.

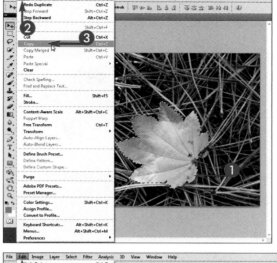

4. Using a selection tool, select where you want to paste the copied element.

If you do not select an area, Photoshop pastes the copy over the original.

5. Click **Edit**.

6. Click **Paste**.

● Photoshop pastes the copy into a new layer, which you can now move independently of the original image.

Note: *See the section "Move a Selection" for more on moving your image.*

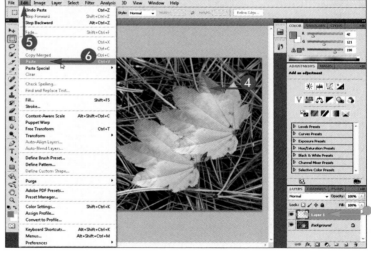

TIPS

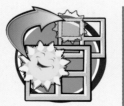

How can I copy a selection from one window to another?

Click the **Move** tool [+] and then click and drag your selection from one window to another. You can also copy selections between windows by using the Copy and Paste commands in the Edit menu. To make multiple windows visible at the same time, see Chapter 2.

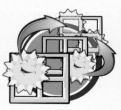

How can I copy content from multiple layers at once?

If your selection overlaps several layers in your image, you can click **Edit** and then **Copy Merged** to combine all the content into a single layer. Using the regular Copy command copies only from the selected layer. For more on layers, see Chapter 8.

Delete a Selection

You can delete a selection to remove an element from your image.

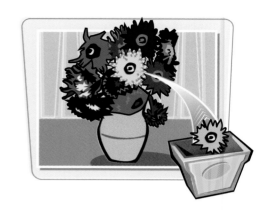

Delete a Selection

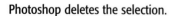

1 Make a selection with a selection tool.

Note: See Chapter 4 for more on the selection tools.

2 Press `Delete`.

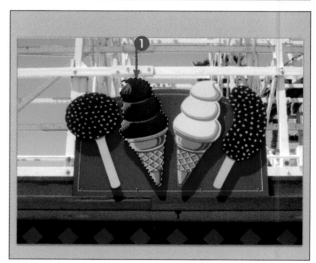

Photoshop deletes the selection.

If you are working in the Background layer, the empty area fills with the background color — in this example, white, the default background color.

If you are working in a layer other than the Background layer, deleting an object turns the selected pixels transparent.

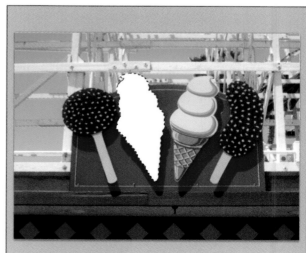

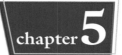

Rotate a Selection

You can rotate a selection to tilt the selected pixels or to turn them upside down in your image.

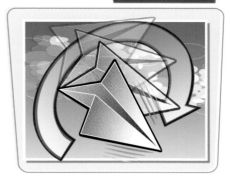

Rotate a Selection

① Make a selection with a selection tool.

Note: See Chapter 4 for more on the selection tools.

② Click **Edit**.

③ Click **Transform**.

④ Click **Rotate**.

A *bounding box*, a rectangular box with handles (□) on the sides and corners, surrounds the object.

⑤ Click and drag to the side of the object.

The object rotates.

Note: You can rotate your selection precisely by typing percentage values in the W and H fields on the Options bar.

⑥ To apply the rotation, click ✓ or press Enter (⌘ + Return on a Mac).

● To cancel, you can click ⊘ or press Esc.

● In this example, a layer containing an astronaut is rotated.

Note: See Chapter 8 for more on layers.

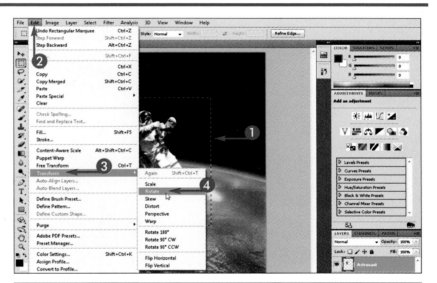

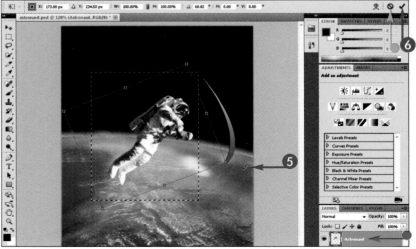

Scale a Selection

You can scale a selection to make the selected area larger or smaller. By scaling, you can emphasize parts of your image.

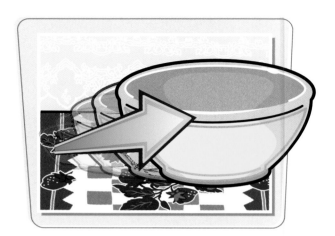

Scale a Selection

1 Make a selection with a selection tool.

Note: See Chapter 4 for more on the selection tools.

2 Click **Edit**.

3 Click **Transform**.

4 Click **Scale**.

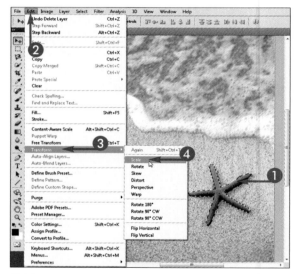

A rectangular bounding box with handles (□) on the sides and corners surrounds the object.

5 Click and drag a corner handle (□) to scale both the horizontal and vertical axes.

Note: You can scale your selection precisely by typing percentage values in the W and H fields on the Options bar.

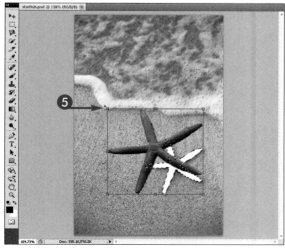

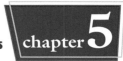

6 Click and drag a side handle (□) to scale one axis at a time.

7 To apply the scaling, click ✓ or press Enter (⌘ + Return on a Mac).

● To cancel, you can click ⊘ or press Esc.

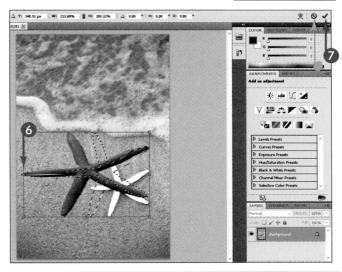

Photoshop scales the object to the new dimensions.

● In this example, an object in the Background layer is scaled.

Note: See Chapter 8 for more on layers.

● The area behind the object is filled with the background color.

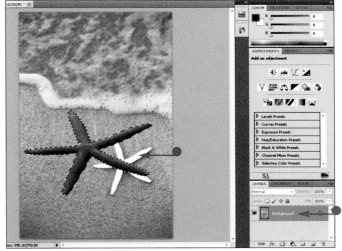

TIPS

How do I scale both dimensions proportionally?

You can press and hold Shift or click the **Maintain Aspect Ratio** icon (⌘) on the Options bar. When you scale your selection, the two axes of your selection grow or shrink proportionally; Photoshop does not distort your image.

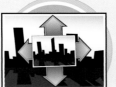

How can I precisely double the size of my selection?

When scaling your selection, type **200%** in the W (width) and H (height) boxes on the Options bar. These boxes enable you to scale your selection to an exact percentage of its original size.

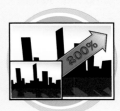

Skew or Distort a Selection

You can transform a selection by using the Skew or Distort command. This enables you to stretch a selected area in your image into interesting shapes.

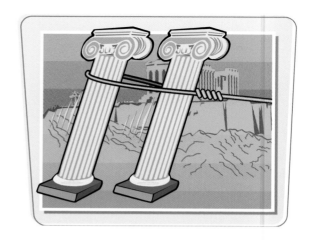

Skew or Distort a Selection

Skew a Selection

① Make a selection with a selection tool.

Note: *See Chapter 4 for more on the selection tools.*

② Click **Edit**.

③ Click **Transform**.

④ Click **Skew**.

● A rectangular bounding box with handles (□) on the sides and corners surrounds the object.

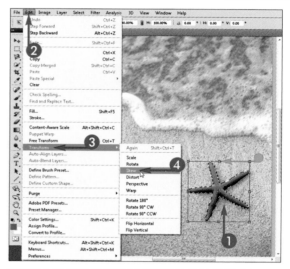

⑤ Click and drag a handle (□) to skew the object.

Because the Skew command works along a single axis, you can drag either horizontally or vertically.

Note: *You can skew your selection precisely by typing percentage values in the W and H fields on the Options bar.*

⑥ To apply the skewing, click ✓ or press Enter (⌘ + Return on a Mac).

● To cancel, you can click ⊘ or press Esc.

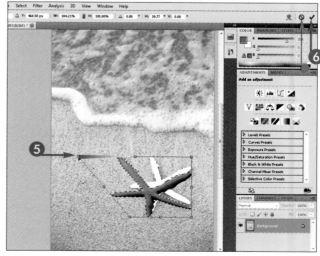

Distort a Selection

① Make a selection with a selection tool.

Note: See Chapter 4 for more on the selection tools.

② Click **Edit**.

③ Click **Transform**.

④ Click **Distort**.

● A rectangular bounding box with handles (☐) on the sides and corners surrounds the object.

⑤ Click and drag a handle (☐) to distort the object.

The Distort command works independently of the selection's different axes; you can drag a handle both vertically and horizontally.

Note: You can distort your selection precisely by typing percentage values in the W and H fields on the Options bar.

⑥ To apply the distortion, click ✓ or press Enter (⌘ + Return on a Mac).

● To cancel, you can click ⊘ or press Esc.

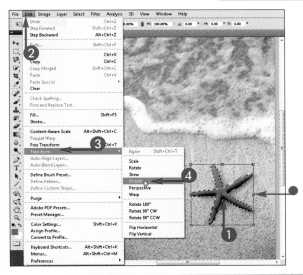

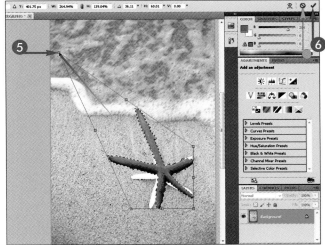

TIPS

How can I undo my skewing or distortion?

You can click **Edit** and then **Undo** to undo the last handle adjustment you made. This is an alternative to clicking ⊘, which cancels the entire Skew or Distort command.

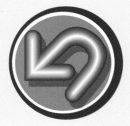

How can I flip my image horizontally or vertically?

You can click **Edit**, **Transform**, and then **Flip Horizontal** or **Flip Vertical**. The Flip Horizontal command makes a selection look like its mirror image.

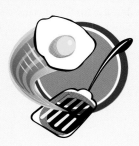

Perform Content-Aware Scaling

You can use Photoshop's content-aware scaling feature to intelligently change the dimensions of an image. Important foreground objects stay the same size, but the less important background shrinks or enlarges.

This feature works best with landscape and beach photos, where important objects stand out clearly from the rest of the scene. It works less well on more complicated images.

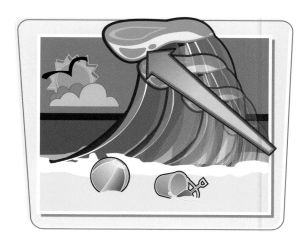

Perform Content-Aware Scaling

1 Click a layer to scale in the Layers panel.

Note: See Chapter 8 for more on layers.

2 Click **Select**.

3 Click **All**.

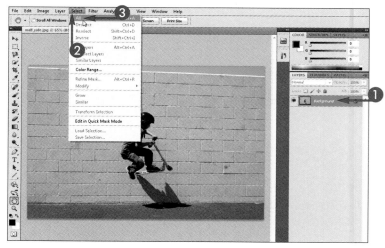

Photoshop selects all the pixels in your image.

4 Click **Edit**.

5 Click **Content-Aware Scale**.

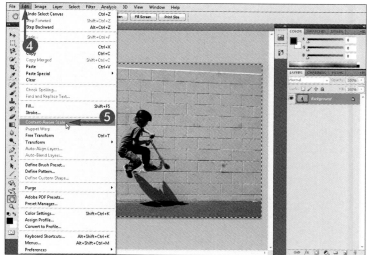

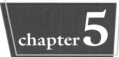

Handles (□) appear on the edges of the selection.

6 Click and drag the handles (□) to shrink or enlarge the image.

In this example, the child against the wall remains unchanged, but the wall scales smaller.

7 To apply the scaling, click ✓ or press Enter (⌘ + Return on a Mac).

● To cancel, you can click ⊘ or press Esc.

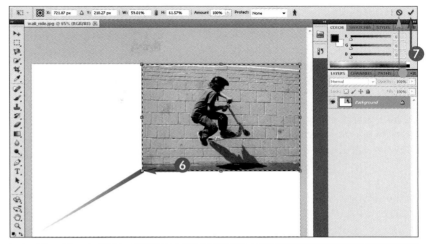

This shows the same example with the regular scale command applied. All the content in the image changes size equally.

Note: See the section "Scale a Selection" for more.

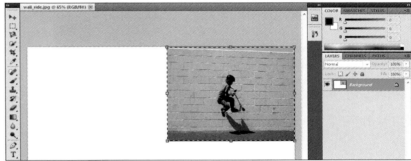

TIP

How can I improve content-aware scaling of images with people in them?

You can use the Protect Skin Tones setting to have Photoshop recognize objects with skin tones and selectively protect those objects.

1 Follow steps 1 to 4 in this section to access content-aware scaling.

2 Click the **Protect Skin Tones** icon (🧍).

3 Click and drag the handles (□) to scale the image.

If objects in the image have skin color, Photoshop protects them as you scale.

In this example, the jumping child is protected, but the rock, water, and other background content scales.

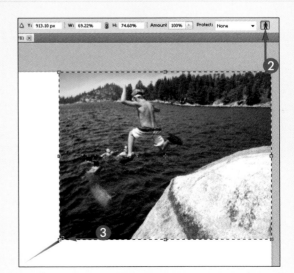

Refine a Selection Edge

You can open the Refine Edge dialog box to make a variety of adjustments to the edge of your selection. For example, you can shift the edge in or out or smooth any sharp angles along an edge.

For more on feathering an edge by using the Refine Edge dialog box, see the section "Feather the Border of a Selection."

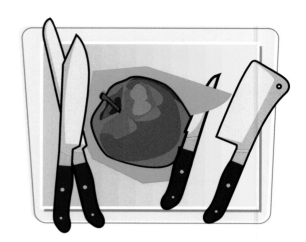

Refine a Selection Edge

① Make a selection with a selection tool.

Note: *See Chapter 4 for more on the selection tools.*

When a selection tool is active, Photoshop displays a Refine Edge button.

② Click **Refine Edge**.

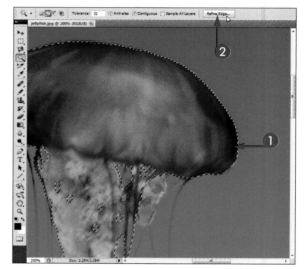

The Refine Edge dialog box opens.

Photoshop displays the selected element to make the selection more apparent.

③ Click and drag the **Radius** slider (🔲) to the right to expand the area considered for automatic selection.

Photoshop examines the color transitions near the edge and adjusts the selection to account for them.

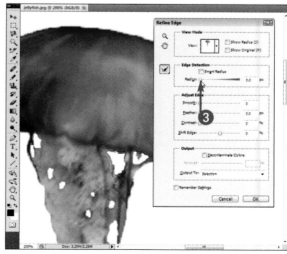

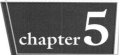

4 Click and drag the **Smooth** slider (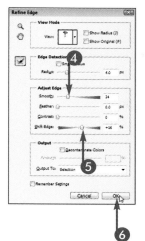) to the right to smooth sharp angles along the edge.

Smoothing can be useful after selecting with the Polygonal Lasso, which can create a selection with sharp points.

5 Click and drag the **Shift Edge** slider (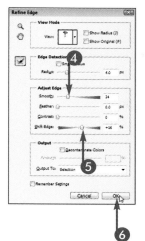) to move the edge in or out from the selected object.

Drag to the left to move the edge in.

Drag to the right to move the edge out.

6 Click **OK**.

Photoshop adjusts the selection.

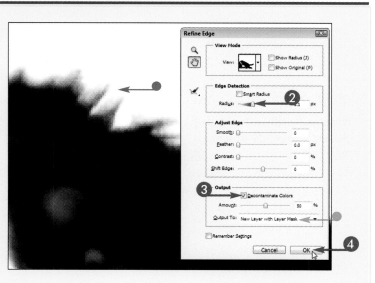

TIP

How do I improve selections along hair and other complex elements?

1 Complete steps **1** and **2** in this section to make a selection and then open the Refine Edge dialog box.

2 Click and drag the **Radius** slider (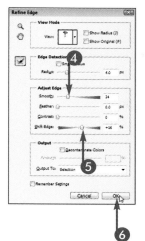) to the right to expand the area considered by the selection tool.

3 Click the **Decontaminate Colors** check box (☐ changes to ☑).

● By default, Photoshop puts the selected content in a new layer.

4 Click **OK**.

● Photoshop adjusts the edge.

Feather the Border of a Selection

You can feather a selection's border to create soft edges around an object in your image.

To soften edges, select an object, feather the selection border, and then delete the part of the image that surrounds your selection.

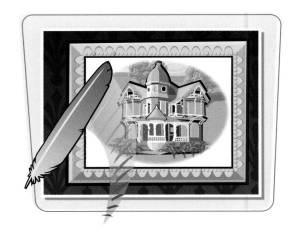

Feather the Border of a Selection

Select and Feather the Image

1. Make a selection with a selection tool.

Note: See Chapter 4 for more on the selection tools.

When a selection tool is active, Photoshop displays a Refine Edge button.

2. Click **Refine Edge**.

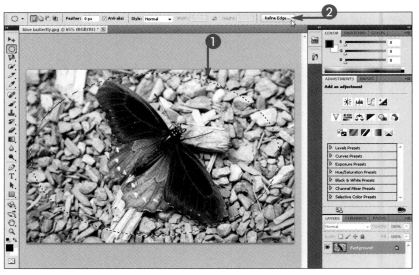

The Refine Edge dialog box opens.

3. Type a pixel value between 0.1 and 250 in the Feather text field to determine the softness of the edge.

The larger the number, the thicker the softened edge.

4. Click **OK**.

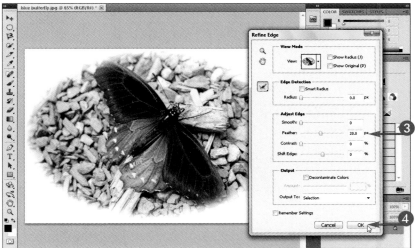

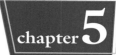

Delete the Surrounding Background

⑤ Click **Select**.

⑥ Click **Inverse**.

The selection inverts but remains feathered.

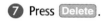

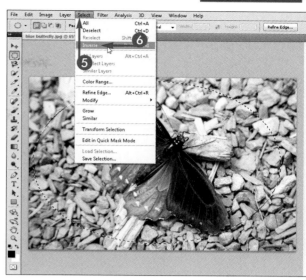

⑦ Press Delete.

Photoshop applies the feathering to the image.

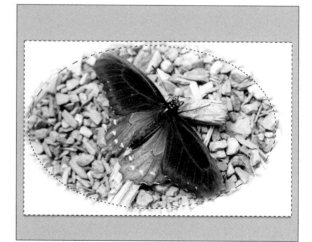

TIPS

What happens if I feather a selection and then apply a command to it?

Photoshop applies the command only partially to pixels near the edge of the selection. For example, if you remove color from a selection by using the Hue/Saturation command, color at the feathered edge of the selection is only partially removed. For more on the Hue/Saturation command, see Chapter 7.

Is there another way to feather my selection?

When selecting with the Marquee or Lasso tool, you can create a feathered selection by first typing a pixel value greater than 0 in the Feather text field on the Options bar. Your resulting selection will have a feathered edge.

Create Vanishing Point Planes

You can model the 3-D characteristics of flat objects in your image by creating planes with the Vanishing Point tool. This can be useful if you work with objects such as the sides of buildings, interior walls, or table surfaces.

After you create vanishing point planes, you can apply special Photoshop commands. See the section "Copy between Vanishing Point Planes" for more.

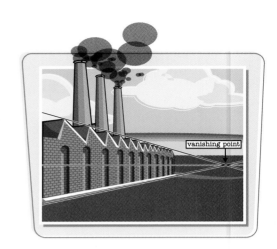

Create Vanishing Point Planes

1. Open an image that includes flat surfaces.

Note: See Chapter 1 for more on opening an image.

2. Click **Filter**.

3. Click **Vanishing Point**.

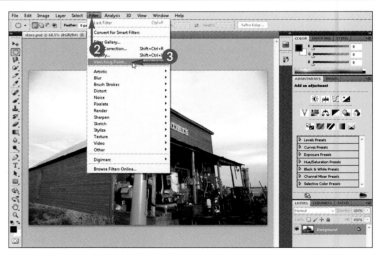

The Vanishing Point dialog box opens.

4. Click the **Create Plane** tool (⬚).

5. Click to mark a corner of a plane.

6. Click a second time to mark another corner.

Photoshop connects the points to create a plane edge.

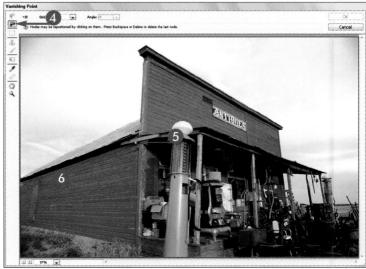

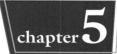

⑦ Click two more times to mark the final two corners of the plane.

Photoshop creates the vanishing point plane.

● You can use the Edit Plane tool () to move a plane or adjust its corners or sides.

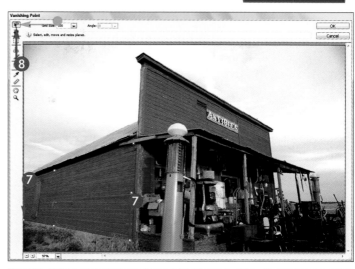

⑧ Click ⊞ again.

⑨ Click four more times to create another vanishing point plane.

Photoshop creates the vanishing point plane, which is oriented differently from the first.

To delete a plane, select it with ⊞ and then press **Delete**.

⑩ Click **OK**.

Photoshop saves your work and closes the dialog box.

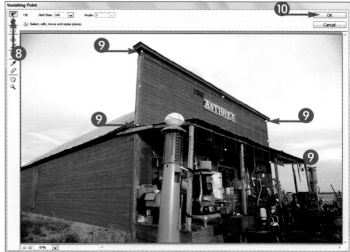

TIP

Why is it called the Vanishing Point tool?
In perspective drawing, the vanishing point is the point on the horizon where receding parallel lines appear to meet. Photoshop uses such parallel lines to represent the planes in the Vanishing Point dialog box.

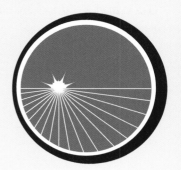

Copy between Vanishing Point Planes

You can copy an object between two vanishing point planes. Photoshop transforms the object as you move it so it conforms to the orientation of the current plane.

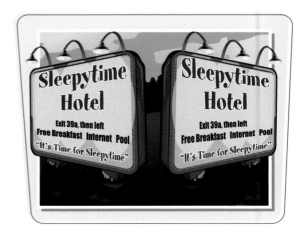

Copy between Vanishing Point Planes

1 Create vanishing point planes in your image.

Note: For more, see the section "Create Vanishing Point Planes."

2 Click **Filter**.

3 Click **Vanishing Point**.

The Vanishing Point dialog box opens, displaying the different planes.

4 Click the **Rectangular Marquee** tool (☐).

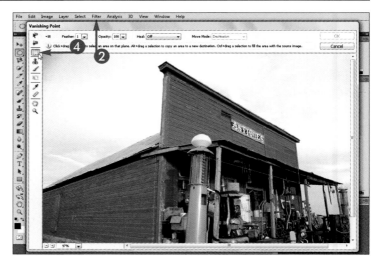

5 Click and drag to select an object inside a plane.

Photoshop draws a marquee whose sides are parallel to those of the plane.

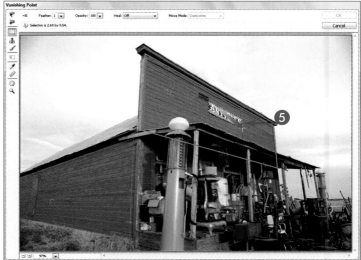

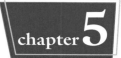

6 Press and hold Alt (Option on a Mac).

7 Click and drag the selection from one plane to another.

Photoshop transforms the selection to orient it with the destination plane.

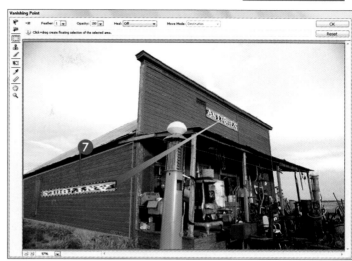

8 Click the **Transform** tool (⊞).

9 Click the **Flip** check box (☐ changes to ☑) to flip the selection horizontally.

10 Click the **Flop** check box (☐ changes to ☑) to flip the selection vertically.

11 Click **OK**.

Photoshop saves your work and closes the dialog box.

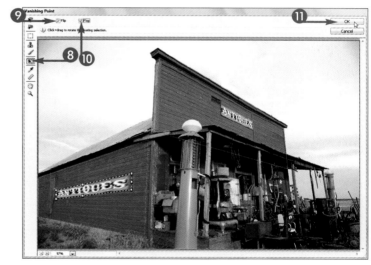

TIPS

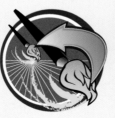

What does the Brush tool (✎) do in the Vanishing Point dialog box?

Like the normal Brush tool, it applies the foreground color to objects in your image. But in the Vanishing Point dialog box, the brush shape conforms to the plane in which you paint.
You can control the characteristics of the brush with the settings at the top of the dialog box.

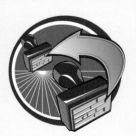

What does the Stamp tool (🖳) do in the Vanishing Point dialog box?

It enables you to clone content from one Vanishing Point plane to another. The cloned pixels conform to the shape of the current plane.

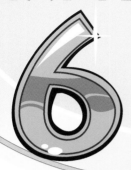
Painting and Drawing with Color

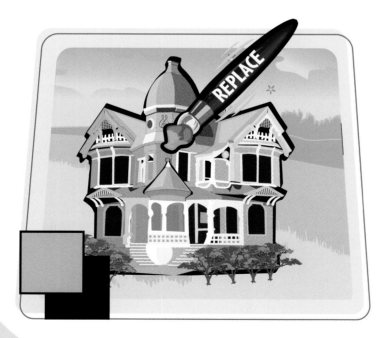

You can add splashes, streaks, or solid areas of color to your image. Photoshop offers a variety of tools with which you can add almost any color or texture imaginable. This chapter introduces you to those tools and shows you how to choose your colors.

Select the Foreground and Background Colors

You can select two colors to work with at a time in Photoshop: a foreground color and a background color. Painting tools, such as the Brush tool, apply the foreground color. You apply the background color when you use the Eraser tool on the Background layer, enlarge the image canvas, or cut pieces out of your image.

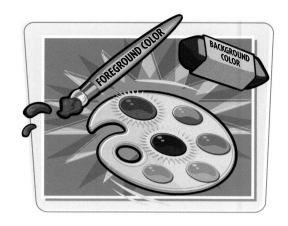

Select the Foreground and Background Colors

Select the Foreground Color

① Click the **Foreground Color** box.

The Color Picker dialog box opens.

● To change the range of colors that appears in the color box, click and drag the slider ( ).

② Click the color you want as the foreground color in the color box.

③ Click **OK**.

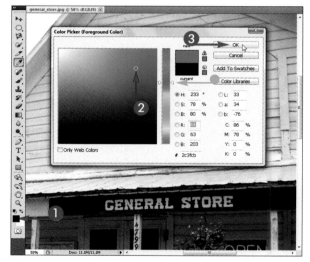

● The selected color appears in the **Foreground Color** box.

④ Click a painting tool in the Toolbox.

This example uses the Brush tool ( ).

Note: For more on painting tools, see the section "Using the Brush Tool."

⑤ Click and drag to apply the color.

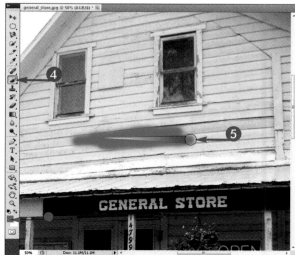

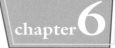

Select the Background Color

1 Click the **Background Color** box.

The Color Picker dialog box opens.

● To change the range of colors that appears in the color box, click and drag the slider (⊳▭◁).

2 To select a background color, click the color you want in the color box.

3 Click **OK**.

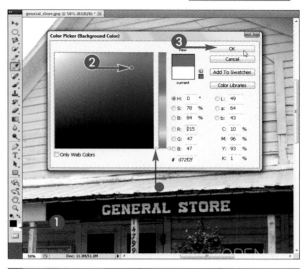

● The selected color appears in the **Background Color** box.

4 Click the **Eraser** tool (⬛).

5 Click and drag the cursor (○).

The tool erases by painting with the background color.

Note: *Painting occurs only when erasing in the Background layer; in other layers, the eraser turns pixels transparent. See Chapter 8 for a full discussion of layers.*

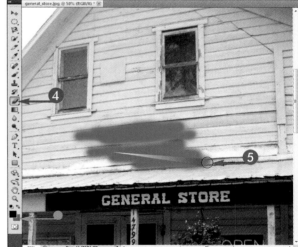

 TIPS

How do I reset the foreground and background colors?
Click the **Default** icon (⬛) to the lower left of the Foreground and Background icons. Doing so resets the colors to black and white.

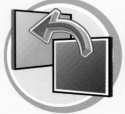

What is a Web-safe color?
Web browsers on some older monitors can display only colors from a specific 216-color palette. These colors are known as Web-safe colors. You can click the **Only Web Colors** check box in the Color Picker dialog box (☐ changes to ☑) to restrict your choices to Web-safe colors.

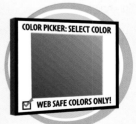

Select a Color with the Eyedropper Tool

You can select a color from an open image with the Eyedropper tool. The Eyedropper tool enables you to paint by using a color already present in your image.

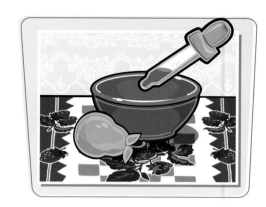

① Click the **Eyedropper** tool (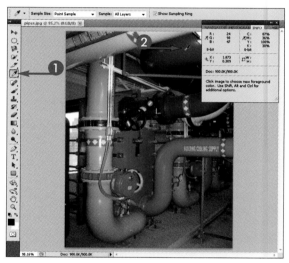).

② Position ✐ over your image.

You can click **Window** and then **Info** to open the Info panel to see color values as you move ✐.

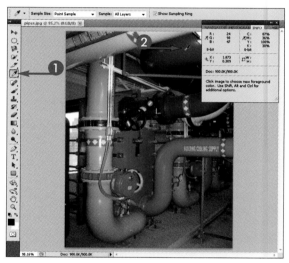

③ Click to select the color of the pixel beneath the tip of ✐.

● The color becomes the new foreground color.

To select a new background color, you can press Alt (Option on a Mac) as you click in step **3**.

You can temporarily employ the Eyedropper tool when using a painting tool, such as the Brush or Paint Bucket, by pressing and holding Alt (Option).

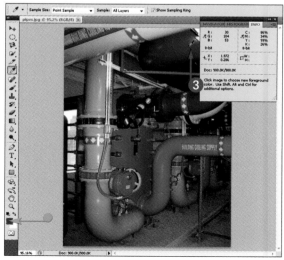

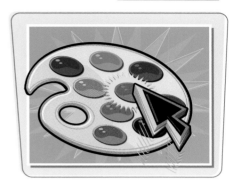

You can select a color with the Swatches panel. The Swatches panel lets you choose from a small set of commonly used colors.

Select a Color with the Swatches Panel

① Click **Window**.

② Click **Swatches**.

③ Position your cursor over a color swatch.

   ⌖ changes to ✐.

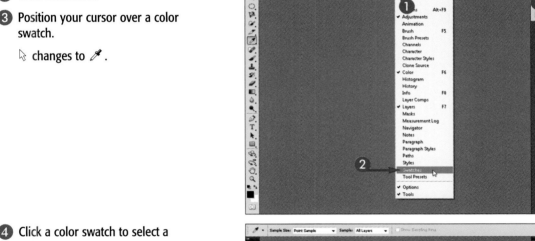

④ Click a color swatch to select a foreground color.

● The color becomes the new foreground color.

   To select a background color, press **Alt** (**Option** on a Mac) as you click in step **3**.

   You can use the Eyedropper tool (✐) to add the current foreground color to the Swatches panel. After selecting the tool, position it over the empty area of the panel and then click.

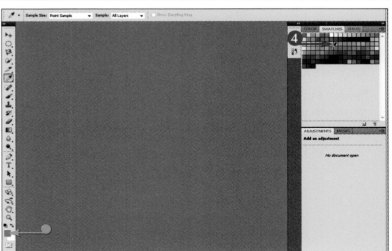

Using the Brush Tool

You can use the Brush tool to add color to your image. You may find the brush useful for applying bands of color.

To limit where the brush applies color, create a selection before painting. For more, see Chapter 4.

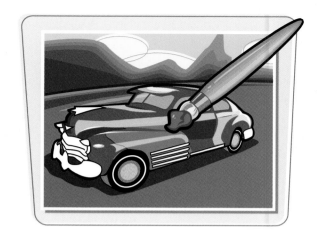

① Click the **Brush** tool (■).

② Click the **Foreground Color** box to select a color with which to paint.

Note: For more, see the section "Select the Foreground and Background Colors."

③ Click here (◻) to open the Brush menu to choose a brush size and type.

Note: To access different brush styles, see the section "Change Brush Styles."

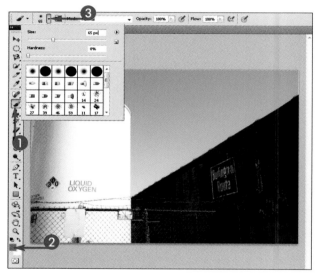

④ Click and drag to apply the foreground color to the image.

To undo the most recent brush stroke, you can click **Edit** and then **Undo Brush**.

Note: To undo more than one brush stroke, see Chapter 2 for more on the History panel.

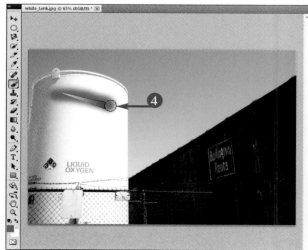

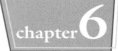

⑤ Type a percentage value to change the opacity of the brush strokes.

● Alternatively, you can click here (⬛) to adjust the Opacity slider.

⑥ Click and drag to apply the semitransparent paintbrush.

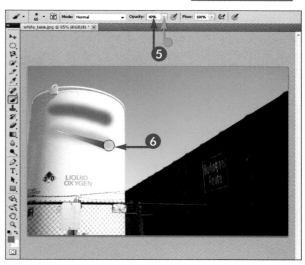

⑦ Type a percentage value to change how much color the brush applies.

● Alternatively, you can click here (⬛) to adjust the Flow slider.

⑧ Click and drag to apply the customized brush.

Photoshop applies color per your specifications.

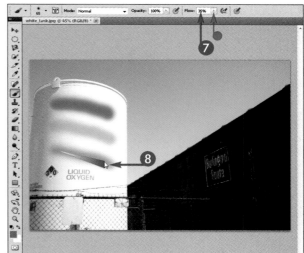

TIPS

What are the Pencil and Airbrush tools?

You can use the Pencil tool to draw hard-edged lines of color. To access the Pencil tool, click and hold the **Brush** tool (⬛) and then click ⬛. The Airbrush tool paints soft lines that get darker the longer you hold down your mouse button. You can convert your brush to an airbrush by clicking the **Airbrush** button (⬛) on the Options bar.

What is a virtual slider?

You can adjust certain slider-based settings, such as the Opacity and Fill settings in the Layers panel, by positioning the cursor over the setting's label and clicking and dragging. For example, you can hover over **Opacity** and then click and drag to the left or right to decrease or increase the currently selected layer's opacity.

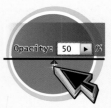

Change Brush Styles

You can select from a variety of brush styles to apply color in different ways. The types of brushes available include calligraphic brushes, texture brushes, and brushes that enable you to add drop shadows to objects.

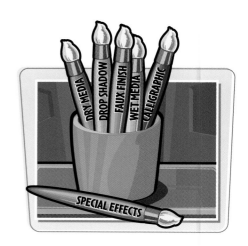

1 Click the **Brush** tool (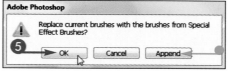).

2 Click here (⊟) to open the Brush menu.

3 Click ▶.

The Brush menu opens.

4 Click a set of brushes.

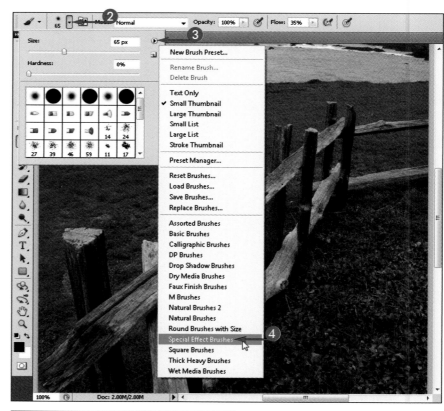

A dialog box opens, asking if you want to replace your brushes.

5 Click **OK**.

● To add the set of brushes to the currently displayed set, click **Append**.

If a dialog box opens asking if you want to save the current brush set, click **No**.

Note: You can reset your brushes to the original set by choosing **Reset Brushes** from the Brush menu.

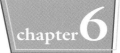

The new set appears in the Brush list.

6 Click a brush style.

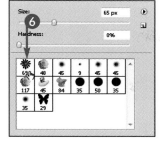

7 Click and drag to apply the new brush.

Photoshop applies color with the brush.

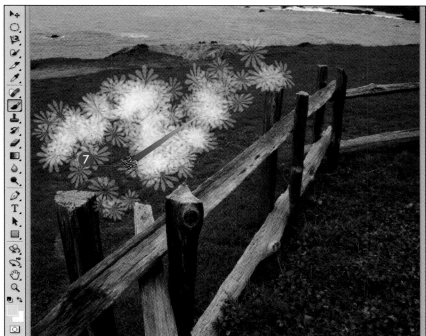

TIP

What are bristle-tip brushes?
Some brushes in the Brush panel have bristles whose settings you can modify. With these bristles, Photoshop models the behavior of real-world bristles to create lifelike strokes.

1 Click **Window** and then **Brush**. The Brush panel opens.

2 In the Brush panel, click a bristle-tip brush.

3 Specify the bristle settings for the brush.

● Photoshop displays the type of stroke that the brush applies.

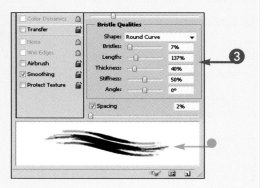

Create a Custom Brush

You can use the Brushes panel to create one-of-a-kind brushes of varying sizes and shapes. You can even specify a brush shape that changes as it paints, allowing you to generate a random design.

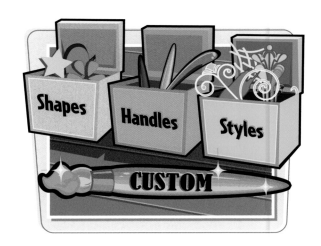

Create a Custom Brush

1. Click the **Brush** tool (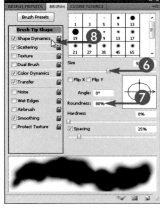).

2. Click **Window**.

3. Click **Brushes**.

   The Brush panel opens.

4. Click **Brush Tip Shape**.

5. Click a brush style to use as a starting point for your custom brush.

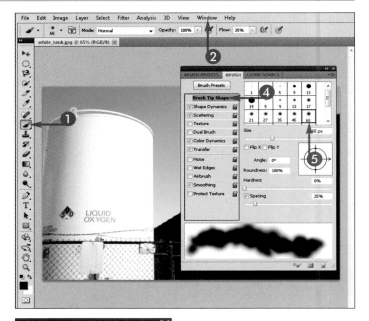

6. Click and drag the **Size** slider (⬜) to change the brush size.

7. Type a Roundness value between 0% and 100%.

   The lower the number, the more oval the brush.

   You can adjust other settings to further define the tip shape.

8. Click the **Shape Dynamics** check box (☐ changes to ☑).

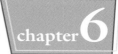

9 Click and drag the **Size Jitter** slider (⬚) to specify the amount your brush varies in size as it paints.

10 Click and drag the **Minimum Diameter** slider (⬚) to specify the smallest size to which the brush scales when Size Jitter is enabled.

11 Click and drag the other sliders (⬚) to control how the brush angle and roundness change.

You can click other categories to define other settings.

12 Click ▶▶ to close the Brush panel.

13 Click and drag inside the image.

Photoshop applies the custom brush.

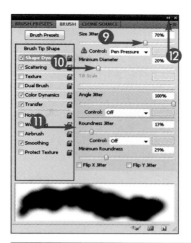

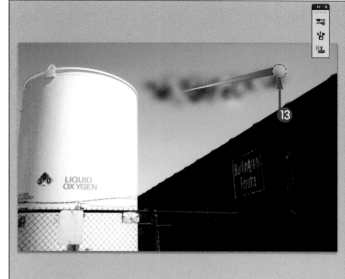

TIP

How do I save my custom brush in the Brush drop-down menu?

1 In the Brush panel, click ▤.

2 Click **New Brush Preset**.

The Brush Name dialog box opens.

3 Type a name in the Brush Name dialog box.

4 Click **OK**.

Photoshop adds your brush to the Brush menu.

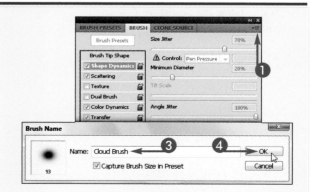

Using the Mixer Brush

The Mixer Brush is a new tool in Photoshop CS5 that mixes colors that you paint, just as wet paint mixes on a real canvas. The tool allows you to produce effects similar to those you can get by using real watercolors and oils.

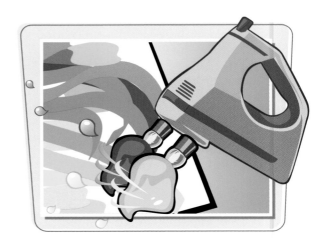

1 Click and hold the **Brush** tool ().

2 In the list that appears, click the **Mixer Brush** tool ().

3 Click here () to choose a brush size.

4 Click here to choose a color with which to paint.

5 Click here () to specify a **Wet** setting.

This controls how much color from the image gets picked up by the brush.

6 Click here () to specify a **Load** setting.

This controls how much color is loaded on the brush prior to applying the brush.

7 Click here () to specify a **Flow** setting.

This controls the rate at which color is deposited on the image by the brush.

● You can select from several presets to combine different brush settings.

8 Click and drag to apply the color.

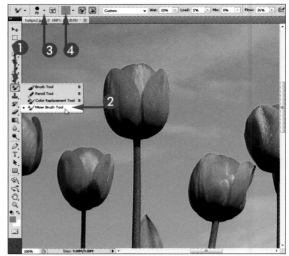

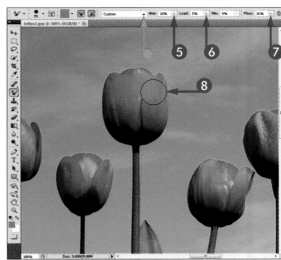

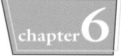

● Photoshop applies the color, mixing it with the colors already in the image.

⑨ Click here to choose a different color to apply.

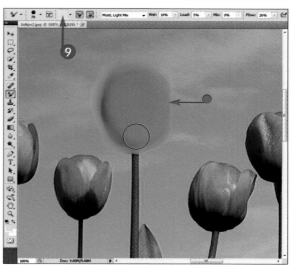

⑩ Click and drag to apply the color to the image.

● Photoshop applies the second color.

The second color is mixed with the first where the colors cross.

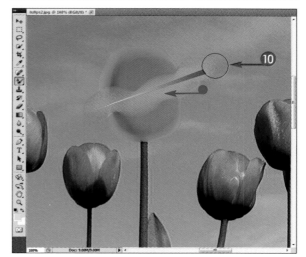

 TIP

What are the different brush settings for the Mixer Brush?

● The Current Brush Load menu enables you to load the brush with the selected color or clean the brush, which removes the loaded color. Applying a clean brush mixes existing colors in the image without applying new color.

● Selecting **Load the Brush after Each Stroke** (☑) adds color to the brush after each stroke. When the option is deselected, the brush dries out over successive strokes.

● Selecting **Clean the Brush after Each Stroke** (☒) removes any color on the brush after each stroke. When the option is deselected, color picked up from the image is applied over successive strokes.

Apply a Gradient

You can apply a *gradient*, which is a transition from one color to another, to your images. This can give objects or areas in your image a shaded or 3-D look.

For another way to add a gradient to your image, see Chapter 8.

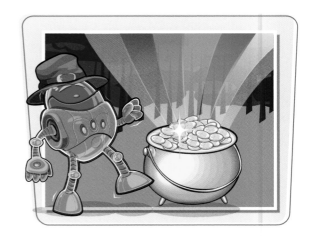

1 Make a selection.

Note: See Chapter 4 for more on making selections.

2 Click the **Gradient** tool (▣).

● A linear gradient is the default. This creates a gradient straight across your selection. You can select different geometries on the Options bar.

3 Click the gradient swatch.

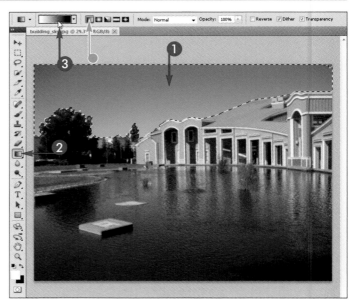

The Gradient Editor opens.

4 Select a gradient type from the Presets area.

● Photoshop shows the settings for the selected gradient below.

You can customize the gradient by changing the settings.

5 Click **OK**.

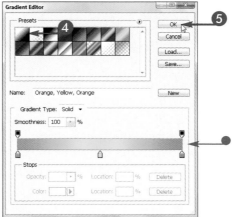

6 Click and drag inside the selection.

The direction and transition of the gradient are defined.

Note: Dragging a long line with the tool produces a gradual transition; dragging a short line produces an abrupt transition.

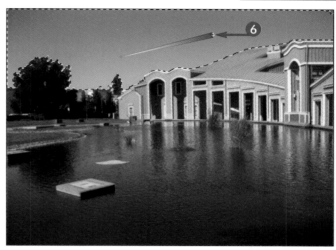

● Photoshop generates a gradient inside the selection.

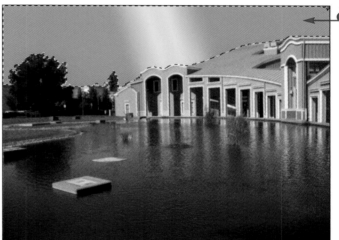

TIP

How can I customize the colors and opacity of my gradient?

The controls at the bottom of the Gradient Editor let you define the colors to use in your gradient, the opacity of those colors, and where the transition occurs.

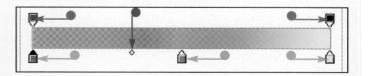

● Click the **Color Stops** to define the colors in a gradient. To add new gradient colors, click along the bottom of the gradient.

● Click the **Opacity Stops** to define the transparency of the gradient colors. To add new opacity settings, click along the top of the gradient.

● You can click and drag the **Midpoint** icon to specify where the gradient's transition occurs.

Using the Paint Bucket Tool

You can fill areas in your image with solid color by using the Paint Bucket tool. The Paint Bucket tool affects only adjacent pixels in the image. You can set the Paint Bucket's Tolerance value to determine what range of colors the paint bucket affects in the image when you apply it.

To fill the pixels of a selected area rather than just adjacent pixels, see the section "Fill a Selection."

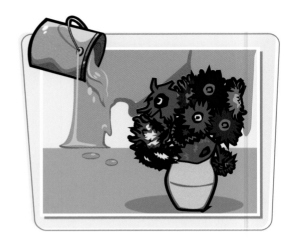

Using the Paint Bucket Tool

Add Color with the Paint Bucket

1. Click and hold the **Gradient** tool (■).

2. In the list that appears, click the **Paint Bucket** tool (■).

   ▷ changes to ◇.

3. Click the **Foreground Color** box to select a color for painting.

Note: For more, see the section "Select the Foreground and Background Colors."

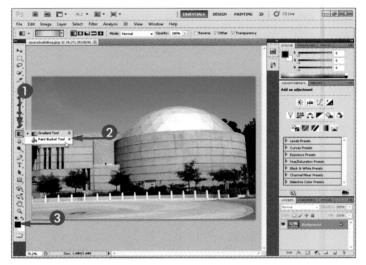

4. Type a Tolerance value from 0 to 255.

   With a low value, the tool fills only adjacent colors that are very similar to that of the clicked pixel.

   A high value fills a broader range of colors.

5. Click inside the image.

   Photoshop fills that area of the image with the foreground color.

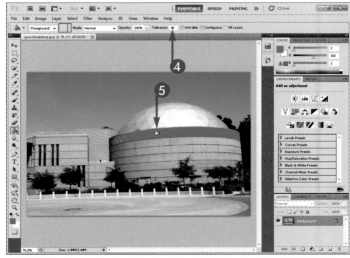

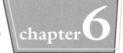

Adjust Opacity

6 To fill an area with a semitransparent color, type a percentage value of less than 100 in the Opacity field.

7 Click inside the image.

Photoshop fills an area with see-through paint.

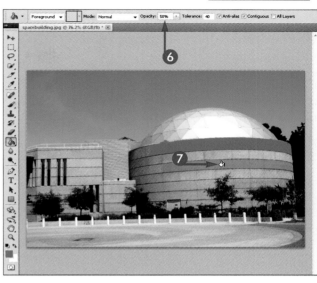

Constrain the Color

8 To constrain where you apply the color, make a selection before clicking.

In this example, the opacity is reset to 100%.

9 Click inside the selection.

The fill effect stays within the boundary of the selection. The tolerance setting also still controls where the effect appears.

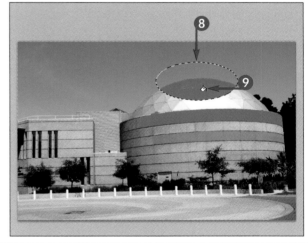

TIPS

How can I reset a tool to its default settings?

Right-click (Control + click) on the tool's icon on the far-left side of the Options bar and then click **Reset Tool** from the menu that appears.

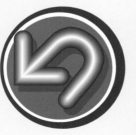

How can I use the Paint Bucket tool to recolor elements throughout an image?

On the Options bar, deselect the **Contiguous** check box (☑ changes to ☐). When you click a color with the Paint Bucket tool, the tool affects similar colors throughout your image.

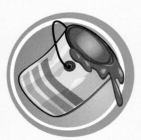

Fill a Selection

You can fill a selection by using the Fill command. The Fill command is an alternative to the Paint Bucket tool. The Fill command differs from the Paint Bucket tool in that it fills the entire selected area, not just adjacent pixels based on a tolerance value. See the section "Using the Paint Bucket Tool" if you want to fill adjacent pixels rather than a selected area.

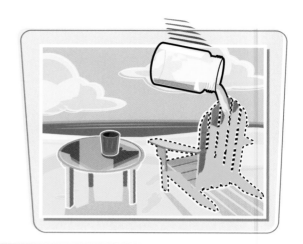

1 Define the area you want to fill by using a selection tool.

Note: See Chapter 4 for more on the selection tools.

2 Click **Edit**.

3 Click **Fill**.

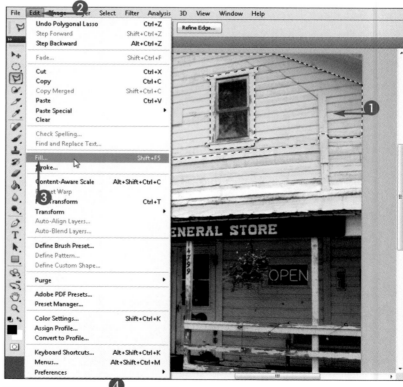

The Fill dialog box opens.

4 Click here (□) to choose a fill option.

● You can also fill your selection with a custom pattern. For more on using this option, see the tip in the section "Using the Pattern Stamp."

To fill the selection with other content from the scene, see the section "Using Content-Aware Fill."

● You can decrease the opacity to fill with a semitransparent color or pattern.

5 Click **OK**.

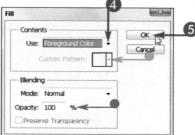

● Photoshop fills the area.

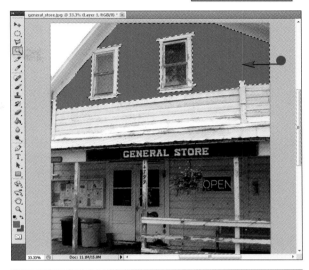

● You can select other areas and then fill them with different colors.

This example uses a fill with the background color set to 30% opacity and the blending mode set to Hard Light.

Note: For more on blending modes, see Chapter 8.

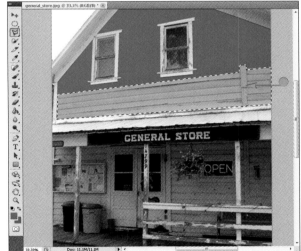

How do I apply a "ghosted" white covering over part of an image?

Use a selection tool to define the area of the image that you want to cover and then apply the Fill command with white selected and the opacity set to less than 50%.

What does the Preserve Transparency option in the Fill dialog box do?

If you click the **Preserve Transparency** check box (☐ changes to ☑), Photoshop does not fill pixels that are transparent in the selected layer. This option enables you to easily color objects that exist by themselves in a layer. This feature is not available when working in the Background layer.

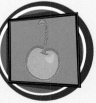

Using Content-Aware Fill

You can use the Content-Aware setting, which is new in Photoshop CS5, with the Fill command to automatically analyze the makeup of your image and intelligently fill the selection with other content in the scene.

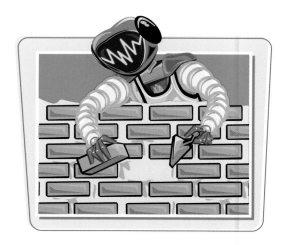

Using Content-Aware Fill

① Define the area you want to fill by using a selection tool.

Note: *See Chapter 4 for more on the selection tools.*

In this example, the dog is selected.

② Click **Edit**.

③ Click **Fill**.

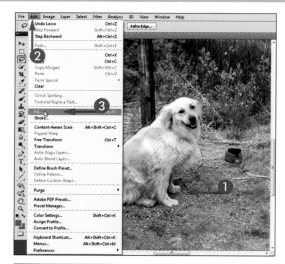

The Fill dialog box opens.

④ Click here (⊡) to choose **Content-Aware**.

⑤ Click **OK**.

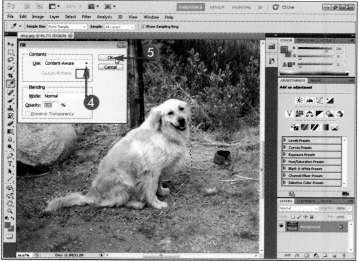

● Photoshop fills the area with
surrounding content.

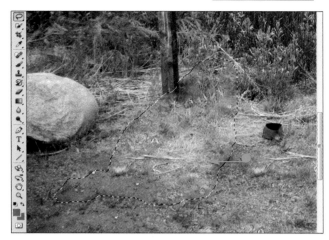

⑥ Click the **Clone Stamp** tool (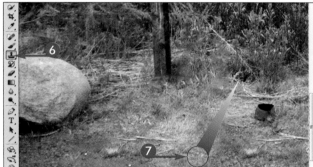).

⑦ You can optionally apply the
Clone Stamp tool to fix areas of
the fill.

*Note: For more on the Clone Stamp tool, see the
section "Using the Clone Stamp."*

TIP

**How do I apply a content-aware fill
with the Spot Healing Brush tool?**

① Click the **Spot Healing Brush** tool (✐).

② Click the **Content-Aware** radio button
(◎ changes to ◉).

③ Click and drag over the object you want to
replace.

Photoshop replaces the object with other
content in the image.

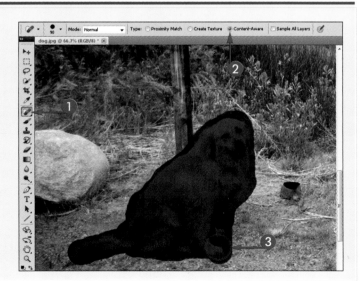

Stroke a Selection

You can use the Stroke command to draw a line along the edge of a selection. This can help you highlight objects in your image.

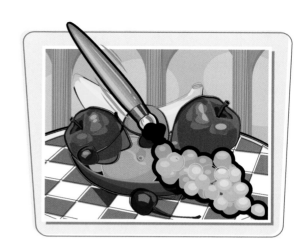

Stroke a Selection

① Select an area of the image with a selection tool.

Note: *See Chapter 4 for more on the selection tools.*

② Click **Edit**.

③ Click **Stroke**.

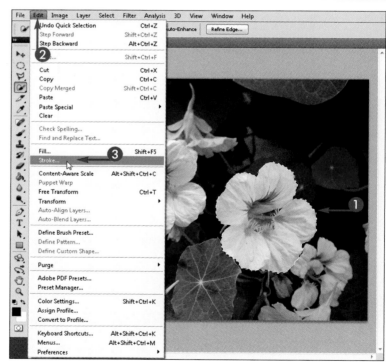

The Stroke dialog box opens.

④ Type a width in pixels.

⑤ Click the **Inside** radio button to stroke a line on the inside of the selection, the **Center** radio button to stroke a line straddling the selection, or the **Outside** radio button to stroke a line on the outside of the selection (◯ changes to ◉).

● You can click the **Color** box to define the color of the stroke.

⑥ Click **OK**.

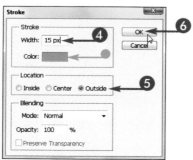

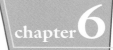

● Photoshop strokes a line along the selection.

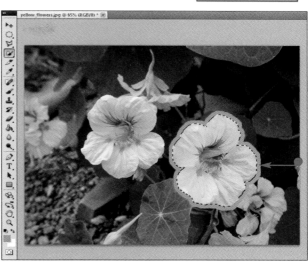

You can select other areas and stroke them by using different settings.

● This stroke was applied to the inside of the selection at 40% opacity.

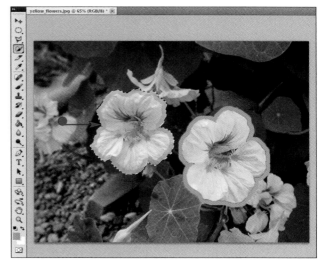

How do I add a colored border to my image?

Click **Select** and then **All**. Apply the Stroke command, clicking the **Inside** radio button as the location (◎ changes to ◉). Photoshop adds a border to the image.

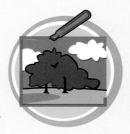

How do I stroke a line a fixed distance outside of an object?

After selecting the object, you can expand your selection and then stroke the line. To expand a selection, click **Select**, **Modify**, and then **Expand**. For more on making selections, see Chapter 4.

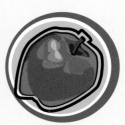

Using the Clone Stamp

You can clean up small flaws or erase elements in your image with the Clone Stamp tool. This tool copies information from one area to another.

For other ways to correct defects in your image, see the sections "Using the Healing Brush" and "Using the Patch Tool."

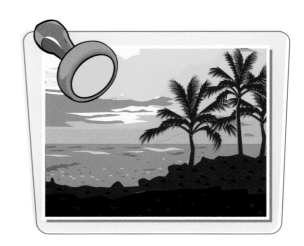

① Click the **Clone Stamp** tool (🖫).

② Click here (⊡) to open the Brush menu to choose a brush size and type.

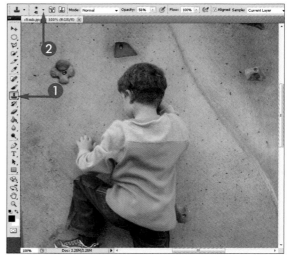

③ Press and hold Alt (Option on a Mac) and then click the area of the image from which you want to copy.

● You can specify an opacity of less than 100% to partially apply the tool.

You do not need to select an area inside the current image; you can Alt + click (Option + click on a Mac) another open image.

This example uses the tool to select an empty area of a climbing wall.

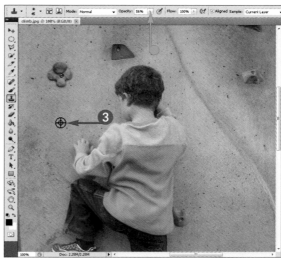

4 Release **Alt** (**Option** on a Mac).

5 Click and drag to apply the Clone Stamp.

Photoshop copies the previously clicked area to where you click and drag.

● As you apply the tool, a preview of the content to be cloned appears inside the brush cursor (○).

● A + appears at the location from which you are cloning.

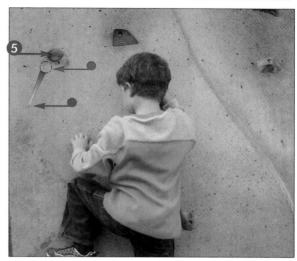

6 Click and drag repeatedly over the image to achieve the desired effect.

As you apply the tool, you can press **Alt** (**Option** on a Mac) and then click again to select a different area from which to copy.

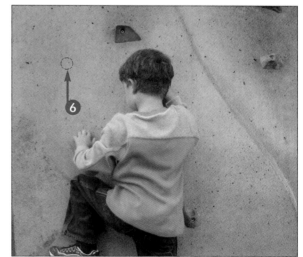

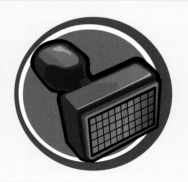

TIP

How can I make the Clone Stamp's effects look seamless?
To erase elements from your image with the Clone Stamp without leaving a trace, try the following:

● Clone between areas of similar color and texture.

● To apply the Clone Stamp more subtly, lower its opacity on the Options bar.

● After you click here (▯) to open the Brush menu, choose a soft-edged brush shape.

Using the Pattern Stamp

You can paint with a pattern by using the Pattern Stamp tool. This tool gives you a free-form way to add repeating elements to your images.

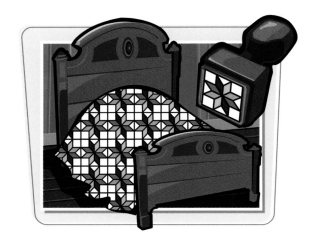

Select a Pattern

① Click and hold the **Clone Stamp** tool (🔲).

② In the list that appears, click the **Pattern Stamp** tool (🔲).

③ Click here (▾) to open the Brush menu to choose a brush size and type.

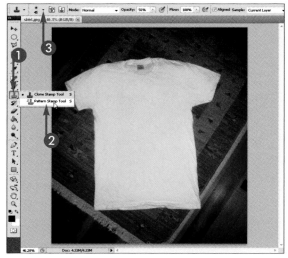

④ Click here (▾) to open the Pattern menu.

⑤ Select a pattern to apply.

● You can click the **Aligned** check box (☐ changes to ☑) to make your strokes paint the pattern as contiguous tiles.

To create a custom pattern, see the tip on the next page.

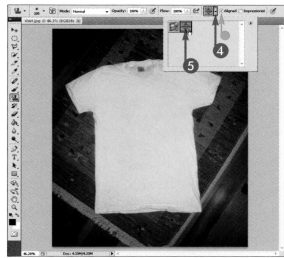

6 Click and drag to apply the pattern.

Photoshop applies the pattern wherever you click and drag.

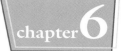

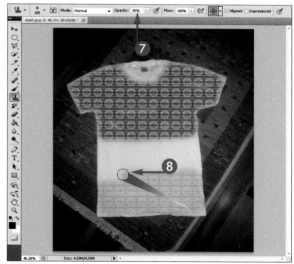

Apply a Different Opacity

7 Type a value of less than 100% in the Opacity box.

8 Click and drag inside the selection to apply the pattern.

Decreasing the opacity causes the brush to apply a semitransparent pattern.

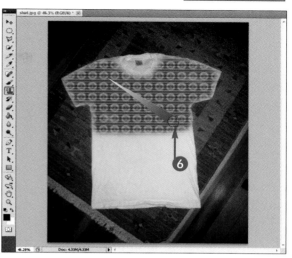

TIP

How do I define my own custom patterns?

1 Click **the Rectangular Marquee** tool (▭).

2 Select an area in your image to use as a pattern.

3 Click **Edit** and then **Define Pattern** to open the Pattern Name dialog box.

● Your pattern appears in the preview in the dialog box.

4 In the Pattern Name dialog box, type a name for your pattern.

5 Click **OK**.

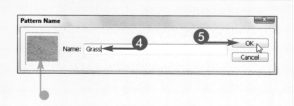

Using the Healing Brush

You can correct defects in your image by using the Healing Brush. The Healing Brush is similar to the Clone Stamp in that it copies pixels from one area of the image to another. However, the Healing Brush takes into account the texture and lighting of the image as it works, which can make its modifications more convincing.

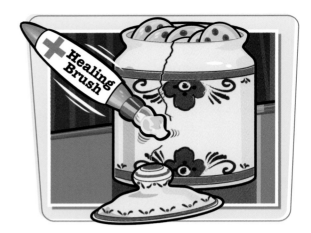

① Click and hold the **Spot Healing Brush** tool (🖌️).

② In the list that appears, click the **Healing Brush** tool (🖌️).

③ Click here (▽) to open the Brush menu to specify your brush settings.

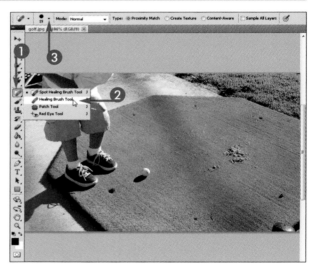

● Make sure to click the **Sampled** radio button (◎ changes to ●).

④ Press and hold Alt (Option on a Mac) and then click the area of the image you want to heal with.

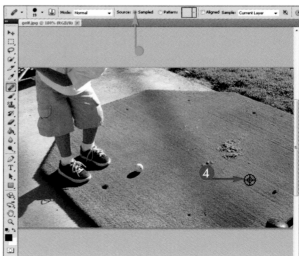

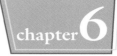

⑤ Release 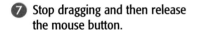 (Option on a Mac).

⑥ Click and drag inside the selection to apply the Healing Brush.

Photoshop copies the selected area wherever you click and drag.

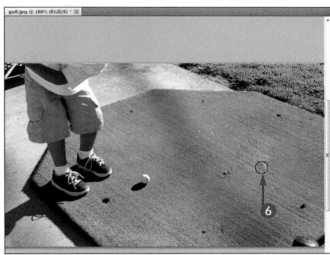

⑦ Stop dragging and then release the mouse button.

Photoshop adjusts the copied pixels to account for the lighting and texture present in the image.

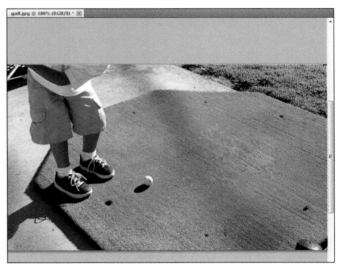

TIP

How does the Spot Healing Brush tool work?
The Spot Healing Brush is a less interactive version of the Healing Brush. With the Brush settings, you specify the diameter of the area that you want to select. When you click an imperfection in your image, Photoshop attempts to automatically heal the selected area. It replaces the imperfection inside the selected area with the surrounding colors. If you click the **Create Texture** radio button (◎ changes to ◉), the tool attempts to also mimic the texture of the selected area.

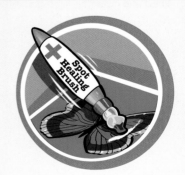

Using the Patch Tool

The Patch tool enables you to correct defects in your image by selecting them and then dragging the selection to an unflawed area of the image. This can be useful if a large part of your image is free of flaws.

For other ways to correct defects in your image, see the sections "Using Content-Aware Fill," "Using the Clone Stamp," and "Using the Healing Brush."

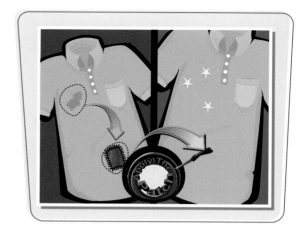

Using the Patch Tool

① Click and hold the **Spot Healing Brush** tool (🖌).

② In the list that appears, click the **Patch** tool (🔘).

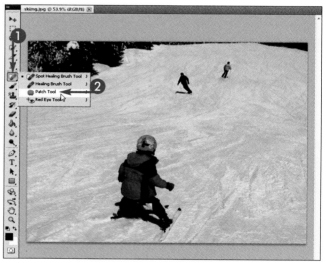

③ Click and drag to select the part of your image that contains the defects you want to patch.

When you make selections, the Patch tool works similar to the Lasso tool.

Note: See Chapter 4 for more on the Lasso tool.

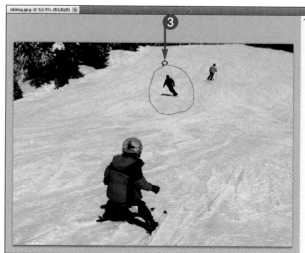

④ Click inside the selection and then drag it to an area that does not have defects.

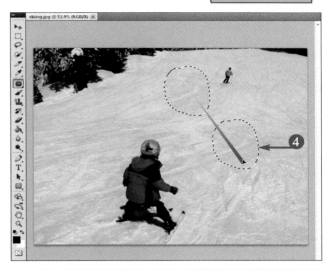

Photoshop uses pixels from the destination selection to patch the defects in the source selection.

● You can click the **Destination** radio button (◎ changes to ◉) to patch defects in the reverse order; flaws in the destination selection are corrected with the pixels from the source selection.

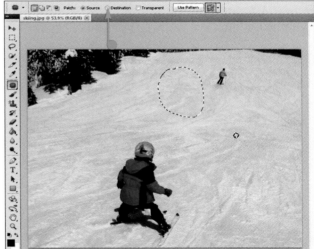

TIPS

How does the Patch tool determine what are defects in my selection?

It does this by comparing the colors and textures in the two selections. The tool then tries to eliminate the differences — the defects — while retaining the overall color and texture.

Can I use other selection tools to create my patch selection?

Yes. You can use selection tools, such as the Marquee tools and the Lasso tools, to define the area you want to patch. Then, you can use the Patch tool (▣) to click and drag the selection to complete the patch.

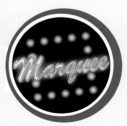

Using the History Brush

You can use the History Brush tool to paint a previous state of your image from the History panel into the current image. This can be useful if you want to revert just a part of your image.

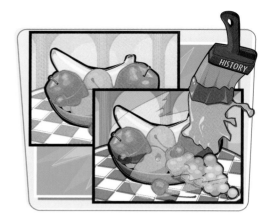

Paint a Previous State

1. Click **Window**.

2. Click **History**.

   The History panel opens.

3. Click the **Create New Snapshot** button (⬚) in the History panel.

● Photoshop puts a copy of the current state of the image into the History panel.

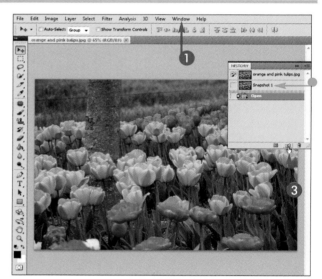

4. Modify your image to make it different from the newly created snapshot.

   In this example, the Fresco filter was applied and the hue adjusted.

5. Click to the left of the snapshot to select it as the History brush source.

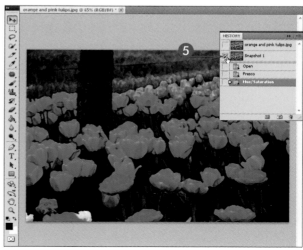

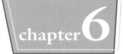

6 Click the **History Brush** tool (🖌).

7 Click here (▾) to open the Brush menu to specify your brush settings.

8 Click and drag inside the image.

Pixels from the previous snapshot are painted into the image.

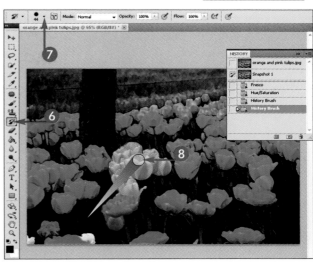

Using the Art History Brush

1 Click and hold the **History Brush** tool (🖌).

2 In the list that appears, click the **Art History Brush** tool (🖌).

With the Art History Brush tool, you can paint in snapshot information with an added impressionistic effect.

3 Click here (▾) to open the Brush menu to specify your brush settings.

4 Click and drag to apply an artistic effect.

 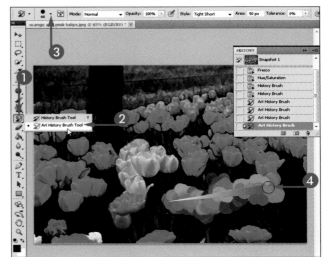

TIP

How do I paint onto a blank image with the History Brush tool?
Start with a photographic image, take a snapshot of it with the Create New Snapshot button (🔲), and then fill the image with a solid color. See the section "Fill a Selection" for more. You can then use the History Brush tool (🖌) to paint in the photographic content.

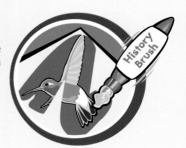

Using the Eraser

You can delete elements from your images by using the Eraser tool. This can be useful when you are trying to separate elements from their backgrounds.

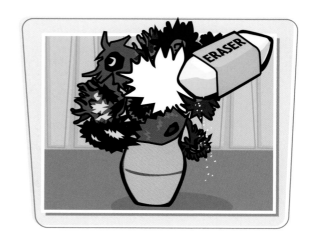

Using the Eraser

In the Background Layer

① Click the Background layer in the Layers panel.

  If you start with a newly scanned image, the Background layer is the only layer.

Note: See Chapter 8 for more on layers.

② Click the **Eraser** tool ().

③ Click here () to open the Brush menu to choose a brush size and type.

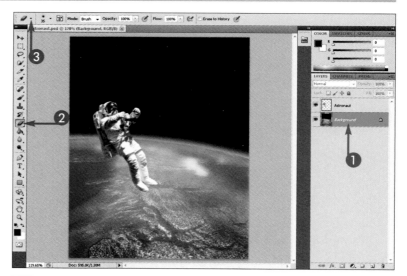

④ Click and drag inside the image.

● Photoshop erases the image by painting with the background color.

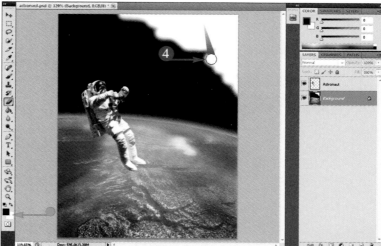

In a Regular Layer

1 Click a layer other than the Background layer in the Layers panel.

Note: See Chapter 8 for more on layers.

2 Click the **Eraser** tool (🖊).

3 Click here (⊟) to open the **Brush** menu to choose a brush size and type.

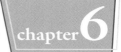
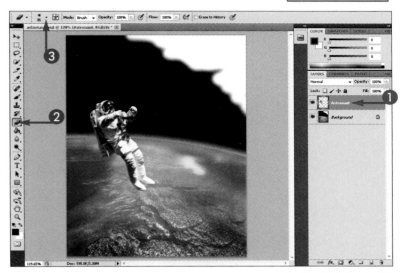

4 Click and drag inside the image.

Photoshop erases elements in the layer by making pixels transparent.

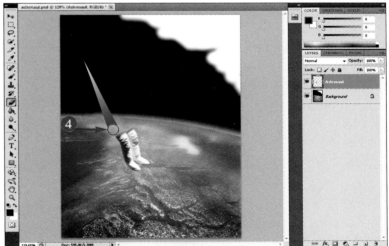

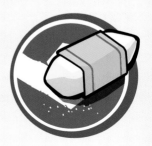

TIP

How can I quickly erase areas of similar color in my image?

If you click and hold the Eraser tool (🖊) in the Toolbox, a list appears, and you can select the Background Eraser (🖊) or the Magic Eraser (🖊). The Background Eraser works by sampling the pixel color beneath the center of the brush and erasing similar colors that are underneath the brush. The Magic Eraser also samples the color beneath the cursor but erases similar pixels throughout the layer. You can adjust the tolerance of both tools on the Options bar to control how much they erase.

Replace a Color

You can replace colors in your image with the current foreground color by using the Color Replacement tool. This gives you a free-form way of recoloring objects in your image while keeping the shading on the objects intact.

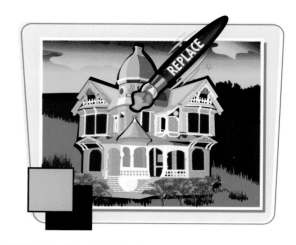

① Click and hold the **Brush** tool (🖌️).

② In the list that appears, click the **Color Replacement** tool (🖌️).

③ Click the **Foreground Color** box to select a color for painting.

Note: For more, see the section "Select the Foreground and Background Colors."

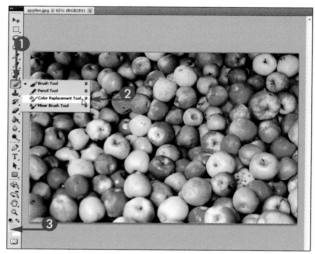

④ Click here (▾) to open the Brush menu to choose a brush size and type.

⑤ Click the **Sampling: Continuous** icon (🖌️).

Sampling: Continuous samples different colors to replace as you paint.

● Sampling: Once (🖌️) samples only the first color you click.

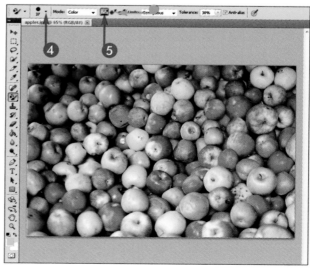

6 Type a tolerance from 1% to 100%.

The greater the tolerance, the greater the range of colors the tool replaces.

7 Click and drag in your image to replace color.

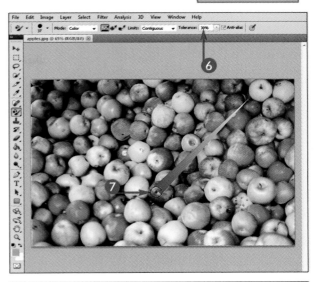

8 Continue to click and drag in your image.

Photoshop replaces more color.

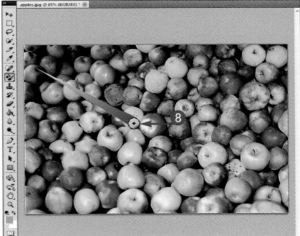

TIP

How does the Color Replacement tool decide what colors to replace?
When you click inside your image, the Color Replacement tool samples the color beneath the cross symbol at the center of the cursor. It then replaces any colors inside the brush that are similar to the sampled color. Photoshop determines similarity based on the Tolerance setting of the tool.

Fix Red Eye in a Photo

You can fix the red eye effect that occurs in pictures taken with flash in low light by using the Red Eye tool. When applied to the eye of your subject, the tool replaces the reddish pixels in the area with pixels of a predefined color.

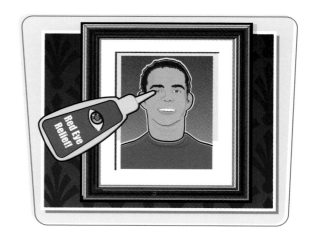

Fix Red Eye in a Photo

① Click and hold the **Spot Healing Brush** tool (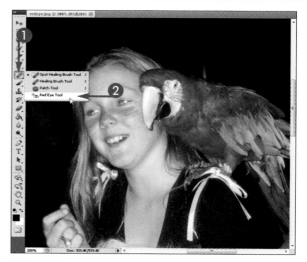).

② In the list that appears, click the **Red Eye** tool (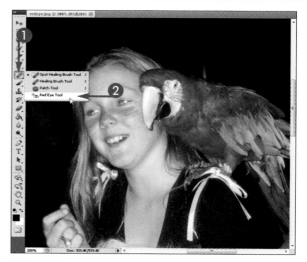).

③ Type a value from 1% to 100% for Pupil Size to determine the size of the area affected.

④ Type a value from 1% to 100% for Darken Amount to determine the darkness of the applied color.

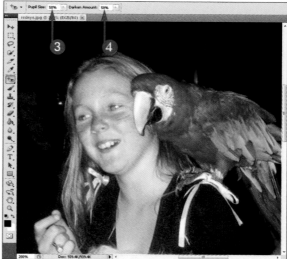

5 Click the center of a pupil.

Photoshop replaces the red pixels with a dark-gray hue.

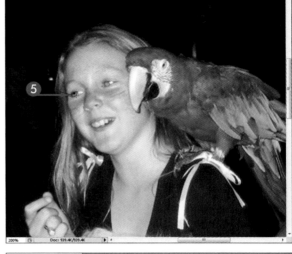

6 Click the other eye.

Photoshop fixes the other eye.

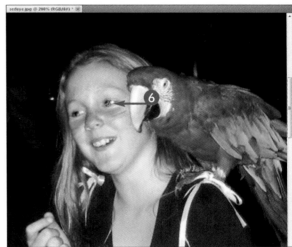

TIPS

What are alternatives to the Red Eye tool?

You can use the Color Replacement tool to fix red eye. First, select the red eye with the **Elliptical Marquee** tool (⬭). Select a dark-gray hue as your foreground color and then apply the foreground color over the eye with the **Color Replacement** tool (🖌). This can also help you fix the blue- and green-eye phenomena that can occur with animals. For more on the Elliptical Marquee tool, see Chapter 4. For more on selecting a foreground color, see the section "Select the Foreground and Background Colors." For more on using the Color Replacement tool, see the section "Replace a Color."

What can cause problems for the Red Eye tool?

If your subject has a reddish skin tone in the photo, the Red Eye tool may apply color to more than just the eyes. To avoid this, you can first select the eyes with the **Elliptical Marquee** tool (⬭). Then, the Red Eye tool leaves the rest of the image alone when you apply it. See Chapter 4 for more.

Adjusting Colors

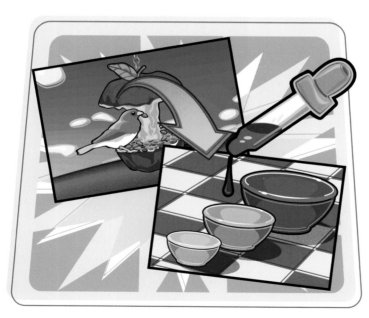

You can fine-tune the colors in your image — darken them, lighten them, or remove them completely. This chapter introduces the tools that do the trick.

Change Brightness and Contrast

The Brightness/Contrast command provides a way to adjust the highlights and shadows in your image. To change the brightness or contrast of small parts of your image, use the Dodge or Burn tool. See the section "Using the Dodge and Burn Tools" for more.

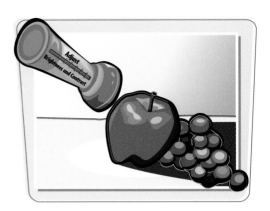

If you make a selection before using the Brightness/Contrast command, changes affect only the selected pixels. Similarly, if you have a multilayered image, your adjustments affect only the selected layer. For more on making selections, see Chapter 4. For more on layers, see Chapter 8.

Change Brightness and Contrast

① Click **Image**.

② Click **Adjustments**.

③ Click **Brightness/Contrast**.

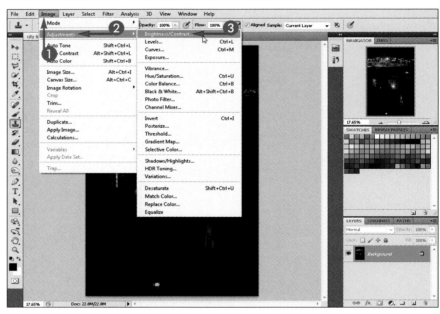

The Brightness/Contrast dialog box opens with sliders set to 0.

④ To display your adjustments in the image window as you make them, click the **Preview** check box (☐ changes to ☑).

⑤ Click and drag the **Brightness** slider (▨).

Drag to the right to lighten the image or drag to the left to darken the image.

● You can also lighten the image by typing a number from 1 to 100 or darken the image by typing a negative number from -1 to -100.

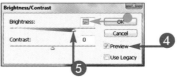

6 Click and drag the **Contrast** slider (⬚).

Drag to the right to increase the contrast or drag to the left to decrease the contrast.

Note: *Increasing contrast can bring out details in your image; decreasing it can soften details.*

● You can also increase the contrast by typing a number from 1 to 100 or decrease the contrast by typing a negative number from -1 to -100.

7 Click **OK**.

Photoshop applies the new brightness and contrast values.

Note: *You can also apply brightness and contrast adjustments to an image with an adjustment layer. For more, see Chapter 8.*

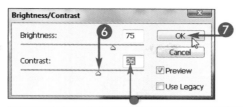

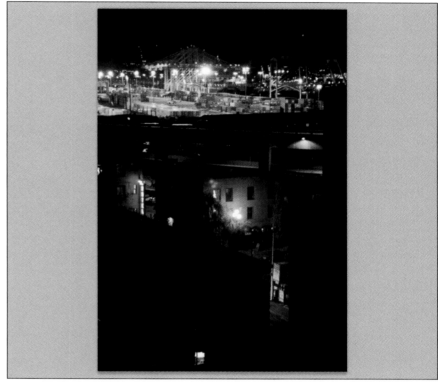

TIP

How can I adjust the contrast of an image automatically?
Click **Image** and then **Auto Contrast**. This converts the lightest pixels in the image to white and the darkest pixels in the image to black. Making the highlights brighter and the shadows darker boosts the contrast, which can improve the appearance of poorly exposed photographs. In this example, you can use the Auto Contrast command to bring out the colors in an ocean scene.

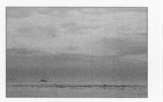

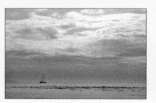

Using the Dodge and Burn Tools

You can use the Dodge and Burn tools to brighten or darken specific areas of an image, respectively. *Dodge* is a photographic term that describes the diffusing of light when developing a film negative. *Burn* is a photographic term that describes the focusing of light when developing a film negative.

These tools are an alternative to the Brightness/Contrast command, which affects the entire image. To brighten or darken the entire image, see the section "Change Brightness and Contrast."

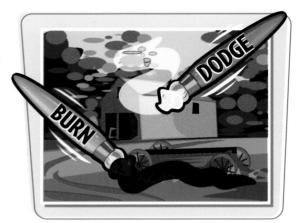

Using the Dodge and Burn Tools

Using the Dodge Tool

1. Click the **Dodge** tool ().

2. Click here () to open the Brush menu.

3. Click the brush you want to use.

● You can also choose the range of colors you want to affect and the tool's exposure or strength.

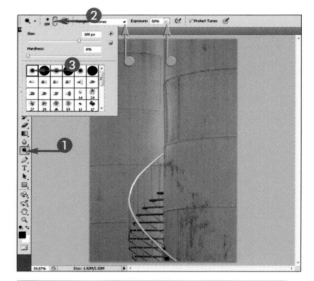

4. Click and drag over the area that you want to lighten.

   Photoshop lightens the area.

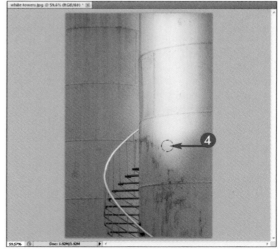

Using the Burn Tool

① Click and hold the **Dodge** tool (🔍).

② Click the **Burn** tool (✊) in the list that appears.

● You can select the brush, the range of colors you want to affect, and the tool's exposure, or strength.

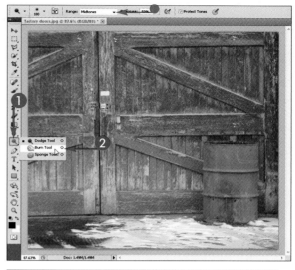

③ Click and drag over the area that you want to darken.

Photoshop darkens the area.

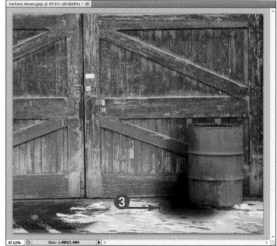

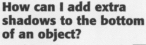

TIPS

How do I invert the bright and dark colors in an image?
Click **Image**, **Adjustments**, and then **Invert**. This makes the image look like a film negative. Bright colors become dark — and vice versa.

How can I add extra shadows to the bottom of an object?
Applying the Burn tool (✊) with the Range set to Shadows offers a useful way to add shadows to the shaded side of an object. Likewise, you can use the Dodge tool (🔍) with the Range set to Highlights to add highlights to the lighter side of an object.

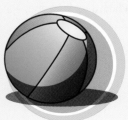

Using the Blur and Sharpen Tools

You can sharpen or blur specific areas of your image with the Sharpen and Blur tools. This enables you to emphasize or de-emphasize objects in a photo.

You can blur or sharpen an entire image by using one of the Blur or Sharpen commands located in Photoshop's Filter menu. For more, see Chapter 10.

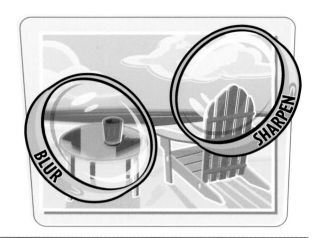

Using the Blur and Sharpen Tools

Using the Blur Tool

1 Click the **Blur** tool (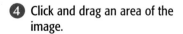).

2 Click here (⊡) to open the Brush menu.

3 Click the brush you want to use.

● To change the strength of the tool, type a value from 1% to 100%.

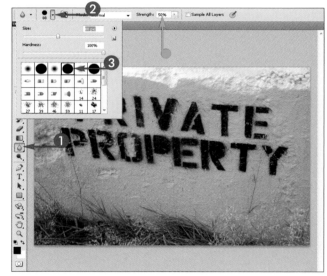

4 Click and drag an area of the image.

Photoshop blurs the area you click and drag over.

Using the Sharpen Tool

① Click and hold the **Blur** tool (⬤).

② Click the **Sharpen** tool (△) in the list that appears.

● You can type a value from 1% to 100% to set the strength of the tool.

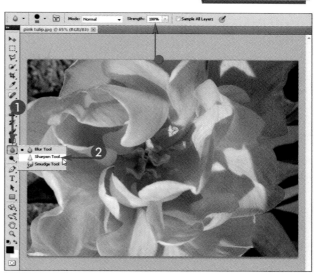

③ Click and drag an area of the image.

Photoshop sharpens the area of the image you click and drag over.

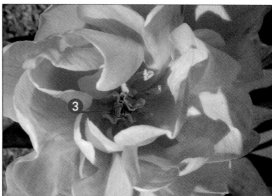

TIP

How do I use the Smudge tool?
The Smudge tool (👆) simulates dragging a finger through wet paint, shifting colors and blurring your image.

① Click and hold the **Blur** tool (⬤).

② Click the Smudge tool (👆) in the list that appears.

You can adjust the tool's brush size and strength on the Options bar.

③ Click and drag over an area of your image to smudge it.

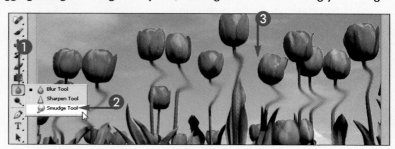

Adjust Levels

You can use the Levels command to make fine adjustments to the highlights, midtones, or shadows in an image. Although more difficult to use, the Levels command offers more control over brightness than the Brightness/Contrast command, covered in the section "Change Brightness and Contrast."

To change only selected pixels, select them before performing the Levels command. Similarly, in a multilayered image, your adjustments affect only the selected layer.

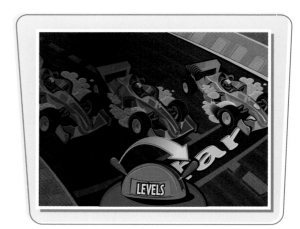

Adjust Levels

1 Click **Image**.

2 Click **Adjustments**.

3 Click **Levels**.

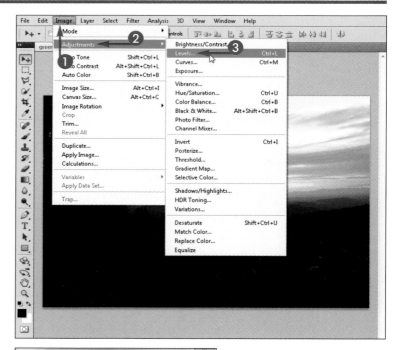

The Levels dialog box opens.

4 To display your adjustments in the image window as you make them, click the **Preview** check box (☐ changes to ☑).

You can use the Input sliders to adjust an image's brightness, midtones, and highlights.

5 Click and drag ◣ to the right to darken shadows and increase contrast.

6 Click and drag ◹ to the left to lighten the bright areas of the image and increase contrast.

7 Click and drag ◭ to adjust the midtones — the shades between the shadows and highlights — of the image.

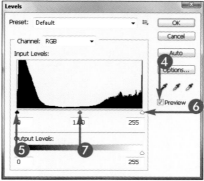

You can use the Output sliders to decrease the contrast while either lightening or darkening the image.

⑧ Click and drag ▣ to the right to lighten the image.

⑨ Click and drag ▨ to the left to darken the image.

⑩ Click **OK**.

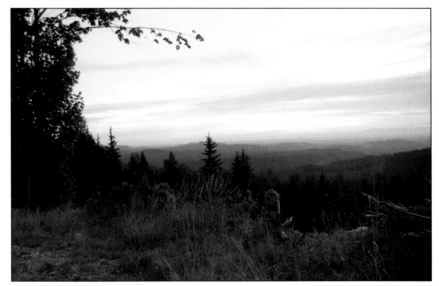

Photoshop makes brightness and contrast adjustments to the image.

In this example, adjusting the Levels has lightened an overly shadowy image to bring out color and detail.

Note: *You can also apply levels adjustments to an image with an adjustment layer. For more, see Chapter 8.*

TIP

How do I automatically adjust the brightness levels of an image?

Click **Image** and then **Auto Tone**. This converts the lightest pixels in the image to white and the darkest pixels to black. This command is similar to the Auto Contrast command and can quickly improve the contrast of an overly gray photographic image. In this example, you can use the Auto Tone command to make the colors in the barn photo crisper.

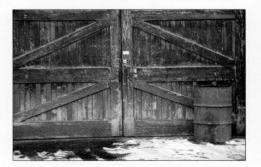

Adjust Curves

You can manipulate the tones and contrast of your image with the Curves dialog box. In the dialog box, colors in the image are represented by a sloping line graph. The top right part of the line represents the highlights, the middle part the midtones, and the bottom left the shadows.

If you make a selection before performing the Curves command, only the selected pixels are affected. Similarly, if you have a multilayered image, your adjustments affect only the selected layer. For more on making selections, see Chapter 4. For more on layers, see Chapter 8.

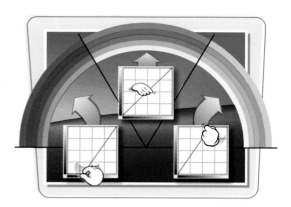

Adjust Curves

1 Click **Image**.

2 Click **Adjustments**.

3 Click **Curves**.

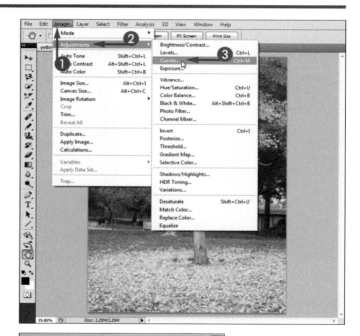

The Curves dialog box opens.

● The dialog box includes a histogram of the existing colors in the image, with the dark colors represented on the left and the light colors on the right.

4 Click the line graph and then drag to adjust the lighting in the image.

Dragging the curve up and to the left lightens the image, and dragging it down and to the right darkens it.

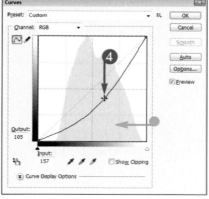

5 Click and drag at additional points on the line graph to fine-tune the lighting.

To boost contrast, you can create a curve with a slight S shape. This lightens the highlights, darkens the shadows, and keeps the midtones relatively unchanged.

6 Click **OK** to apply the adjustments and close the dialog box.

● To reset the line graph, you can press **Alt** and then click **Cancel**, which changes to **Reset**.

Photoshop adjusts the tones in the image.

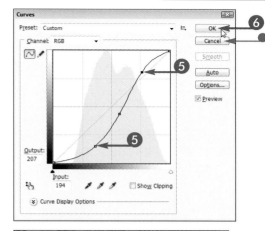

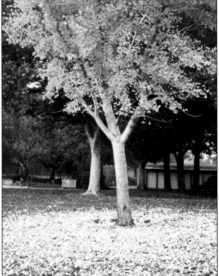

TIP

How do I apply automatic adjustments to my image with the Curves dialog box?

The Curves dialog box offers several presets that you can select from to apply common adjustments.

1 In the Curves dialog box, click a setting in the Preset menu.

Photoshop adjusts the shape of the line graph and adjusts the colors in the image.

2 Click **OK** to apply the adjustment.

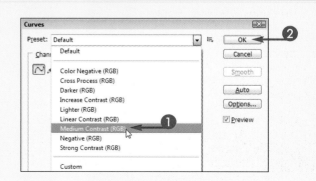

Adjust Hue and Saturation

You can change the hue to shift the component colors of an image. You can change the saturation to adjust the color intensity in an image.

If you make a selection before performing the Hue/Saturation command, only the selected pixels are affected. Similarly, if you have a multilayered image, your adjustments affect only the selected layer. For more on making selections, see Chapter 4. For more on layers, see Chapter 8.

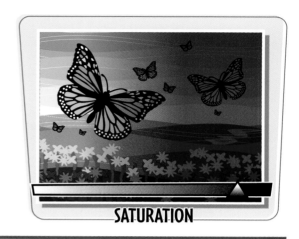

SATURATION

Adjust Hue and Saturation

① Click **Image**.

② Click **Adjustments**.

③ Click **Hue/Saturation**.

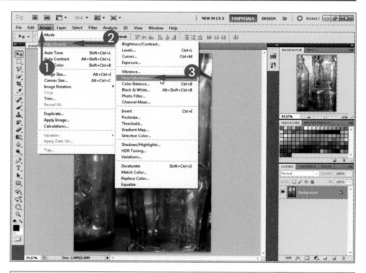

The Hue/Saturation dialog box opens.

④ To display your adjustments in the image window as you make them, click the **Preview** check box (☐ changes to ☑).

⑤ Click and drag the **Hue** slider (◻) to shift the colors in the image.

Dragging left or right shifts the colors in different — and sometimes bizarre — ways.

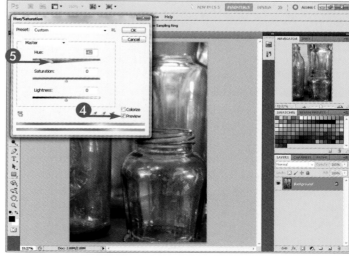

⑥ Click and drag the **Saturation** slider (⬚).

Dragging to the right or to the left increases or decreases the intensity of the image's colors, respectively.

● Clicking the **Colorize** check box (⬚ changes to ☑) partially desaturates the image and adds a single color. You can adjust the color with the sliders.

⑦ Click **OK**.

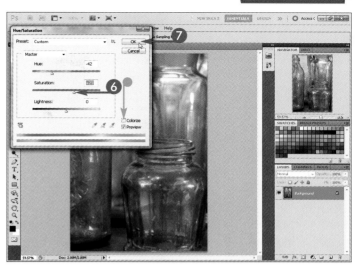

Photoshop makes the color adjustments to the image.

Note: You can also apply hue and saturation adjustments to an image with an adjustment layer. See Chapter 8 for more.

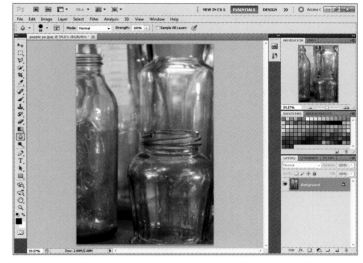

TIPS

How does Photoshop adjust an image's hues?

When you adjust an image's hues in Photoshop, its colors shift according to their position on the color wheel. The color wheel is a graphical way of presenting all the colors in the visible spectrum. Making adjustments with the Hue slider shifts the colors in a clockwise or counterclockwise direction around the wheel.

How can the Hue/ Saturation command enhance my digital photos?

Boosting the saturation can improve photos whose colors appear faded or washed out. Increasing the saturation by 10 to 20 points is often enough to enhance the colors without making them look artificially bright.

Using the Sponge Tool

You can use the Sponge tool to adjust the color saturation, or color intensity, of a specific area of an image. This can help bring out the colors in washed-out areas of photos or mute colors in areas that are too bright.

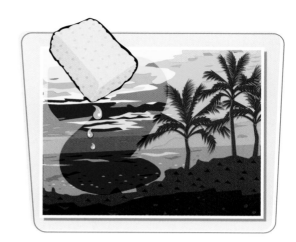

Decrease Saturation

① Click and hold the **Dodge** tool (🔍).

② Click the **Sponge** tool (🧽) in the list that appears.

③ Click here (⊡) to open the Brush menu and then choose the brush you want to use.

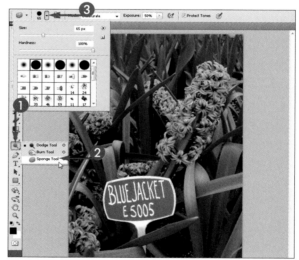

④ Click here (⊡) to choose **Desaturate**.

⑤ Click and drag the mouse (○) to decrease the saturation of an area of the image.

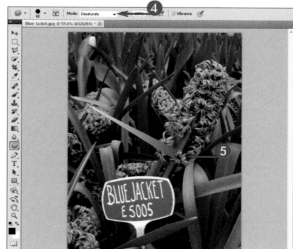

Increase Saturation

1. Perform steps **1** to **3** on the previous page.

2. Click here (⊟) to choose **Saturate**.

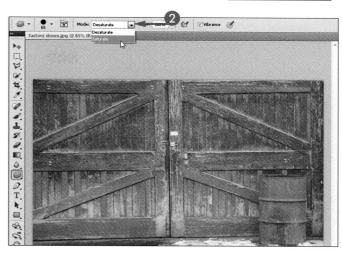

3. Click and drag the mouse (○) over an area of the image.

Photoshop increases the saturation of that area of the image.

You can adjust the strength of the Sponge tool by typing a new Flow setting from 1% to 100%.

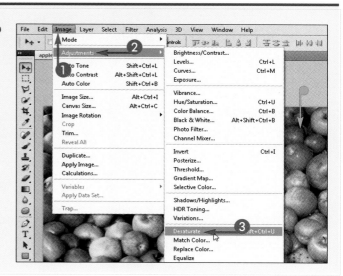

TIP

How can I easily convert a color image to a grayscale image?

1. Click **Image**.

2. Click **Adjustments**.

3. Click **Desaturate**.

● Photoshop sets the saturation value of the image to 0, effectively converting it to a grayscale image.

In a multilayer image, only the selected layer is desaturated.

Note: For more control over your conversion, see the section "Convert to Black and White."

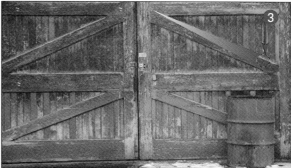

Adjust Color Balance

You can use the Color Balance command to change the amounts of specific colors in your image. This can be useful if you need to remove a colorcast introduced by a scanner or by age.

If you make a selection before performing the Color Balance command, only the selected pixels are affected. Similarly, if you have a multilayered image, your adjustments affect only the selected layer. For more on making selections, see Chapter 4. For more on layers, see Chapter 8.

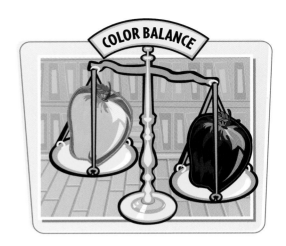

Adjust Color Balance

1 Click **Image**.

2 Click **Adjustments**.

3 Click **Color Balance**.

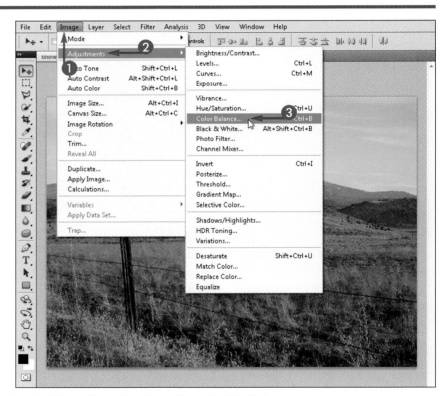

The Color Balance dialog box opens.

4 To display your adjustments in the image window as you make them, click the **Preview** check box (☐ changes to ☑).

5 Choose the tones in the image that you want to affect (◉ changes to ◉).

6 Click and drag a slider (◻) toward the color you want to add more of.

To add a warm cast to your image, you can drag toward red or magenta.

To add a cool cast, you can drag toward blue or cyan.

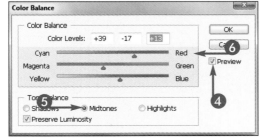

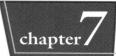

7 Choose another Color Balance option.

8 Type a number from -100 to 100 in one or more of the Color Levels fields.

Note: Step 8 is an alternative to dragging a slider.

9 Click **OK**.

Photoshop makes color adjustments to the image.

Note: You can also apply color balance adjustments to an image with an adjustment layer. See Chapter 8 for more.

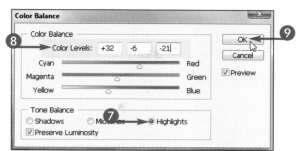

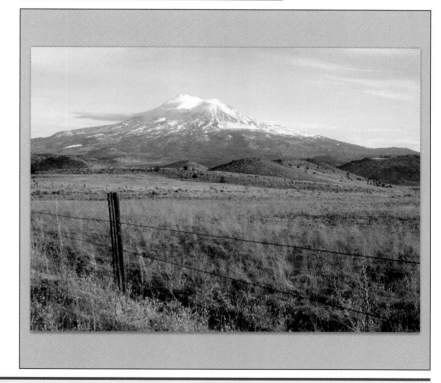

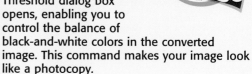

TIPS

How can the Color Balance command help me improve poorly lit digital photos?

The Color Balance command can help eliminate the colorcast that can sometimes permeate a digital photo. For example, some indoor incandescent or fluorescent lighting can add a yellowish or bluish tint to your images. You can remove these tints by adding blue or red, respectively, to your images by using this command.

How can I convert my image to black and white pixels?

Click **Image**, **Adjustments**, and then **Threshold**. The Threshold dialog box opens, enabling you to control the balance of black-and-white colors in the converted image. This command makes your image look like a photocopy.

Using the Variations Command

The Variations command includes a user-friendly interface that enables you to adjust the color in your image.

If you make a selection before performing the Variations command, only the selected pixels are affected. Similarly, if you have a multilayered image, your adjustments affect only the selected layer. For more on making selections, see Chapter 4. For more on layers, see Chapter 8.

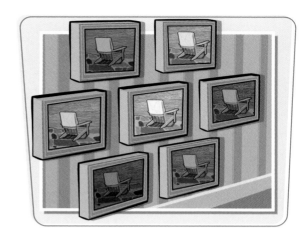

For more on making selections, see Chapter 4. For more on layers, see Chapter 8.

Using the Variations Command

1 Click **Image**.

2 Click **Adjustments**.

3 Click **Variations**.

The Variations dialog box opens.

4 Choose a tonal range to adjust (◎ changes to ◉).

● Alternatively, you can choose **Saturation**, or strength of color (◎ changes to ◉).

5 Click and drag the slider (▭) left to perform small adjustments or right to make large adjustments.

6 To add a color to your image, click one of the **More** thumbnails.

● The result of the adjustments appears in the Current Pick thumbnails.

To increase the effect, you can click the **More** thumbnail again.

● You can increase the brightness of the image by clicking **Lighter**.

● You can decrease the brightness of the image by clicking **Darker**.

7 Click **OK**.

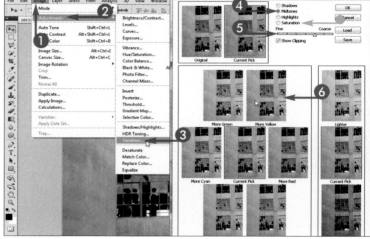

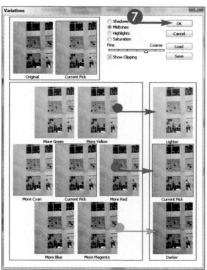

Photoshop makes the color adjustments to the image.

In this example, some of the blue colorcast is replaced with yellow.

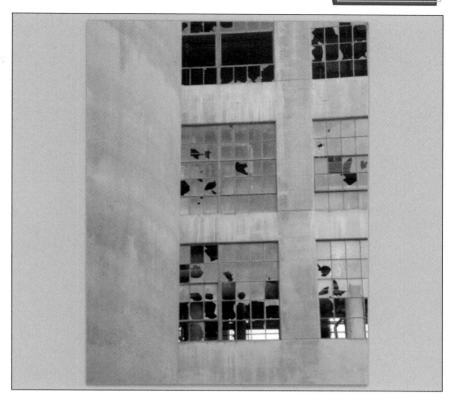

TIP

How can I undo color adjustments while using the Variations dialog box?

If you clicked one of the **More** thumbnail images to increase a color, you can click the **More** thumbnail image opposite to undo the effect.

When you add colors in equal amounts to an image, the colors opposite one another — for example, Green (●) and Magenta (●) — cancel each other out.

Clicking the Original image in the upper-left corner also returns the image to its original state.

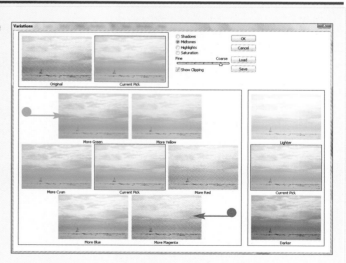

Match Colors between Images

You can use the Match Color command to match the colors in one image with the colors from another. For example, you can apply the colors from a bluish shoreline to a reddish desert to give the desert image a cooler appearance.

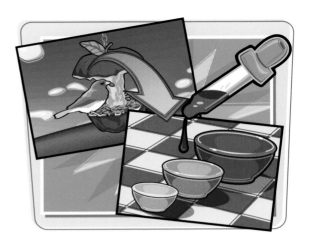

① Open a source image from which you want to match colors.

② Open a destination image whose colors you want to change.

Make sure the image window for the destination image is selected.

③ Click **Image**.

④ Click **Adjustments**.

⑤ Click **Match Color**.

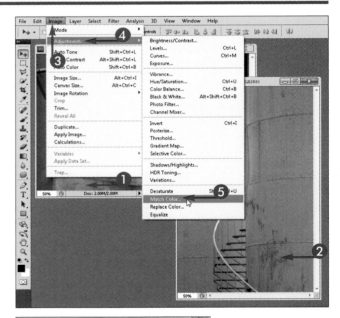

The Match Color dialog box opens.

⑥ Click here (⊡) to choose the file name of the source image.

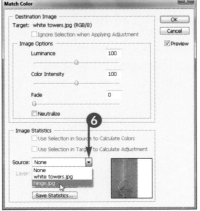

⑦ Click and drag the sliders (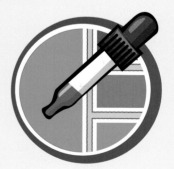) to control how the new colors are applied.

Luminance controls the brightness.

Color Intensity controls the saturation.

Fade controls how much color Photoshop replaces; you can increase the Fade value to greater than 0 to only partially replace the color.

⑧ Click **OK**.

Photoshop replaces the colors in the destination image with those in the source image.

● In this example, Photoshop applies the reds from a photo of rusty metal to a less colorful photo of an industrial tank.

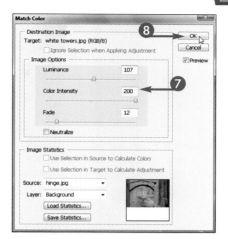

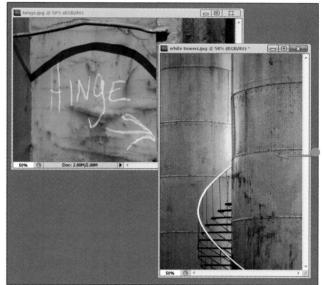

TIP

How do I match colors by using colors from only a selected part of my source image?

Make a selection before performing steps **3** to **5** in this section and then click the **Use Selection in Source to Calculate Colors** check box (☐ changes to ☑) in the Match Color dialog box. Photoshop uses only colors from inside the selection to determine color replacement.

Correct Shadows and Highlights

You can quickly correct images with overly dark or light areas by using the Shadows/Highlights command. This command can help correct photos that have a shadowed subject because of backlighting.

If you make a selection before performing the Shadows/Highlights command, only the selected pixels are affected. Similarly, if you have a multilayered image, your adjustments affect only the selected layer. For more on making selections, see Chapter 4. For more on layers, see Chapter 8.

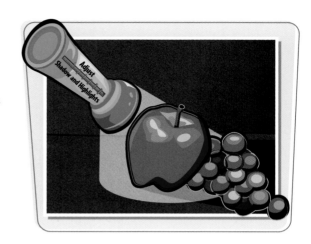

Correct Shadows and Highlights

1 Click **Image**.

2 Click **Adjustments**.

3 Click **Shadows/Highlights**.

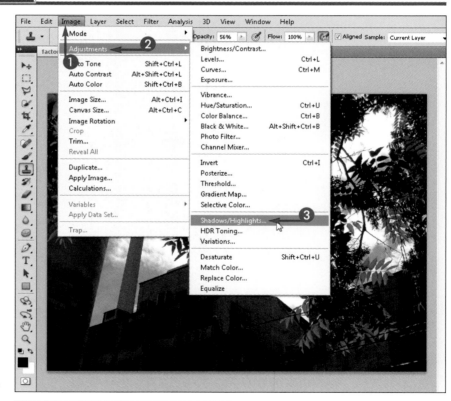

The Shadows/Highlights dialog box opens.

4 Click and drag the **Amount** slider ( ) in the Shadows section.

The farther you drag to the right, the more the shadows lighten.

● You can also adjust the shadows by typing a number from 0 to 100.

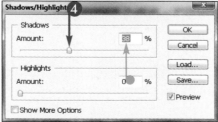

⑤ Click and drag the **Amount** slider (⬜) in the Highlights section.

The farther you drag to the right, the more the highlights darken.

● You can also adjust the highlights by typing a number from 0 to 100.

⑥ Click **OK**.

Photoshop adjusts the shadows and highlights in the image.

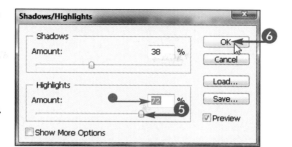

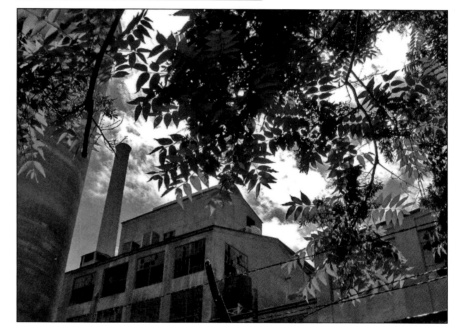

TIP

How do I get more control over how the Shadows/Highlights command affects my shadows and highlights?
Click the **Show More Options** check box in the Shadows/Highlights dialog box (⬜ changes to ☑). Additional settings appear. Adjusting the Tonal Width sliders helps you control what parts of the image are considered shadows and highlights. The Radius sliders help you control the contrast in the adjusted shadows and highlights.

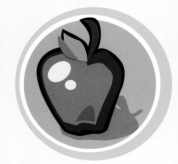

Create a Duotone

You can convert a grayscale image to a duotone. This is an easy way to add some color to a black-and-white photo.

A *duotone* is essentially a grayscale image with a color tint.

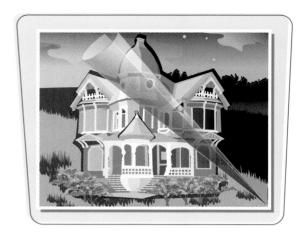

1 Click **Image**.

2 Click **Mode**.

3 Click **Grayscale**.

4 In the message box that appears, click **Discard**.

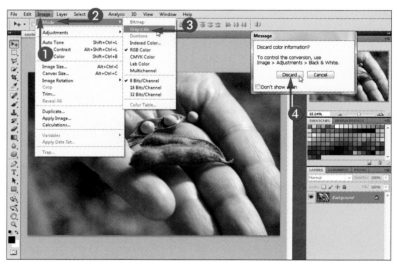

Photoshop converts your image to grayscale.

5 Click **Image**.

6 Click **Mode**.

7 Click **Duotone**.

The Duotone Options dialog box opens.

8 Click here (⏷) to choose **Duotone**.

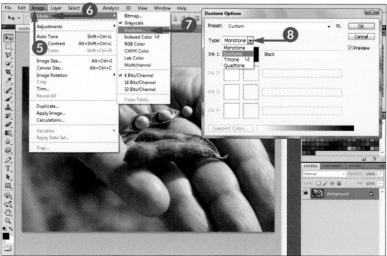

⑨ Click the first color swatch.

The Select ink color dialog box opens.

⑩ Click inside the window to choose your first duotone color.

● You can click and drag the slider (▷□◁) to change the color selection.

⑪ Click **OK**.

⑫ Type a name for the color.

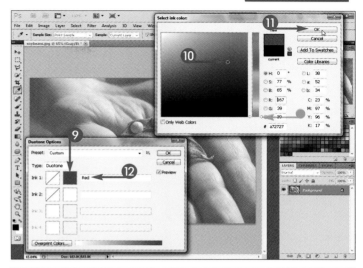

⑬ Click the second color swatch.

The Color Libraries dialog box opens.

⑭ Click inside the window to choose your second duotone color.

⑮ Click **OK** in the Color Libraries dialog box.

⑯ Click **OK** in the Duotone Options dialog box.

Photoshop uses the two selected colors to create the tones in the image.

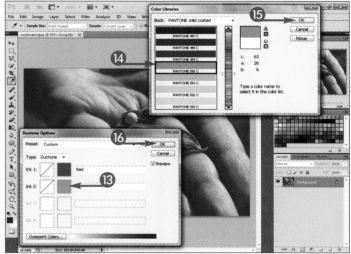

 TIPS

How can I use duotones to enliven a project?

Duotones offer a quick and easy way to add color to a Web page or printed publication when all you have available are grayscale images.

Can I combine more than two colors to create the tones in my grayscale image?

Yes. You can combine three colors to create a tritone or four colors to create a quadtone. Choose **Tritone** or **Quadtone** in step **7** to create these types of images. You can also choose **Monotone** to create your image tones by using a single color.

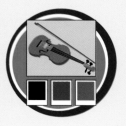

Convert to Black and White

You can use the Black and White interface to remove colors in a photo and then adjust various sliders to control the lightness and darkness of the different areas of the photo.

If you make a selection before performing the Black & White command, only the selected pixels are affected. Similarly, if you have a multilayered image, your adjustments affect only the selected layer. For more on making selections, see Chapter 4. For more on layers, see Chapter 8.

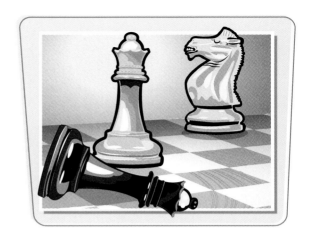

Convert to Black and White

Adjust Lighting with Sliders

1 Click **Image**.

2 Click **Adjustments**.

3 Click **Black & White**.

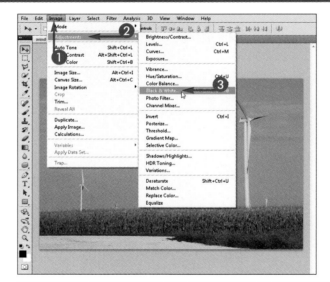

The Black and White dialog box opens.

Photoshop converts your image to grayscale.

4 Click and drag a slider (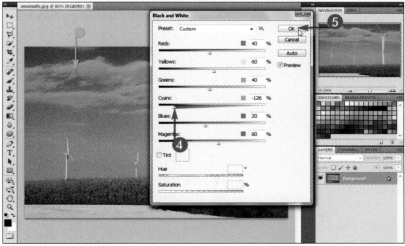) to adjust the lightness of a color in the image.

The sliders correspond to the colors in the original image.

Drag to the left to darken a color.

Drag to the right to lighten a color.

Photoshop adjusts the color.

● In this example, the sky is darkened by clicking and dragging the **Cyans** slider to the left.

5 Click **OK** to apply the adjustments.

Adjust Lighting with the Mouse

1. With the Black and White dialog box open, click inside the image and then hold down the mouse button ($\mathrel{\leftthumbsup}$ changes to $\mathscr{I}$).

● Photoshop reads the clicked color and then highlights the relevant color in the dialog box.

2. With the mouse button down, drag the cursor to the left or right to adjust the color lightness ($\mathscr{I}$ changes to $\mathrel{\leftthumbsup}$).

3. Click **OK** to apply the adjustment.

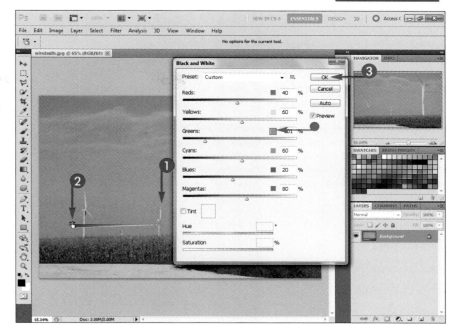

TIP

How can I tint my image by using the Black and White tool?

1. In the Black and White dialog box, click the **Tint** check box (☐ changes to ☑).

   Photoshop tints the image.

2. Click and drag the **Hue** slider (◻) to control the color of the tint.

● You can also click the color box to choose a tint color.

3. Click and drag the **Saturation** slider (◻) to control the intensity of the tint.

   You can also type values for the hue and saturation.

4. Click **OK** to apply the adjustments.

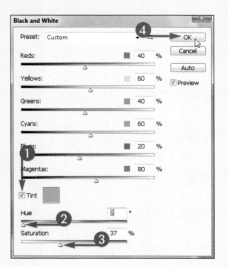

Adjust Vibrance

The Vibrance command can boost the intensity of the colors in an image, helping you improve the look of a faded or washed-out photo. You can also use the command to mute an overly colorful image.

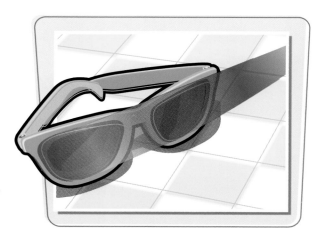

If you make a selection before performing the Vibrance command, only the selected pixels are affected. Similarly, if you have a multilayered image, your adjustments affect only the selected layer. For more on making selections, see Chapter 4. For more on layers, see Chapter 8.

Adjust Vibrance

1 Click **Image**.

2 Click **Adjustments**.

3 Click **Vibrance**.

The Vibrance dialog box opens.

4 To display your adjustments in the image window as you make them, click the **Preview** check box (☐ changes to ☑).

5 Click and drag the **Vibrance** slider (▢) to adjust the intensity of the colors.

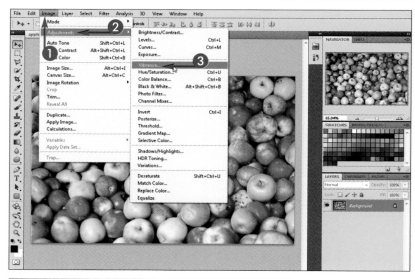

The Vibrance setting takes into account the current saturation of the colors, emphasizing colors that are less intense.

6 Click and drag the **Saturation** slider (▢) to adjust the intensity of the colors in the image.

The Saturation setting changes the intensity evenly across all colors.

7 Click **OK**.

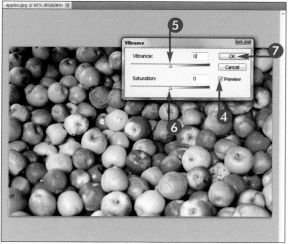

Photoshop applies the
adjustments.

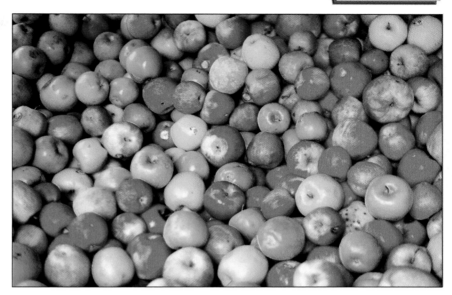

TIP

**How can I improve an under- or
overexposed image?**
You can fix exposure problems by using the
Exposure command.

① Click **Image**, **Adjustments**, and then
Exposure to open the Exposure
dialog box.

② Make exposure adjustments by dragging the
sliders (🔲).

You can drag the **Exposure** slider to adjust
highlights.

You can drag the **Offset** slider to adjust
shadows and midtones.

You can drag the **Gamma Correction** slider
to adjust the gamma brightness function, which can correct for varying monitor brightnesses.

③ Click **OK** to apply the adjustments.

Note: To locally adjust exposure, see the section "Using the Dodge and Burn Tools."

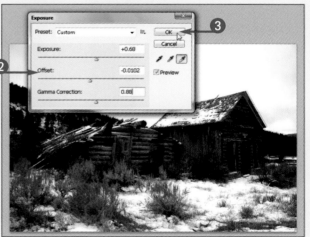

CHAPTER 8

Working with Layers

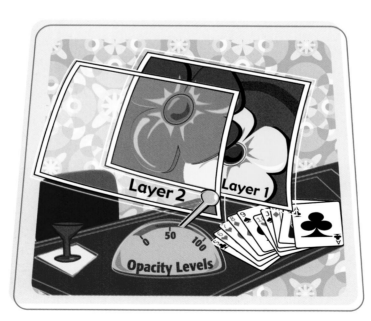

You can separate the elements in your image so you can move and transform them independently of one another. You can accomplish this by placing them in different layers.

What Are Layers?

A Photoshop image can consist of multiple layers, with each layer containing different objects in the image. When you open a digital-camera photo or a newly scanned image in Photoshop, it exists as a single layer known as the Background layer. You can add new layers on top of the Background layer as you work.

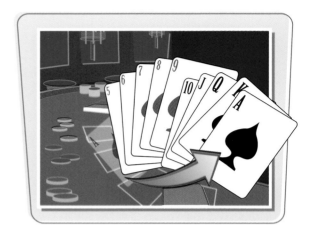

Layer Independence

Layered Photoshop files act like several images combined into one. Each layer of an image has its own set of pixels that you can move and transform independently of the pixels in other layers.

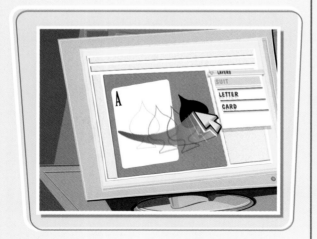

Apply Commands to Layers

Most Photoshop commands affect only the layer that you select. For example, if you click and drag with the Move tool ( ), the selected layer moves while the other layers stay in place. If you apply a color adjustment, only colors in the selected layer change.

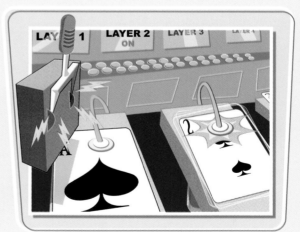

Manipulate Layers

You can combine, duplicate, and hide layers in an image as well as shuffle their order. You can also link particular layers so they move in unison or blend content from different layers in creative ways. You manage all this in Photoshop's Layers panel.

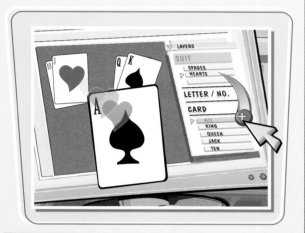

Transparency

Layers can have transparent areas, where the elements in the layers below can show through. When you perform a Cut or Erase command on a layer, the affected pixels become transparent. You can also make a layer partially transparent by decreasing its opacity or its fill.

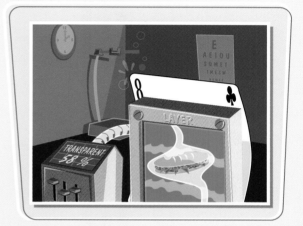

Adjustment Layers

Adjustment layers are special layers that contain information about color or tonal adjustments. An adjustment layer affects the pixels in all the layers below it. You can increase or decrease an adjustment layer's intensity to get precisely the effect you want.

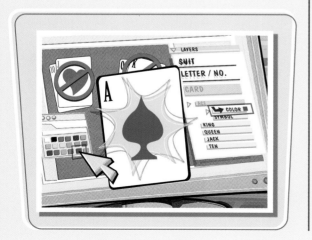

Save Layered Files

You can save multilayered images only in the Photoshop, PDF, and TIFF file formats. To save a layered image in another file format — for example, BMP, GIF, or JPEG — you must combine the image's layers into a single layer, a process known as *flattening*. For more on saving files, see Chapter 14.

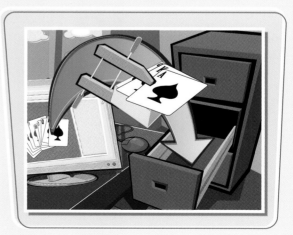

Create and Add to a Layer

To keep elements in your image independent of one another, you can create separate layers and add objects to them.

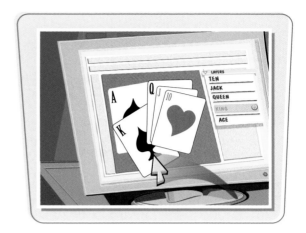

Create a Layer

1. Click the **Layers** tab to open the Layers panel.

   If the Layers tab is hidden, you can click **Window** and then **Layers** to open the Layers panel.

2. Click the layer above which you want to add the new layer.

3. In the Layers panel, click the **New Layer** button (⬜).

   Alternatively, you can click **Layer**, **New**, and then **Layer**.

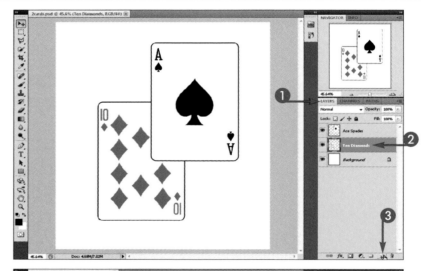

● Photoshop creates a new transparent layer.

Note: *To change the name of a layer, see the section "Rename a Layer."*

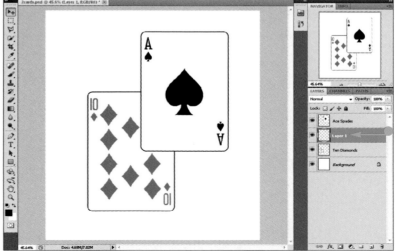

Copy and Paste into a Layer

Note: *This example shows how to add content to the new layer by copying and pasting from another image file.*

1 Open another image.

2 Using a selection tool, select the content you want to copy into the other image.

Note: *For more on opening an image, see Chapter 1. For more on the selection tools, see Chapter 4.*

3 Click **Edit**.

4 Click **Copy**.

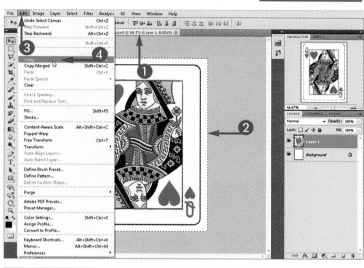

View the image where you created the new layer.

5 Click the new layer in the Layers panel.

6 Click **Edit**.

7 Click **Paste**.

● The selected content from the other image appears in the new layer.

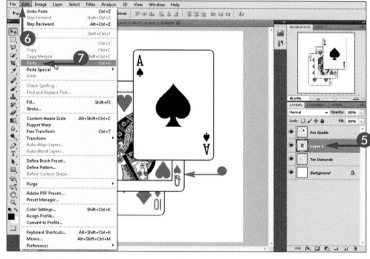

TIPS

What is the Background layer?

The Background layer is the default bottom layer that appears when you create a new image that has a nontransparent background color or when you import an image from a scanner or a digital camera. You can create new layers on top of a Background layer but not below it. Unlike other layers, a Background layer cannot contain transparent pixels.

How can I copy layers between images?

If you have multiple images open in Photoshop, you can click and drag a layer from the Layers panel of one image into the window of a different image. Photoshop copies the layer into the second image. You can move multiple layers by **Ctrl** + clicking (⌘ + clicking on a Mac) them and then dragging them to a different image window.

You can hide a layer to temporarily remove elements in that layer from view. Hidden layers do not appear when you print or use the Save for Web command.

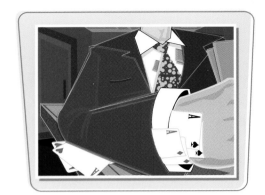

1 Click the **Layers** tab to open the Layers panel.

If the Layers tab is hidden, you can click **Window** and then **Layers** to open the Layers panel.

2 Click the visibility icon (👁) for a layer.

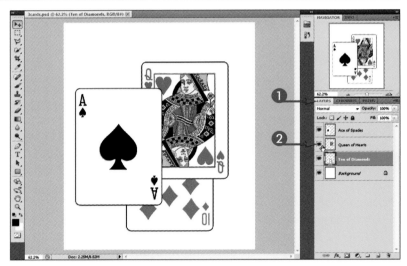

● The icon disappears.

Photoshop hides the layer.

To show one layer and hide all the others, you can press Alt (Option on a Mac) and then click 👁 for the layer you want to show. Pressing Alt (Option) and then clicking again makes the other layers reappear.

Note: You can also delete a layer. See the section "Delete a Layer" for more.

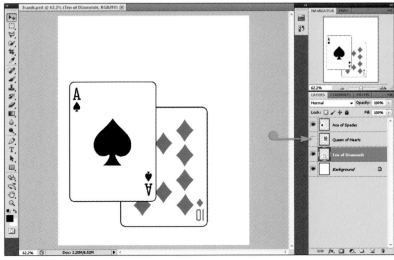

Move a Layer

You can use the Move tool to reposition the elements in one layer without moving those in others.

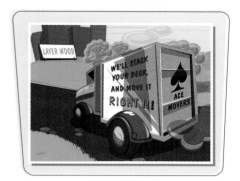

Move a Layer

① Click the **Layers** tab to open the Layers panel.

If the Layers tab is hidden, you can click **Window** and then **Layers** to open the Layers panel.

② Click a layer.

③ Click the **Move** tool (▶️➕).

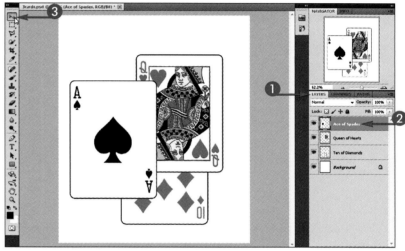

④ Click and drag inside the window.

Content in the selected layer moves.

Content in the other layers does not move.

Note: To move several layers at the same time, see the section "Link Layers."

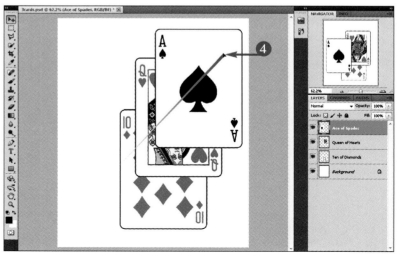

By duplicating a layer, you can manipulate elements in an image while keeping a copy of their original state.

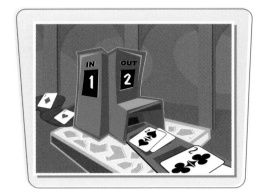

Duplicate a Layer

① Click the **Layers** tab to open the Layers panel.

If the Layers tab is hidden, you can click **Window** and then **Layers** to open the Layers panel.

② Click a layer.

③ Click and drag the layer to 🔳.

Alternatively, you can click **Layer** and then **Duplicate Layer**; a dialog box opens, asking you to name the duplicate layer.

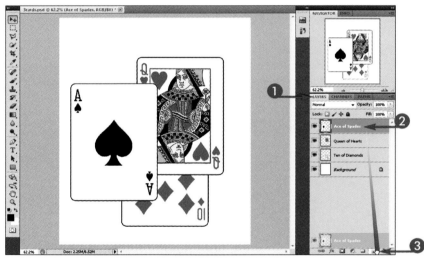

● Photoshop duplicates the selected layer.

Note: To rename the duplicate layer, see the section "Rename a Layer."

● You can see that Photoshop has duplicated the layer by selecting the new layer, clicking the **Move** tool 📩, and then clicking and dragging the layer.

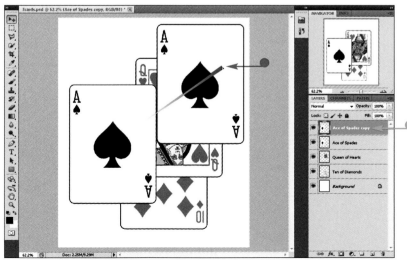

Delete a Layer

You can delete a layer when you no longer have a use for its contents.

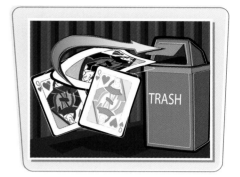

Delete a Layer

① Click the **Layers** tab to open the Layers panel.

If the Layers tab is hidden, you can click **Window** and then **Layers** to open the Layers panel.

② Click a layer.

③ Click and drag the layer to the Trash icon (🗑).

Alternatively, you can click **Layer** and then **Delete Layer** or you can select a layer and click 🗑. In both cases, a confirmation dialog box opens.

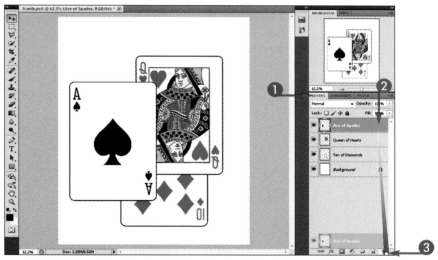

Photoshop deletes the selected layer, and the content in the layer disappears from the image window.

Note: You can also hide a layer. See the section "Hide a Layer" for more.

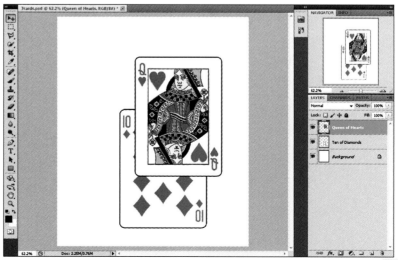

Reorder Layers

You can change the stacking order of layers to move elements forward or backward.

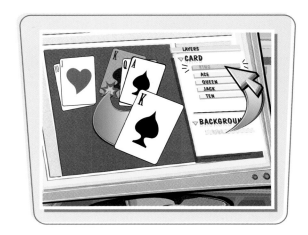

Reorder Layers

Using the Layers Panel

1 Click the **Layers** tab to open the Layers panel.

If the Layers tab is hidden, you can click **Window** and then **Layers** to open the Layers panel.

2 Click a layer other than the Background layer.

3 Click and drag the layer to change its position in the stack.

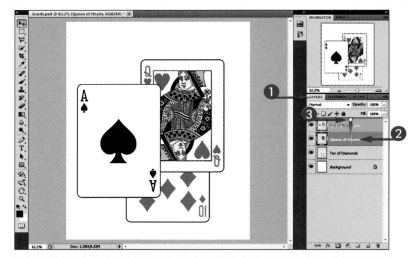

● The layer assumes its new position in the stack.

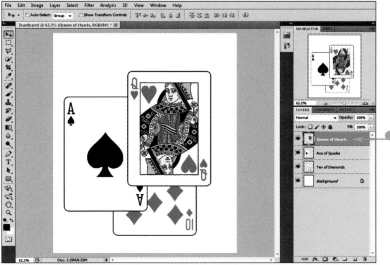

Using the Arrange Commands

① In the Layers panel, click a layer other than the Background layer.

② Click **Layer**.

③ Click **Arrange**.

④ Click the command for how you want to move the layer.

You can choose **Bring to Front**, **Bring Forward**, **Send Backward**, **Send to Back**, or **Reverse**.

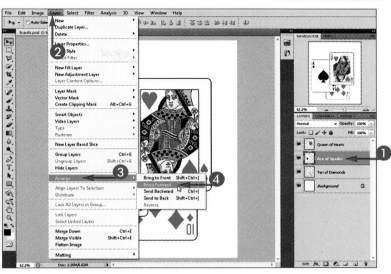

In this example, Bring Forward is chosen.

● The layer assumes its new position in the stack.

Note: *You cannot move a layer below the default Background layer.*

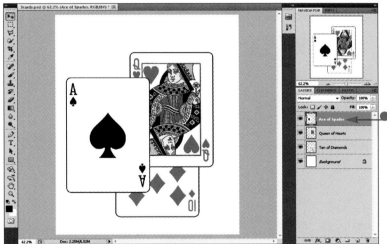

 TIP

Are there shortcuts for changing the order of layers?
You can shift layers forward and backward in the stack by pressing the following shortcuts keys:

Move...	Windows Shortcut	Mac Shortcut
...forward one step	Ctrl +]	⌘ +]
...backward	Ctrl + [	⌘ + [
...to the very front	Shift + Ctrl +]	Shift + ⌘ +]
...to the very back	Shift + Ctrl + [	Shift + ⌘ + [

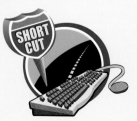

Change the Opacity of a Layer

Adjusting the opacity of a layer can let elements in the layers below show through. *Opacity* is the opposite of transparency. Decreasing the opacity of a layer increases its transparency.

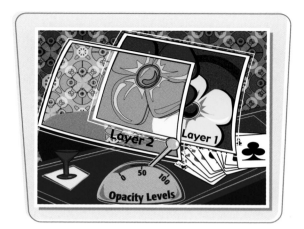

Change the Opacity of a Layer

1 Click the **Layers** tab to open the Layers panel.

If the Layers tab is hidden, you can click **Window** and then **Layers** to open the Layers panel.

2 Click a layer other than the Background layer.

Note: *You cannot change the opacity of the Background layer.*

● The default opacity is 100%, which is completely opaque.

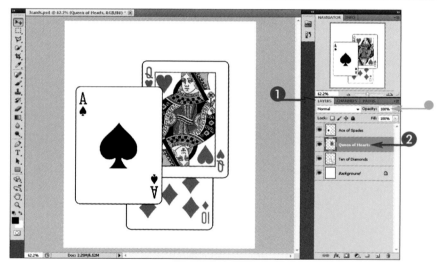

3 Type a new value in the Opacity field and then press Enter (Return on a Mac).

● Alternatively, you can click ⬚ and then drag the slider (⬚).

A layer's opacity can range from 0% to 100%.

● The layer changes in opacity.

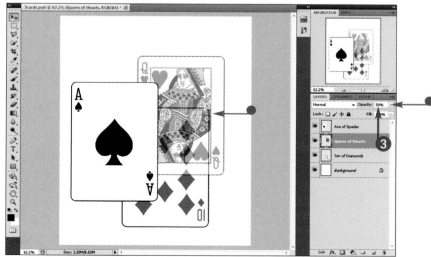

A shortcut for changing a layer's opacity is to click the layer and then press a number key.

● In this example, 3 is pressed, which changes the opacity to 30%.

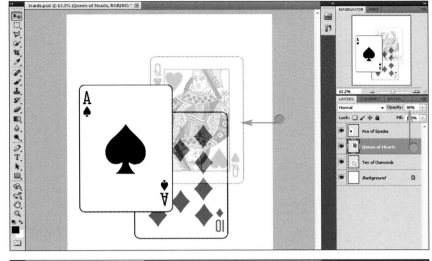

You can make multiple layers in your image semitransparent by changing their opacities.

● In this example, both the Queen of Hearts and Ten of Diamonds layers are semitransparent.

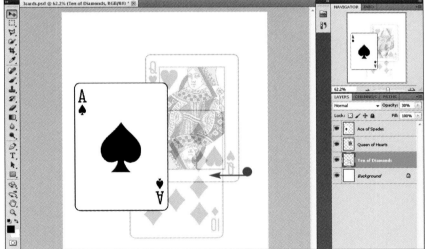

TIP

What is the Fill setting in the Layers panel?
It is similar to the Opacity setting, except that lowering it does not affect any blending options or layer styles applied to the layer. For example, if you apply a drop shadow to a layer, lowering the Fill setting makes the layer object more transparent but does not affect the shadow behind the object. Lowering the Opacity setting does affect blending options and layer styles. For more on blending options, see the section "Blend Layers." For more on layer styles, see Chapter 9.

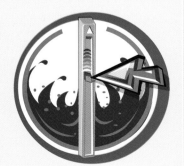

Merge Layers

Merging layers enables you to permanently combine information from two or more separate layers. Flattening an image combines all the layers of an image into one.

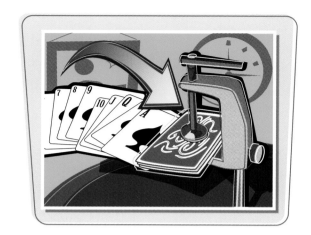

Merge Layers

1. Click the **Layers** tab to open the Layers panel.

   If the Layers tab is hidden, you can click **Window** and then **Layers** to open the Layers panel.

2. Click a layer.

3. While pressing **Ctrl** (⌘ on a Mac), click one or more layers to merge with the selected layer.

4. Click **Layer**.

5. Click **Merge Layers**.

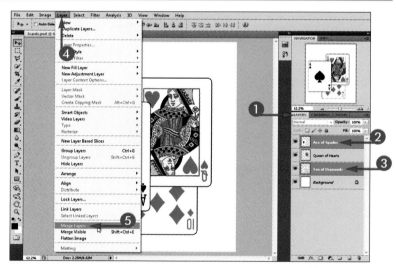

- The layers merge.

  Photoshop keeps the name of the uppermost layer. The merged layers also assume the position of the uppermost layer.

- To see the result of the merge, select the new layer, click the **Move** tool (⊹), and then click and drag the merged layer.

  The elements that were previously in separate layers now move together.

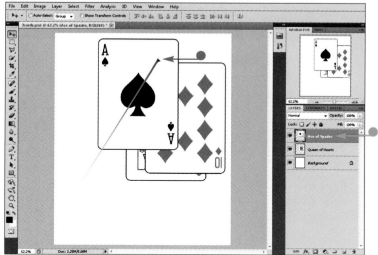

Flatten an Image

1 Click **Layer**.

2 Click **Flatten Image**.

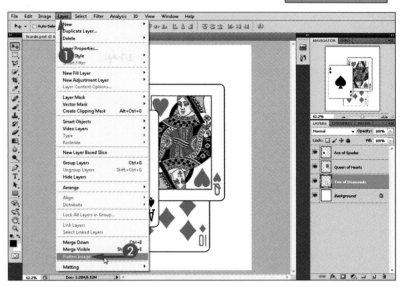

● All the layers merge into one Background layer.

● You can also access Merge and Flatten commands in the Layers panel menu. Click the panel menu (◾) to access it.

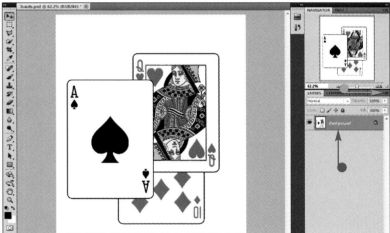

TIPS

Why would I want to merge layers?
Merging layers enables you to save computer memory. The fewer layers a Photoshop image has, the less space it takes up in RAM and on your hard drive when you save it. Merging layers also lets you permanently combine elements of your image when you are happy with how you have arranged them relative to one another. If you want the option of rearranging all the original layers in the future, save a copy of your image before you merge layers.

What happens to layers when I save an image for the Web?
When creating a JPEG, nonanimated GIF, or PNG file for publishing on the Web, Photoshop automatically flattens the layers of an image before creating the new file. Your original Photoshop image retains its layers. For more on saving images, see Chapter 14.

You can rename a layer to give it a name that describes its content. Giving your layers names can be helpful when you are managing many layers in a single image.

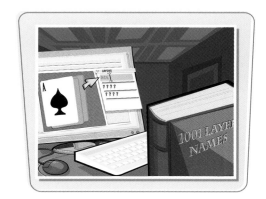

① Click the **Layers** tab to open the Layers panel.

If the Layers tab is hidden, you can click **Window** and then **Layers** to open the Layers panel.

② Click a layer.

③ Click **Layer**.

④ Click **Layer Properties**.

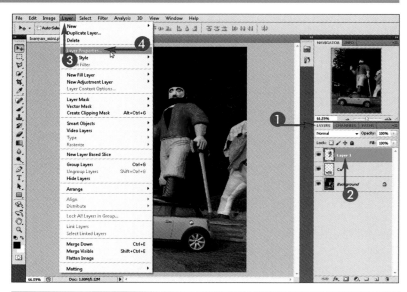

The Layer Properties dialog box opens.

⑤ Type a new name for the layer.

⑥ Click **OK**.

● The name of the layer changes in the Layers panel.

You can also double-click the name of the layer in the Layers panel to edit the name.

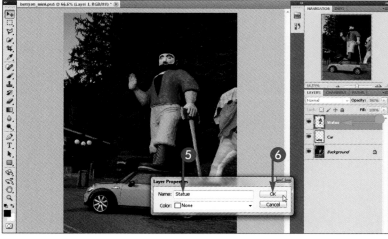

Transform a Layer

You can use a transform tool to change the shape of the objects in a layer. When you transform a layer, the rest of your image remains unchanged.

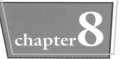
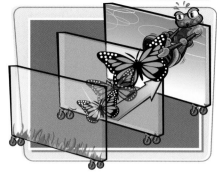

Transform a Layer

① Click the **Layers** tab to open the Layers panel.

If the Layers tab is hidden, you can click **Window** and then **Layers** to open the Layers panel.

② Click **Edit**.

③ Click **Transform**.

④ Click a transform command.

You can also click the **Move** tool (▶⊕) and then click **Show Transform Controls** on the Options bar.

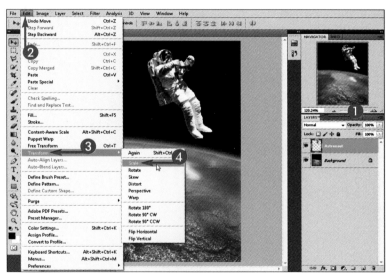

⑤ Click and drag the side and corner handles (□) to transform the shape of the layer (▷ changes to ↗).

⑥ Click ✓ or press Enter (⌘ + Return on a Mac) to apply the change.

● You can click ⊘ or press Esc to cancel the change.

Photoshop changes your image according to the transform command you selected.

Note: For more on transforming your images, see Chapter 5.

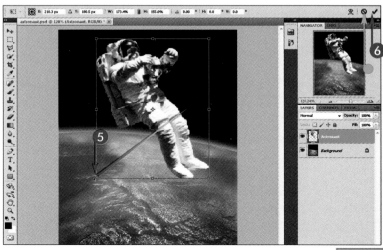

Create a Solid Fill Layer

You can create a solid fill layer to place an opaque layer of color throughout your image. You can use fill layers that contrast with the objects in layers above them to make those objects stand out.

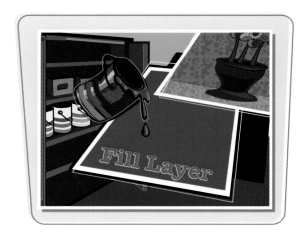

Create a Solid Fill Layer

1 Click the **Layers** tab to open the Layers panel.

If the Layers tab is hidden, you can click **Window** and then **Layers** to open the Layers panel.

2 Click the layer above which you want to add solid color.

3 Click **Layer**.

4 Click **New Fill Layer**.

5 Click **Solid Color**.

● You can also click the **Create New Fill or Adjustment Layer** button (image) and then choose **Solid Color**.

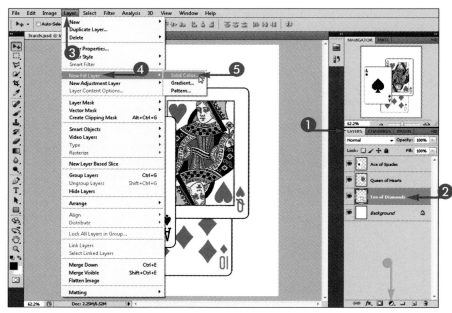

The New Layer dialog box opens.

6 Type a name for the layer.

● You can specify a blend mode or opacity setting for the layer.

Note: See the section "Blend Layers" or "Change the Opacity of a Layer" for more.

7 Click **OK**.

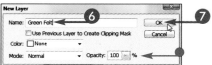

The Color Picker dialog box opens.

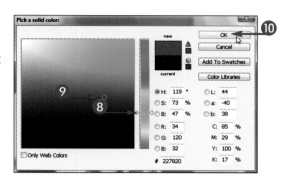

8 To change the range of colors that appears in the window, click and drag the slider (⊲▭⊲).

9 To choose a fill color, click in the color window.

10 Click **OK**.

● Photoshop creates a new layer filled with a solid color.

Layers below the new fill layer are covered, while the layers above the new layer are not affected.

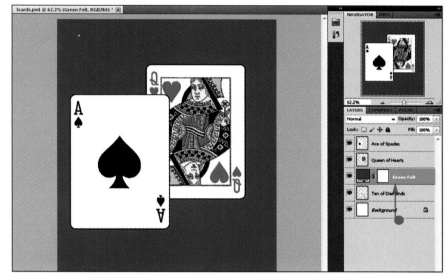

TIPS

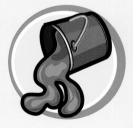

How do I add solid color to just part of a layer?
Make a selection with a selection tool before creating the solid fill layer. Photoshop adds color only inside the selection.

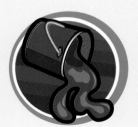

What other types of fill layers can I create?
You can add a gradient fill layer that shows a transition from one color to another by clicking **Layer**, **New Fill Layer**, and then **Gradient**. You can add a pattern fill layer that displays a repeated design by clicking **Layer**, **New Fill Layer**, and then **Pattern**.

Create an Adjustment Layer

Adjustment layers let you store color and tonal changes in a layer instead of having them permanently applied to your image. The information in an adjustment layer is applied to the pixels in the layers below it.

You can use adjustment layers to test an editing technique without applying it to the original layer. Adjustment layers are especially handy for experimenting with colors, tones, and brightness settings.

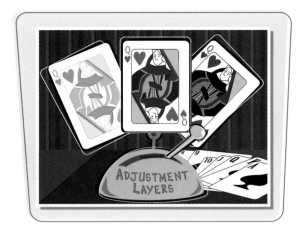

Create an Adjustment Layer

1 Click the **Layers** tab to open the Layers panel.

If the Layers tab is hidden, you can click **Window** and then **Layers** to open the Layers panel.

2 Click the **Adjustments** tab to open the Adjustments panel.

If a panel tab is not visible, you can click **Window** and then the panel name to open the panel.

3 Click the layer above which you want to create an adjustment layer.

4 Click an adjustment layer button.

Note: See the Tip on the next page for a description of the adjustment types.

● Photoshop places the new adjustment layer above the selected layer.

● You can specify a blend mode or opacity setting for the layer.

Note: See the section "Blend Layers" or "Change the Opacity of a Layer" for more.

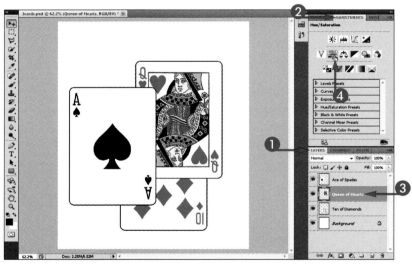

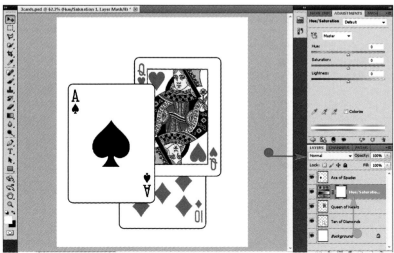

● The settings for the adjustment command appear in the Adjustments panel.

⑤ Click and drag the sliders (⬚) or type values to adjust the settings.

In this example, an adjustment layer is created that changes the hue and saturation.

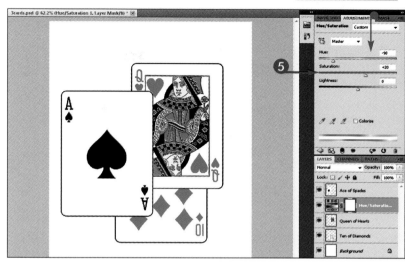

Photoshop applies the effect to the layers below the adjustment layer, including the Background layer.

● In this example, the adjustment layer affects the card layers below it while leaving the card layer above it unaffected.

● You can click **Clip to Layer** (⬚) to have the adjustment layer affect only the layer directly below it.

⑥ Click **Return to Adjustment List** (⬚) to show a list of adjustments in the Adjustments panel.

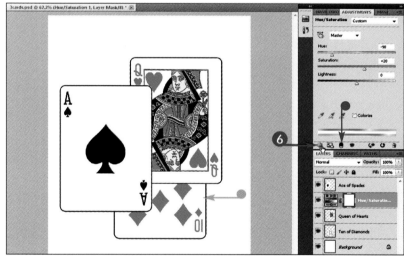

TIP

What types of adjustments can I apply to my image?

The adjustments are also available as commands, accessible by clicking **Image** and then **Adjustments**. Some of these commands are covered in Chapter 7. For the others, see the Photoshop help documentation.

⬚	Brightness/Contrast	⬚	Hue/Saturation	⬚	Invert
⬚	Levels	⬚	Color Balance	⬚	Posterize
⬚	Curves	⬚	Black & White	⬚	Threshold
⬚	Exposure	⬚	Photo Filter	⬚	Gradient Map
⬚	Vibrance	⬚	Channel Mixer	⬚	Selective Color

Edit an Adjustment Layer

You can modify the color and tonal changes that you defined in an adjustment layer. This enables you to fine-tune your adjustment layer to get the effect you want.

You can decrease the opacity of an adjustment layer to lessen its effect on the layers below it.

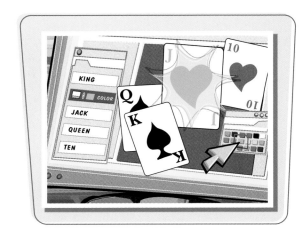

Edit an Adjustment Layer

① Click the **Layers** tab to open the Layers panel.

   If the Layers tab is hidden, you can click **Window** and then **Layers** to open the Layers panel.

② Click the **Adjustments** tab to open the Adjustments panel.

   If a panel tab is not visible, you can click **Window** and then the panel name to open the panel.

③ Click the adjustment layer you want to edit.

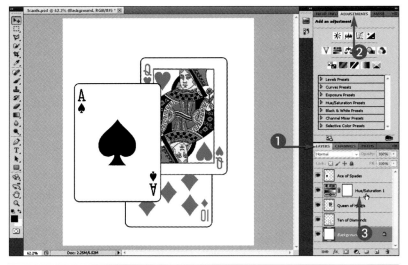

   The settings corresponding to the adjustment command appear in the Adjustments panel.

④ Click and drag the sliders (▢) to change the settings in the panel.

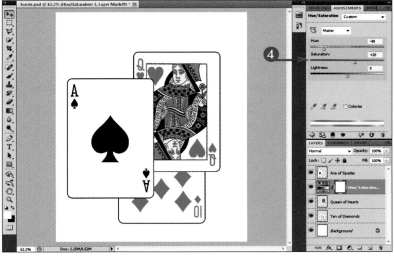

Photoshop applies your changes.

In this example, the hue is changed, which shifts the color in the layers below the adjustment layer.

● You can lessen the effect of an adjustment layer by decreasing the layer's opacity to less than 100%.

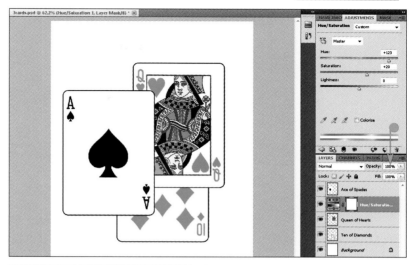

● In this example, the opacity was decreased to 60%, which reverses the decrease in saturation. Some of the original color in the cards returns.

● You can click here (🗑) to delete the selected adjustment layer.

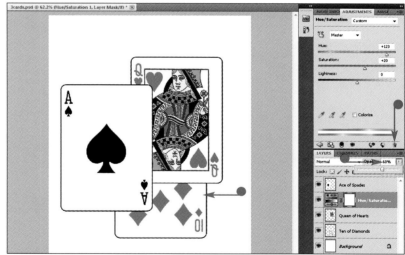

TIP

How do I merge an adjustment layer with a regular layer?

❶ Place the adjustment layer above the layer with which you want to merge it.

❷ Click **Layer** and then **Merge Down**.

Photoshop applies the adjustment layer's effects to the layer below it. The adjustment layer is removed from the Layers panel.

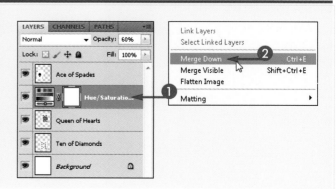

Apply an Adjustment-Layer Preset

Photoshop offers a variety of ready-to-use adjustment layers that apply common color-correction techniques and special effects. After you apply them, you can make changes to their settings in the Adjustments panel.

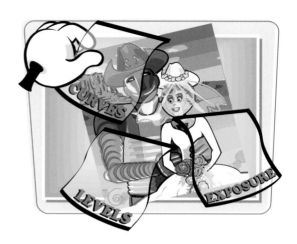

Apply an Adjustment-Layer Preset

① Click the **Layers** tab to open the Layers panel.

If the Layers tab is hidden, you can click **Window** and then **Layers** to open the Layers panel.

② Click the **Adjustments** tab to open the Adjustments panel.

If a panel tab is not visible, you can click **Window** and then the panel name to open the panel.

③ Click the layer above which you want to create an adjustment layer.

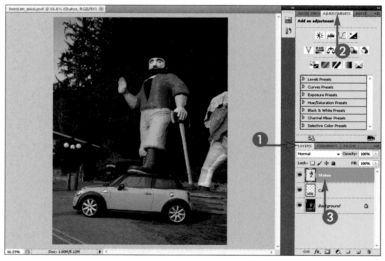

④ Click ▶ to open a list of adjustment-layer presets (▶ changes to ▽).

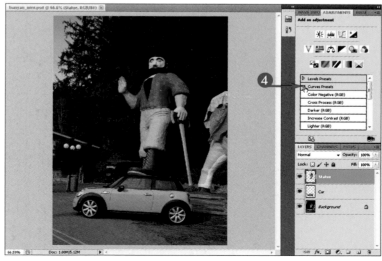

5 Click a preset.

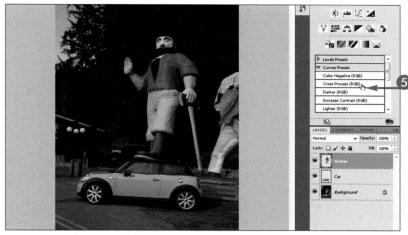

● Photoshop creates a new adjustment layer for the preset.

● The settings appear in the Adjustments panel.

The settings affect the layers below the adjustment layer, including the Background layer.

● You can click **Clip to Layer** (⬤) to have the adjustment layer affect only the layer directly below it.

6 Click **Return to Adjustment List** (🔲) to show a list of adjustments in the Adjustments panel.

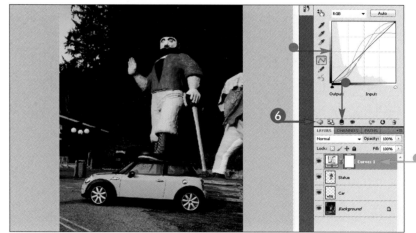

 TIP

How do I save an adjustment layer as a preset?
You can save your own adjustment layers as presets and then apply those layers to future projects.

1 Create an adjustment layer and then select it in the Layers panel.

2 Click the panel menu (▤) in the Adjustments panel.

3 Click **Save Preset**. The command name differs depending on the type of adjustment layer you are saving.

The Save dialog box opens, enabling you to name and save the preset.

After saving, your preset appears in the Adjustments panel preset list.

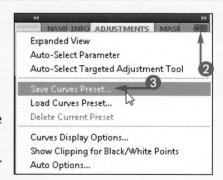

Link Layers

Linking causes different layers to move in unison when you rearrange them with the Move tool. You may find linking useful when you want to keep elements of an image aligned with one another but do not want to merge their layers. See the section "Merge Layers" for more on merging. Keeping layers unmerged enables you to apply effects independently to each one.

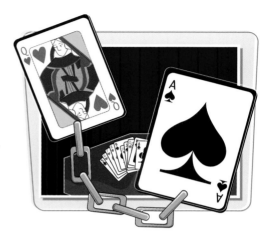

Create a Link

1 Click the **Layers** tab to open the Layers panel.

If the Layers tab is hidden, you can click **Window** and then **Layers** to open the Layers panel.

2 While pressing and holding Ctrl (⌘ on a Mac), click the layers you want to link.

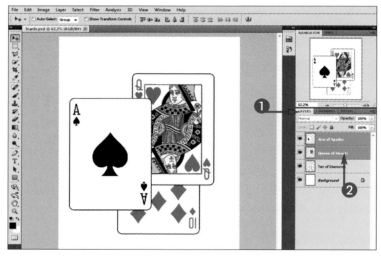

3 Click **Layer**.

4 Click **Link Layers**.

● Doing so turns on a linking icon (🔗).

The layers link together.

● You can also click Link Layers (🔗) in the Layers panel.

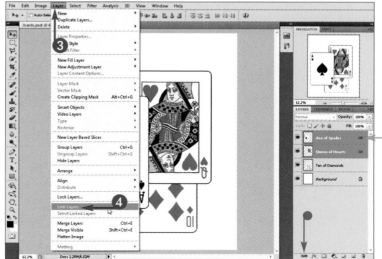

Move Linked Layers

1 Click the **Move** tool (▶+).

2 Click and drag inside the image window.

The linked layers move together.

Unlink Layers

1 While pressing **Ctrl** (⌘ on a Mac), click the layers you want to unlink.

2 Click **Layer**.

3 Click **Unlink Layers**.

Photoshop removes the link.

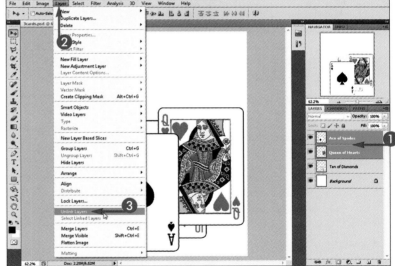

TIP

How do I keep from changing a layer after I have it the way I want it?

You can lock the layer by selecting the layer and then clicking the **Lock All** icon (🔒) in the Layers panel. You cannot move, delete, or otherwise edit a locked layer. You can click the **Lock Transparent Pixels** icon (▢) to prevent a user from editing the transparent pixels in the layer. Click the **Lock Image Pixels** icon (✏) to lock the nontransparent pixels in a layer, and click the **Lock Position** icon (⊞) to keep a layer from moving.

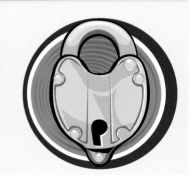

Blend Layers

You can use Photoshop's blending modes to specify how pixels in a layer should blend with the layers below. You can blend layers to create all kinds of visual effects in your photos.

In the following example, two photos are combined in one image file as two separate layers and then the layers are blended together. To copy a photo into a layer, see the section "Create and Add to a Layer."

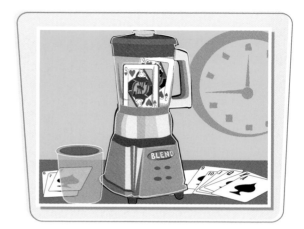

Blend Layers

Blend a Regular Layer

① Click the **Layers** tab to open the Layers panel.

If the Layers tab is hidden, you can click **Window** and then **Layers** to open the Layers panel.

② Click the layer that you want to blend.

③ Click here (▾) to choose a blend mode.

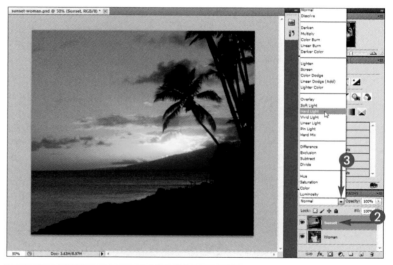

Photoshop blends the selected layer with the layers below it.

This example blends a sunset layer with a layer of a woman by using the Hard Light mode.

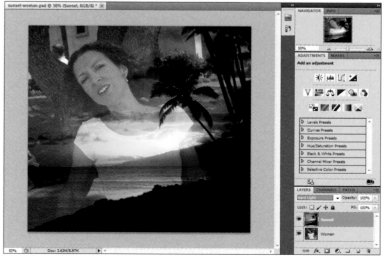

Blend an Adjustment Layer

① Click the **Layers** tab to open the Layers panel.

If the Layers tab is hidden, you can click **Window** and then **Layers** to open the Layers panel.

② Click the adjustment layer that you want to blend.

③ Click here (⊟) to choose a blend mode.

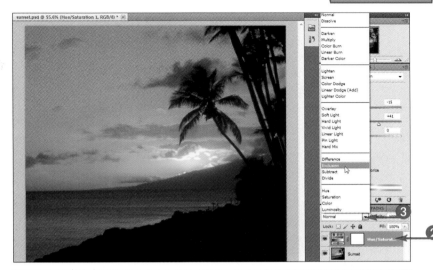

Photoshop blends the selected layer with the layers below it.

This example shows the Exclusion mode applied to a Hue and Saturation adjustment layer, which creates a photo-negative effect where the layers overlap.

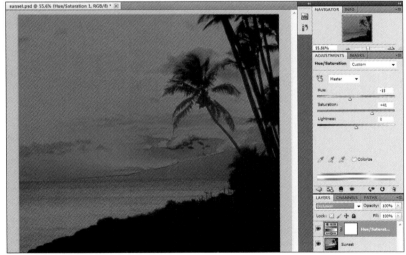

TIP

What effects do some of the different blending modes have?

- **Multiply:** Darkens the colors where the selected layer overlaps layers below it
- **Screen:** The opposite of Multiply. It lightens colors where layers overlap.
- **Color:** Takes the selected layer's colors and blends them with the details in the layers below it
- **Luminosity:** The opposite of Color. It takes the selected layer's details and mixes them with the colors below it.

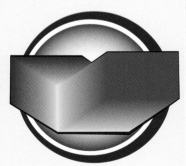

Work with Smart Objects

You can convert a layer into a Smart Object. Unlike a regular layer, Photoshop remembers the original composition of a Smart Object, so you can resize and perform other operations on it without its quality degrading.

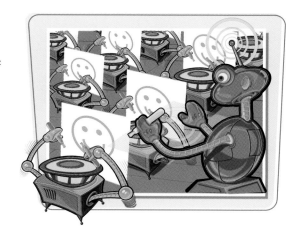

Create a Smart Object

1 Click the layer you want to convert into a Smart Object.

2 Click **Layer**.

3 Click **Smart Objects**.

4 Click **Convert to Smart Object**.

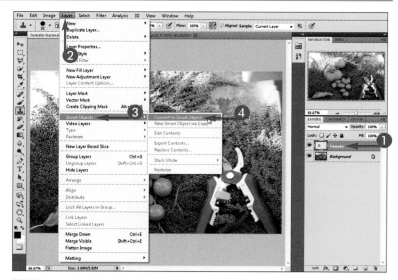

● Photoshop converts the layer to a Smart Object.

Smart Objects are designated with a special icon (🗗) in the Layers panel.

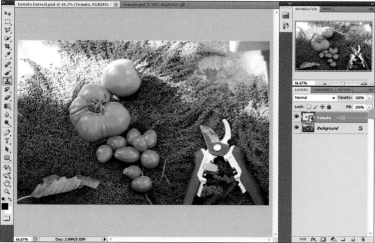

Duplicate a Smart Object

1 Click a Smart Object in the Layers panel.

2 Click **Layer**.

3 Click **Smart Objects**.

4 Click **New Smart Object via Copy**.

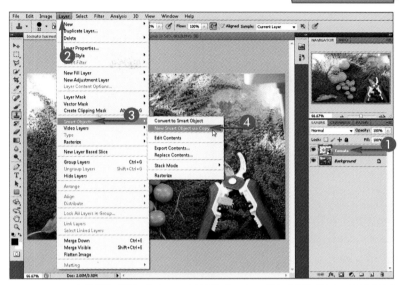

● Photoshop duplicates the Smart Object, and the new Smart Object appears in the Layers panel.

5 Click the **Move** tool (⊕).

6 Click and drag to view the new Smart Object.

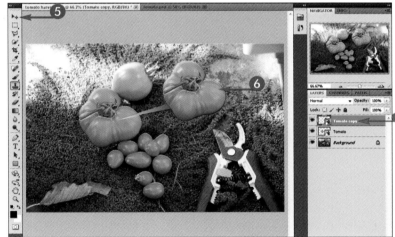

TIP

How do I convert a Smart Object back to a regular layer?

1 Click the Smart Object in the Layers panel.

2 Click **Layer** and then **Smart Objects**.

3 Click **Rasterize**.

Photoshop converts the Smart Object back to a layer.

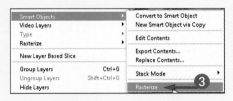

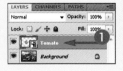

Work with Smart Objects (continued)

Because Photoshop remembers the original composition of a Smart Object, you can transform the object multiple times without it degrading in quality like a normal object would.

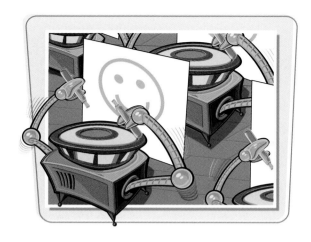

Scale a Smart Object

1 Click the Smart Object in the Layers panel.

2 Click **Edit**.

3 Click **Transform**.

4 Click **Scale**.

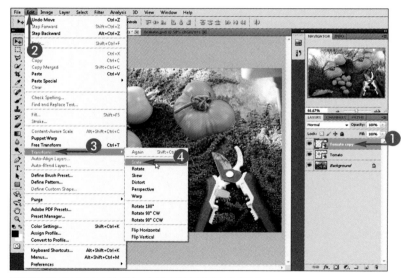

A rectangular bounding box with handles (☐) on the sides and corners surrounds the object.

5 Click and drag the handles (☐) to shrink the object (↖ changes to ↗).

6 Click ✔ or press Enter (⌘ + Return on a Mac) to commit the scaling.

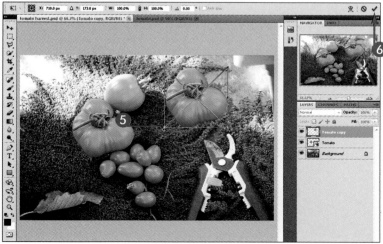

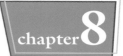

- Photoshop shrinks the object.

7 Repeat steps **2** to **4**.

8 Click and drag the handles (□) to enlarge the object (↖ changes to ↗).

9 Click ✓ or press **Enter** (⌘ + **Return** on a Mac) to commit the scaling.

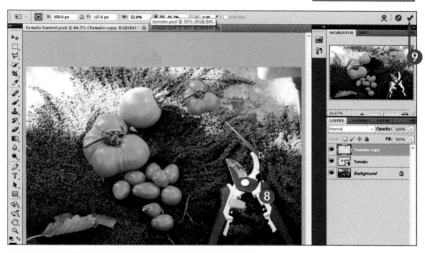

- Photoshop enlarges the object.

  Because Photoshop remembers the pixel information associated with the original object, the quality of the Smart Object is not degraded when you rescale it to its original size.

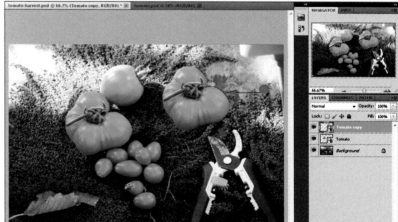

TIP

How can I insert another image into my project as a Smart Object?

You can use the **Place** command to insert a separate image as a Smart Object:

1 Click **File** and then **Place**.

2 In the Place dialog box that opens, click the image file you want to use.

3 Click **Place**.

4 Press **Enter** (**Return** on a Mac) to complete the Place command. Photoshop adds the image as a Smart Object.

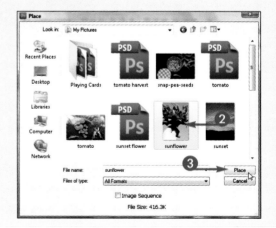

Create a
Layer Group

You can create a layer group to organize related layers together in the Layers panel. By selecting a layer group, you can execute commands on all the layers in the group at once. For example, you can hide, show, move, or reorder the layers in a layer group.

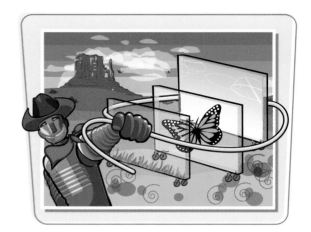

Create a Layer Group

① Click a layer in the Layers panel.

② Click **Create a New Group** (□).

● Photoshop creates a layer group above the selected layer.

You can double-click the layer group text to rename the layer group.

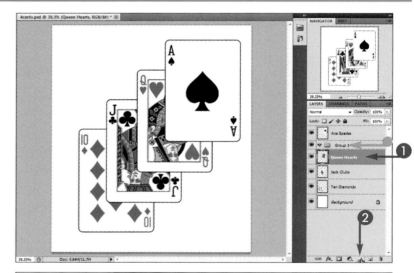

Add to a Layer Group

③ Click and drag a layer in the Layers panel to the layer group.

To add multiple layers at once, you can Ctrl + click to select the layers before dragging.

④ Release the mouse button.

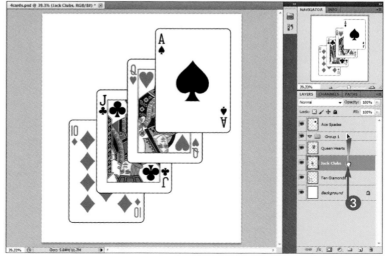

● Photoshop adds the layer to the group.

● You can repeat steps **3** and **4** to add more layers to the group.

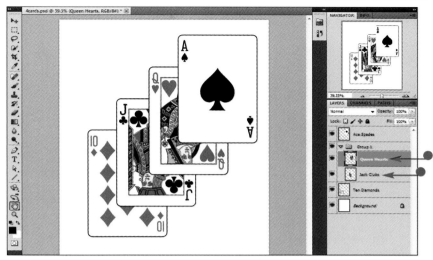

Execute Commands on a Layer Group

5 Click a layer group.

6 Click the visibility icon (👁).

● Photoshop hides all the layers in the layer group.

● You can click the **Move** tool (🔛) to move all the layers in a selected layer group.

● You can click here (▽) to close the layer group to free up space in the Layers panel (▽ changes to ▷).

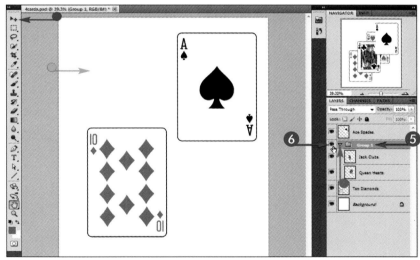

TIPS

How do I delete a layer group?

You can click a layer group in the Layers panel and then click 🗑. A dialog box opens, enabling you to delete the group and all its contents or just the group.

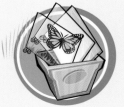

How can I control the opacity of several layers at once?

You can add the layers to a layer group, select the group, and then change the opacity of the group just as you would a single layer. For more, see the section "Change the Opacity of a Layer."

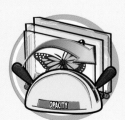

Applying Layer Styles

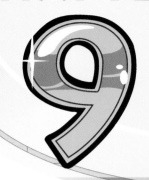

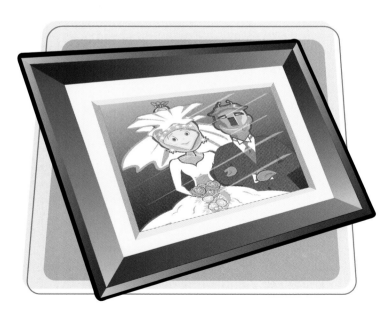

You can apply special effects to layers by using Photoshop's built-in layer styles. With these styles, you can add shadows, glows, and 3-D appearances to your layers. Photoshop's Styles panel enables you to easily apply predefined combinations of styles to your image or create your own styles.

Apply a Drop Shadow

You can apply a drop shadow to make a layer look as though it is floating above the canvas.

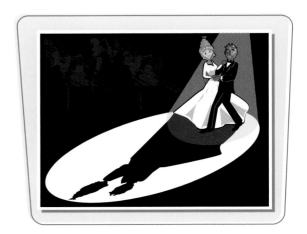

1 Click the **Layers** tab to open the Layers panel.

If the Layers tab is hidden, you can click **Window** and then **Layers** to open the Layers panel.

2 Click the layer to which you want to add the effect.

3 Click **Layer**.

4 Click **Layer Style**.

5 Click **Drop Shadow**.

● You can also click the **Add a Layer Style** button (fx) and then choose **Drop Shadow** from the menu.

The Layer Style dialog box opens.

Note: Perform steps **6** to **11** if you want to enter your own settings. If you want to use the default settings, you can skip to step **12**.

6 Type an Opacity value to specify the shadow's transparency.

7 Click the color swatch to select a shadow color.

Note: The default shadow color is black.

8 Type an Angle value to specify in which direction the shadow is displaced.

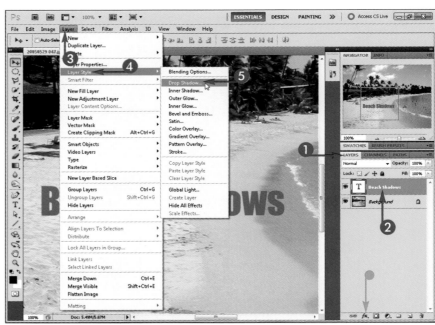

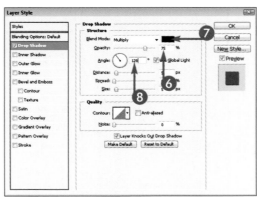

9 Type a Distance value to specify how far the shadow is displaced.

10 Type a Spread value to specify the fuzziness of the shadow's edge.

11 Type a Size value to specify the size of the shadow's edge.

You can also drag a slider () to change the distance, spread, and size values.

12 Click **OK**.

● Photoshop creates a shadow in back of the selected layer.

● Photoshop displays the name of the style under the affected layer in the Layers panel.

Note: In this example, the effect is applied to a text layer. For more on text, see Chapter 12.

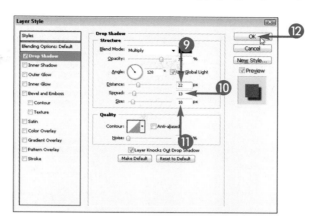

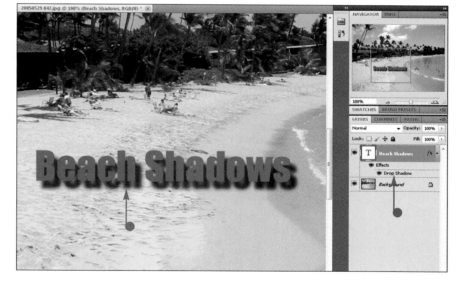

TIP

How do I add an inner shadow to a layer?
An inner shadow creates a *cutout* effect, with the selected layer appearing to drop behind the image canvas. To apply it, follow these steps:

1 Click a layer in the Layers panel.

2 Click **Layer**, **Layer Style**, and then **Inner Shadow**.

● Photoshop applies the style to objects in the layer. You can adjust the appearance of the inner shadow in the Layer Style dialog box that opens.

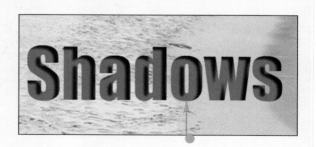

Apply an Outer Glow

The Outer Glow effect adds faint coloring to the outside edge of a layer.

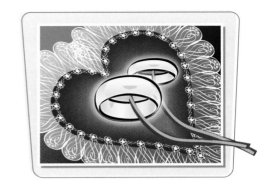

① Click the **Layers** tab to open the Layers panel.

If the Layers tab is hidden, you can click **Window** and then **Layers** to open the Layers panel.

② Click the layer to which you want to add the style.

③ Click **Layer**.

④ Click **Layer Style**.

⑤ Click **Outer Glow**.

● You can also click the **Add a Layer Style** button (*fx.*) and then choose **Outer Glow**.

The Layer Style dialog box opens.

Note: *Perform steps 6 to 10 if you want to enter your own Outer Glow settings. If you want to use the default settings, you can skip to step 11.*

⑥ Type an Opacity value to specify the glow's darkness.

⑦ Specify a Noise value to add speckling to the glow.

You can also drag the sliders (⬚) to change the opacity and noise values.

⑧ Click the color swatch to choose the color of the glow (◎ changes to ◉).

● You can also choose from a series of preset color gradients by clicking here (⊡).

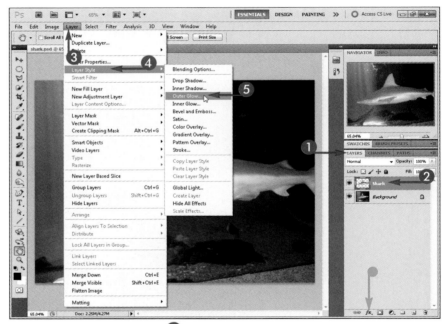

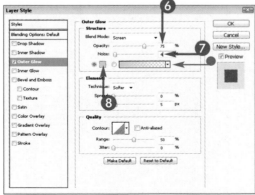

⑨ Type a Spread value to determine the fuzziness of the glow.

⑩ Type a Size value to specify the size of the glow.

You can also drag the sliders (▶▶) to change the spread and size values.

⑪ Click **OK**.

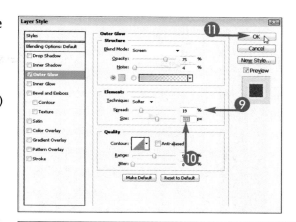

● Photoshop creates a glow around the outer edge of objects in the selected layer.

● Photoshop displays the name of the style under the affected layer in the Layers panel.

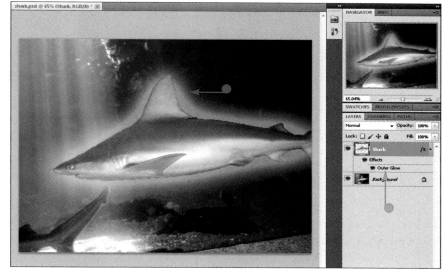

How do I give elements in a layer an inner glow?
The Inner Glow style adds color to the inside edge of a layer. To apply it, follow these steps:

① Click a layer in the Layers panel.

② Click **Layer**, **Layer Style**, and then **Inner Glow**.

● Photoshop applies the style to objects in the layer.

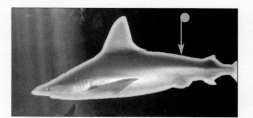

Apply Beveling and Embossing

You can bevel and emboss a layer to give it a three-dimensional look. This can make objects in the layer stand out and seem to rise off or sink into the screen.

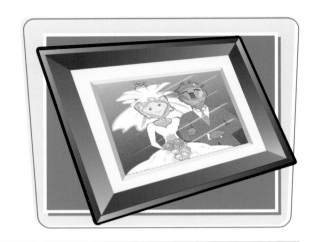

① Click the **Layers** tab to open the Layers panel.

If the Layers tab is hidden, you can click **Window** and then **Layers** to open the Layers panel.

② Click the layer to which you want to add the style.

③ Click **Layer**.

④ Click **Layer Style**.

⑤ Click **Bevel and Emboss**.

● You can also click the **Add a Layer Style** button ([fx]) and then choose **Bevel and Emboss**.

The Layer Style dialog box opens.

Note: Perform steps 6 to 9 if you want to enter your own settings. If you want to use the default settings, you can skip to step 10.

⑥ Click here ([·]) to choose an effect style.

Choosing **Inner Bevel** creates a three-dimensional look.

⑦ Specify the direction of the style's shadowing (○ changes to ●).

⑧ Type Depth and Size values to control the magnitude of the style.

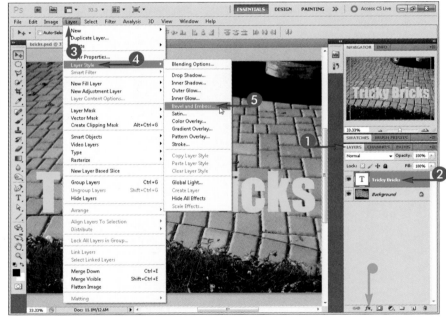

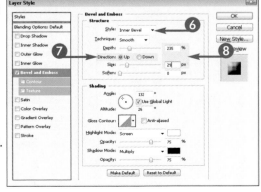

9 Specify the direction of the shading by changing the Angle and Altitude values.

● You can click here (⬚) to choose one of the Gloss Contour settings to apply abstract styles to your layer.

10 Click **OK**.

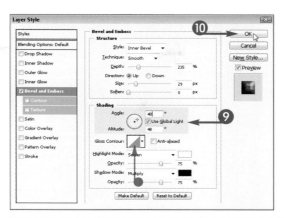

● Photoshop applies the Bevel and Emboss settings to the layer.

● Photoshop displays the name of the style under the affected layer in the Layers panel.

Note: In this example, the style is applied to a text layer. For more on text, see Chapter 12.

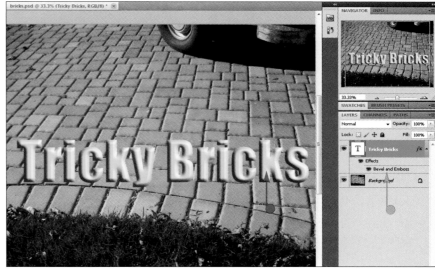

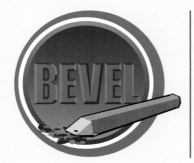

TIPS

When would I use the Bevel and Emboss style?

The style can be useful for creating three-dimensional buttons for Web pages or multimedia applications. For example, to create a 3-D button, you can apply Bevel and Emboss to a colored rectangle and then add type over it.

How else can I enhance the 3-D effect of Bevel and Emboss?

You can click the **Contour** check box (⬚ changes to ☑) in the left-hand column of the Layer Style dialog box to darken the shading or click the **Texture** check box (⬚ changes to ☑) to add shadowing that is slightly wavy.

Apply Multiple Styles to a Layer

You can apply multiple styles to layers in your image. This enables to you to enhance the look of your layers in complex ways.

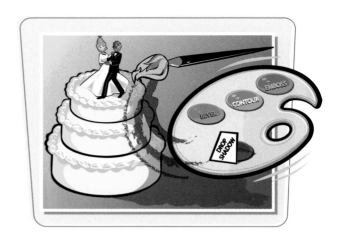

Apply the First Style

1 Click the **Layers** tab to open the Layers panel.

If the Layers tab is hidden, you can click **Window** and then **Layers** to open the Layers panel.

2 Click the layer to which you want to add the style.

3 Click **Layer**.

4 Click **Layer Style**.

5 Click the name of the first style you want to apply.

In this example, Gradient Overlay is applied to the layer.

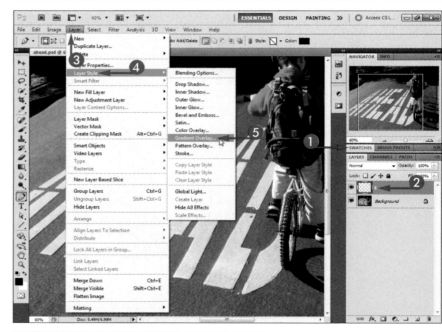

The Layer Style dialog box opens.

6 Specify the settings for the first style.

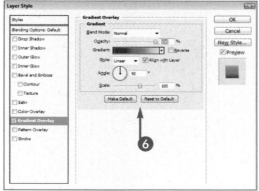

Apply the Second Style

7 Click the check box for the next style you want to apply (□ changes to ☑).

In this example, the Bevel and Emboss style is also applied to the layer, with the Technique set to Smooth.

8 Specify the settings for this style.

You can apply other styles to the layer by repeating steps **7** and **8**.

9 Click **OK**.

● Photoshop applies the styles to the layer.

● The effects appear below the selected layer in the Layers panel.

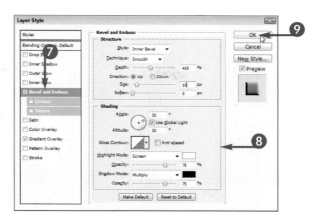

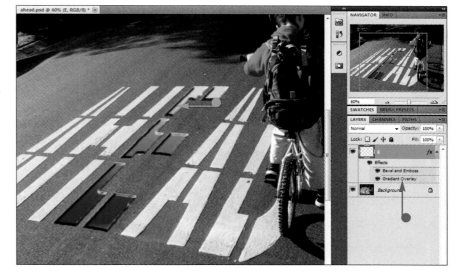

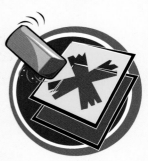

TIPS

How do I turn off layer effects that I have applied?

When you apply a style to a layer, Photoshop adds the style to the Layers panel. You may have to click ▸ to see a layer's effects. You can temporarily turn off an effect by clicking the visibility icon (👁) in the Layers panel. You can turn the effect on by clicking the now-empty box again to make 👁 reappear.

Is there a quick way to remove the styles from a layer?

Select the layer and then click **Layer**, **Layer Style**, and **Clear Layer Style**. Photoshop removes all the styles currently applied to the layer.

219

Edit a Layer Style

You can edit a layer style that you have applied to your image. This enables you to fine-tune the effect to achieve the appearance you want.

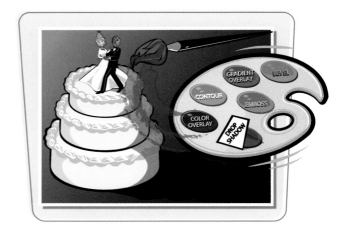

① Click the **Layers** tab to open the Layers panel.

If the Layers tab is hidden, you can click **Window** and then **Layers** to open the Layers panel.

In this example, the color overlay of a layer object is edited.

② Click the layer that has the style you want to edit.

③ Click **Layer**.

④ Click **Layer Style**.

⑤ Click the style you want to edit.

● You can also double-click the style's name in the Layers panel.

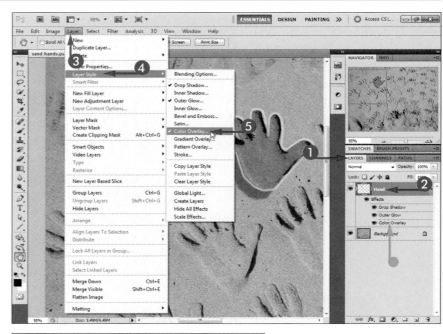

The Layer Style dialog box opens.

● Photoshop displays the current configuration values for the style.

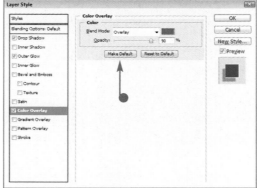

⑥ Edit the values in the Layer Style dialog box.

This example changes a color overlay.

● You can click the check box for another style in the Layer Style list to edit it (☐ changes to ☑).

⑦ Click **OK**.

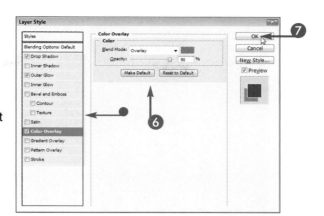

● Photoshop applies the edited style to the layer.

You can edit a style as many times as you want.

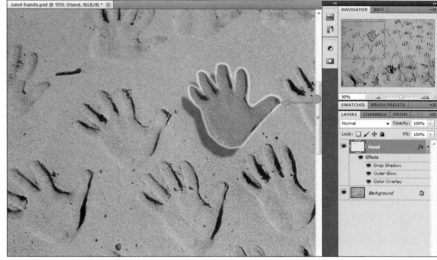

 TIPS

How do I keep a layer effect from accidentally being changed?

You can lock a layer and its styles by selecting the layer and then clicking the **Lock** icon (🔒) in the Layers panel; the button depresses and becomes highlighted. The layer is then locked, which means you cannot change its styles or apply additional Photoshop commands to it. You can click the Lock icon again to unlock the layer.

Can I copy styles between layers?

Yes. Select the layer you want to copy from and then click **Layer**, **Layer Styles**, and **Copy Layer Style**. To paste the style, select the destination layer and then click **Layer**, **Layer Styles**, and **Paste Layer Style**. You can also press Alt (Option on a Mac) and then click and drag a style from one layer to another in the Layers panel to copy it.

Using the Styles Panel

You can apply a custom combination of Photoshop styles to a layer to give it a colorful or textured look. The Styles panel offers an easy way to apply such complex effects.

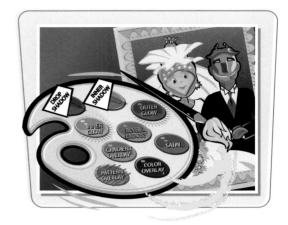

Apply a Style from the Styles Panel

1 Click the **Layers** tab to open the Layers panel.

If the Layers tab is hidden, you can click **Window** and then **Layers** to open the Layers panel.

2 Click the **Styles** tab to display Photoshop's styles.

If the Styles tab is hidden, you can click **Window** and then **Styles** to open the Styles panel.

3 Click the layer to which you want to apply the style.

4 Click a style.

● Photoshop applies the style to the selected layer.

● The style appears as a set of effects in the Layers panel.

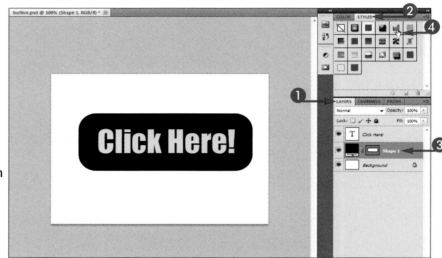

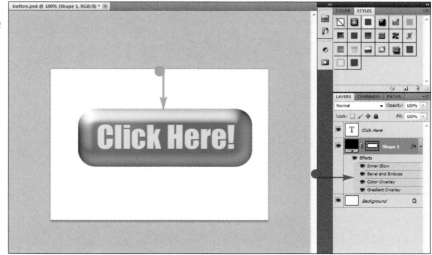

Access More Styles

1 Click the Styles panel icon (▤).

2 Click a set of styles.

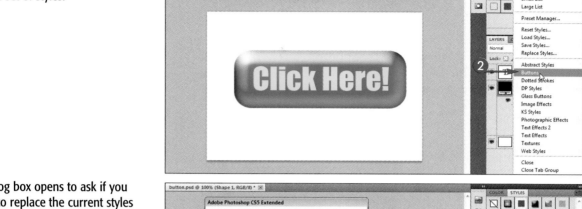

A dialog box opens to ask if you want to replace the current styles with the new set or append the new set.

3 Click **OK** or **Append**.

● Photoshop places the new styles in the Styles panel.

In this example, the new styles have been appended to the current ones.

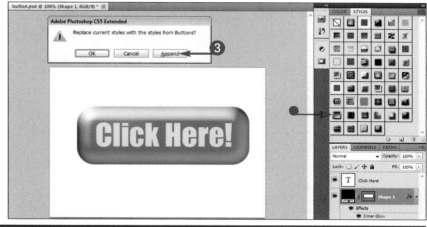

TIP

How do I create my own custom styles?

1 Perform the techniques covered in this chapter to apply one or more effects to a layer in your image.

2 Select the layer in the Layers panel.

3 Click ▤ and then choose **New Style**.

4 In the New Style dialog box that opens, type a name for your new style.

5 Click **OK**.

● An icon for your new style appears in the Styles panel.

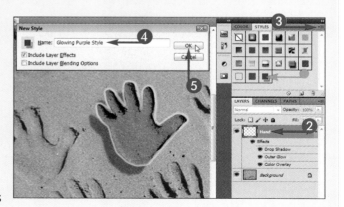

10

Applying Filters

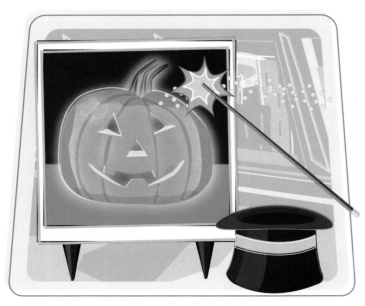

With Photoshop's filters, you can quickly and easily apply enhancements to your image, including artistic effects, texture effects, and distortions. Filters can help you correct defects in your images or enable you to turn a photograph into something resembling an impressionist painting. Photoshop comes with more than 100 filters; this chapter highlights only a few. For more on all the filters, see the Help documentation.

Turn an Image into a Painting

You can use many of Photoshop's artistic filters to make your image look as though it was created with a paintbrush. The Dry Brush filter, for example, applies a painted effect by converting similarly colored areas in your image to solid colors.

The Dry Brush filter uses the Filter Gallery interface. For more on the Filter Gallery, see the section "Apply Multiple Filters."

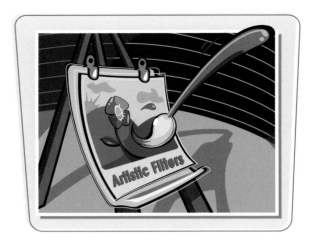

Turn an Image into a Painting

① Select the layer to which you want to apply the filter.

In this example, the image has a single Background layer.

To apply the filter to just part of your image, make a selection with a selection tool.

Note: For more on layers, see Chapter 8. For more on the selection tools, see Chapter 4.

② Click **Filter**.

③ Click **Artistic**.

④ Click **Dry Brush**.

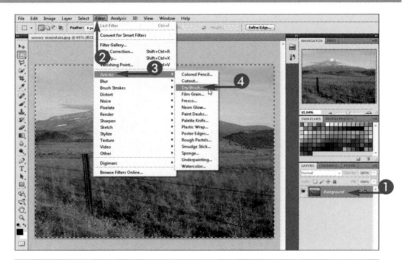

The Filter Gallery dialog box opens with the Dry Brush filter selected.

The left pane displays a preview of the filter's effect.

The middle pane enables you to select a different artistic or another type of filter.

● You can also select a different filter by clicking ⊟ in the right pane.

⑤ Fine-tune the filter effect by typing values for Brush Size, Brush Detail, and Texture.

● You can also move the sliders (⬚) to choose values.

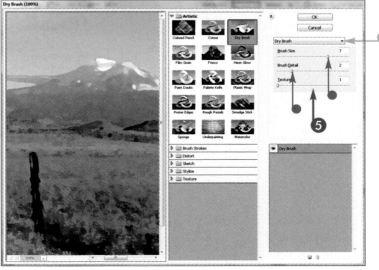

● You can close the middle pane by clicking 🔼.

On a Mac, you can close the middle pane by clicking ▲ (▲ changes to ▼).

This example shows how to thicken the Dry Brush effect by increasing Brush Size and decreasing Brush Detail.

⑥ Click **OK**.

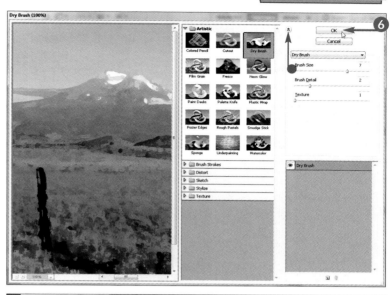

Photoshop applies the filter.

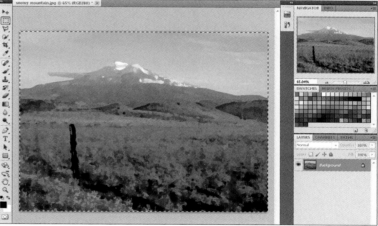

TIPS

What does the Sponge filter do?
The Sponge filter reduces detail and modifies the shapes in an image to create the effect you get when applying a damp sponge to a wet painting. Apply it by clicking **Filter**, **Artistic**, and then **Sponge**. This effect is different from that of the Sponge tool (🔘), which changes the intensity of colors in an image. See Chapter 7 for more on the Sponge tool.

How can I make the objects in my image look like they are molded from plastic?
The Plastic Wrap filter gives objects a shiny appearance, as if wrapped in heat-shrink plastic. To apply this effect, click **Filter**, **Artistic**, and then **Plastic Wrap**. You can adjust how well the plastic wrap reflects light, its shininess, and its smoothness.

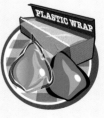

Blur an Image

Photoshop's blur filters reduce the amount of detail in your image. The Gaussian Blur filter has an advantage over other blur filters in that you can control the amount of blur added.

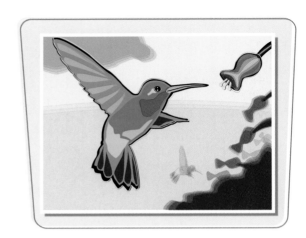

1. Select the layer to which you want to apply the filter.

   To apply the filter to just part of your image, make a selection with a selection tool.

   Note: *For more on layers, see Chapter 8. For more on the selection tools, see Chapter 4.*

   ● In this example, the scenery around a leaf has been selected.

2. Click **Filter**.

3. Click **Blur**.

4. Click **Gaussian Blur**.

   The Gaussian Blur dialog box opens.

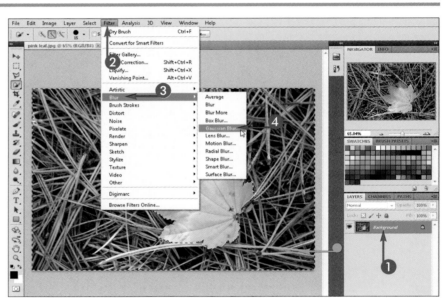

5. Click the **Preview** check box (changes to ✓).

   ● A preview of the filter's effect appears here.

   ● You can click ＋ or － to zoom in or out.

6. Click and drag the **Radius** slider ( ) to control the amount of blur added.

   You can also type a value in the Radius field.

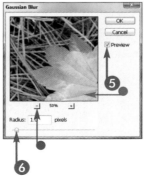

In this example, boosting the
Radius value increases the amount
of blur.

7 Click **OK**.

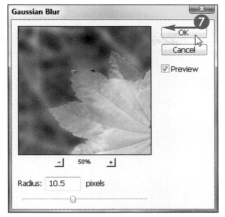

Photoshop applies the filter.

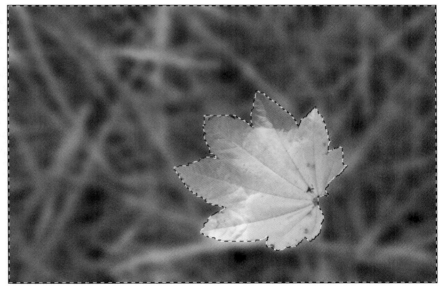

How do I add directional blurring to an image?

You can add directional blur to your image with the Motion Blur filter. This can add a sense of motion to your image. To apply the filter:

1 Click **Filter**, **Blur**, and then **Motion Blur**.

2 In the Motion Blur dialog box, adjust the angle and distance to customize the blur's direction and intensity.

3 Click **OK** to apply the filter.

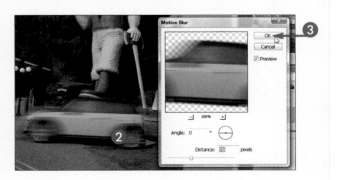

Sharpen an Image

Photoshop's sharpen filters intensify the detail and reduce blurring in your image. The Unsharp Mask filter has advantages over other sharpen filters in that you can control the amount of sharpening you apply.

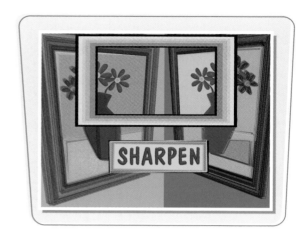

① Select the layer to which you want to apply the filter.

In this example, the filter is applied to the statue layer.

To apply the filter to just part of your image, you can make a selection with a selection tool.

Note: *For more on layers, see Chapter 8. For more on the selection tools, see Chapter 4.*

② Click **Filter**.

③ Click **Sharpen**.

④ Click **Unsharp Mask**.

The Unsharp Mask dialog box opens.

⑤ Click the **Preview** check box (☐ changes to ☑).

● A preview of the filter's effect appears here.

● You can click ⊞ or ⊟ to zoom in or out.

⑥ Click and drag the sliders (◻) to control the amount of sharpening you apply to the image.

You can also type values for the amount of sharpening.

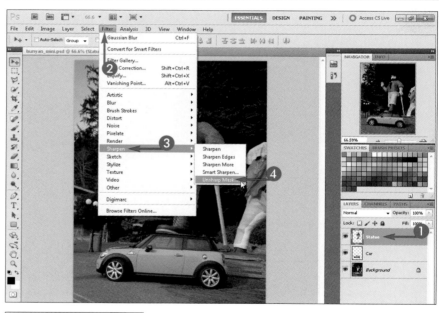

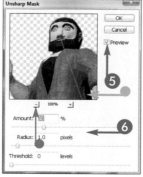

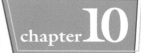

Amount controls the overall amount of sharpening.

Radius controls whether sharpening is confined to edges in the image (low Radius setting) or added across the entire image (high Radius setting).

Threshold controls the amount of contrast that must be present for an edge to be recognized and sharpened.

⑦ Click **OK**.

Photoshop applies the filter.

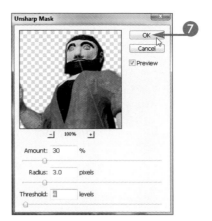

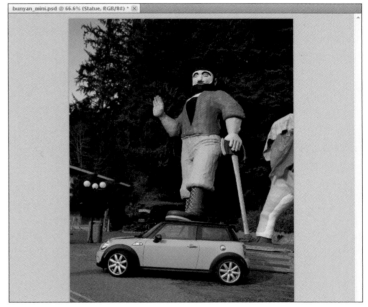

When should I apply sharpening?

It is a good idea to sharpen an image after you enlarge it because enlarging can cause blurring. Applying the Unsharp Mask filter can also help clarify scanned images.

How can I remove a specific type of blurring from my image?

The Smart Sharpen filter gives you additional control over the sharpening applied to your image. You can specify that it remove blurring applied by the Gaussian Blur, Lens Blur, or Motion Blur filter. To access it, click **Filter**, **Sharpen**, and **Smart Sharpen**. You can also add blurring in the first place as a Smart Filter, which gives you the option of removing the filter later. For more, see the section "Using Smart Filters."

Distort an Image

Photoshop's distort filters stretch and squeeze areas of your image. For example, the Spherize filter produces a fun house effect, making your image look like it is being reflected in a mirrored sphere. You can also distort an image by using the Distort command, located under the Edit menu. See Chapter 5 for more.

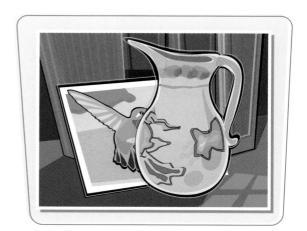

Distort an Image

① Select the layer to which you want to apply the filter.

To apply the filter to just part of your image, make a selection with a selection tool.

Note: *For more on layers, see Chapter 8. For more on the selection tools, see Chapter 4.*

● In this example, one of the glass jars is selected.

② Click **Filter**.

③ Click **Distort**.

④ Click **Spherize**.

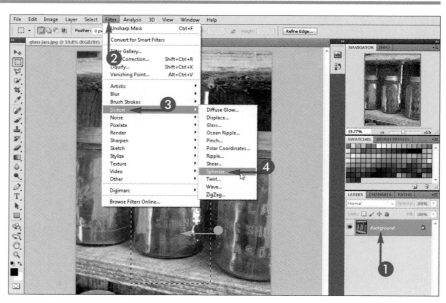

The Spherize dialog box opens.

● A preview of the filter's effect appears here.

● You can click ⊞ or ⊟ to zoom in or out.

⑤ Click and drag the **Amount** slider (▣) to control the amount of distortion added.

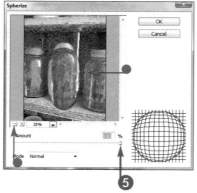

In this example, the amount of the spherize effect has been decreased.

6 Click **OK**.

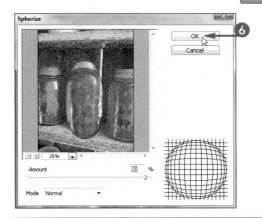

Photoshop applies the filter.

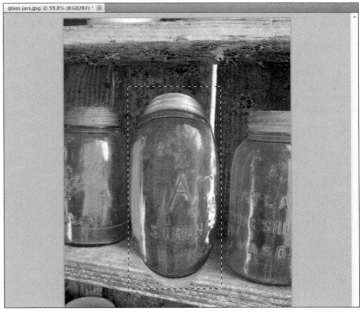

What happens when I type a negative value in the Amount field of the Spherize dialog box?

A negative value squeezes the shapes in your image instead of expanding them. The Pinch filter — which you can also find under the Filter and Distort menu selections — produces a similar effect.

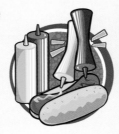

How can I quickly add wild special effects to my images?

Many of the filters in the Stylize menu produce out-of-this-world effects. The Emboss and Solarize filters are two examples. Click **Filter** and then click **Stylize** to access them.

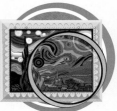

Add Noise to an Image

Filters in the Noise menu add or remove graininess. You can add graininess to your image with the Add Noise filter. Although photographers usually try to avoid graininess in their photos, the filter can be useful to apply an abstract texture to a scene.

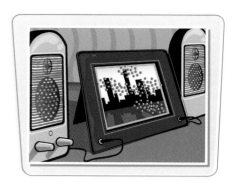

Add Noise to an Image

① Select the layer to which you want to apply the filter.

This image has a single Background layer.

To apply the filter to just part of your image, make a selection with a selection tool.

Note: For more on layers, see Chapter 8. For more on the selection tools, see Chapter 4.

② Click **Filter**.

③ Click **Noise**.

④ Click **Add Noise**.

The Add Noise dialog box opens.

⑤ Click the **Preview** check box (☐ changes to ☑).

● A preview appears here.

● You can click ➕ or ➖ to zoom in or out.

⑥ Click and drag the **Amount** slider (▣) to control the amount of noise added.

You can also type a value for the amount of noise.

⑦ Select the way you want the noise distributed (◯ changes to ◉).

The Uniform option spreads the noise more evenly than the Gaussian option.

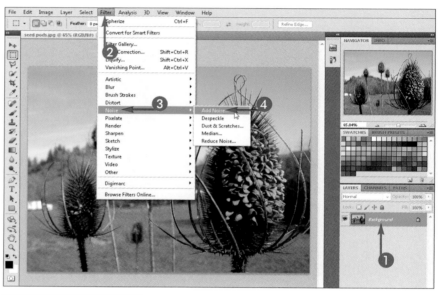

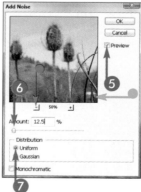

In this example, the Amount value has been increased.

8 Click **OK**.

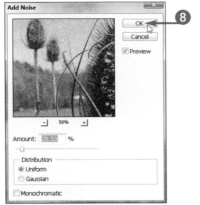

Photoshop applies the filter.

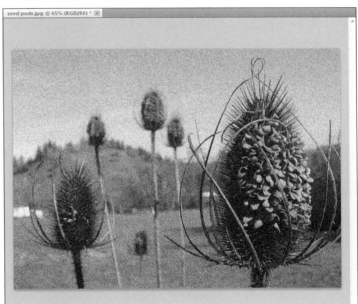

TIP

What does the Monochromatic setting in the Add Noise dialog box do?
If you click **Monochromatic** (☐ changes to ☑), Photoshop adds noise by lightening or darkening pixels in your image. Pixel hues stay the same. At high settings with the Monochromatic setting on, the filter produces a television-static effect.

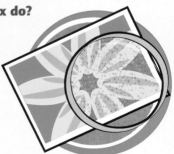

Turn an Image into Shapes

The Pixelate filters divide areas of your image into solid-colored dots or shapes. The Crystallize filter — one example of a pixelate filter — re-creates your image by using colored polygons.

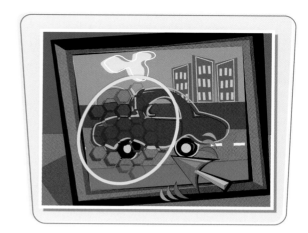

1 Select the layer to which you want to apply the filter.

In this example, the image has a single Background layer.

To apply the filter to just part of your image, make a selection with a selection tool.

Note: *For more on layers, see Chapter 8. For more on the selection tools, see Chapter 4.*

2 Click **Filter**.

3 Click **Pixelate**.

4 Click **Crystallize**.

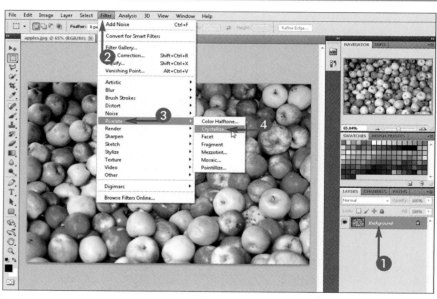

The Crystallize dialog box opens.

● A preview of the filter's effect appears here.

● You can click ⊞ or ⊟ to zoom in or out.

5 Click and drag the **Cell Size** slider (▢) to adjust the size of the shapes.

You can also type a value for the size.

The size can range from 3 to 300.

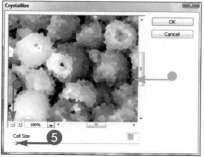

In this example, the Cell Size value has been increased.

6 Click **OK**.

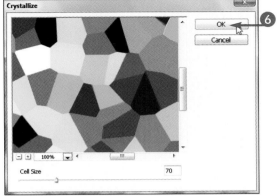

Photoshop applies the filter.

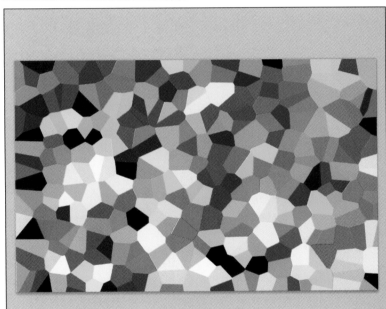

TIPS

What does the Mosaic filter do?

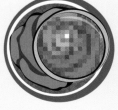

The Mosaic filter converts your image to a set of solid-color squares. You can control the size of the squares in the filter's dialog box. Apply the filter by clicking **Filter**, **Pixelate**, and then **Mosaic**.

What does the Stained Glass filter do?

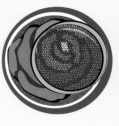

The Stained Glass filter converts small areas of your image to different solid-color shapes, similar to those you may see in a stained-glass window. A foreground-color border separates the shapes. You can adjust the thickness of the border, along with cell size and light intensity. Apply this filter by clicking **Filter**, **Texture**, and then **Stained Glass**.

Turn an Image into a Charcoal Sketch

The Sketch filters add outlining effects to your image. The Charcoal filter, for example, makes an image look as if you sketched it by using charcoal on paper.

The Charcoal filter uses the Filter Gallery interface. For more on the Filter Gallery, see the section "Apply Multiple Filters."

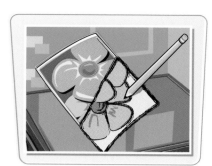

Turn an Image into a Charcoal Sketch

① Select the layer to which you want to apply the filter.

In this example, the image has a single Background layer.

To apply the filter to just part of your image, make a selection with a selection tool.

Note: *For more on layers, see Chapter 8. For more on the selection tools, see Chapter 4.*

② Click **Filter**.

③ Click **Sketch**.

④ Click **Charcoal**.

The Filter Gallery dialog box opens with the Charcoal filter selected.

The left pane displays a preview of the filter's effect.

The middle pane enables you to select a different Sketch or other type of filter.

● You can also select a different filter by clicking ⊡ in the right pane.

⑤ Click and drag the sliders (▣) to control the filter's effect.

You can also type values in these fields.

● You can close the middle pane by clicking ☒.

On a Mac, you can close the middle pane by clicking ▲ (▲ changes to ▼).

⑥ Click **OK**.

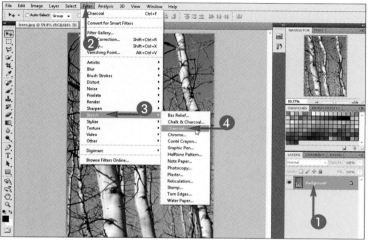

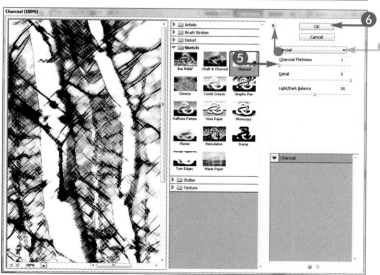

Photoshop applies the filter.

In this example, the thickness of the charcoal strokes has been increased, and the Light/Dark Balance setting has also been increased.

● Photoshop uses the current foreground color as the charcoal and the current background color as the canvas.

Note: *For more on choosing the foreground and background colors, see Chapter 6.*

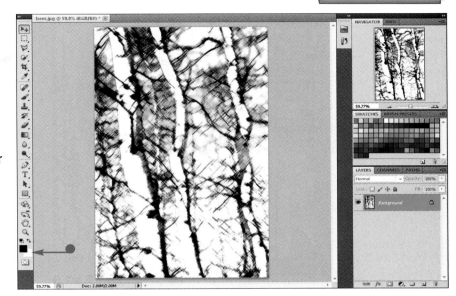

TIP

What does the Photocopy filter do?

The Photocopy filter converts shadows and midtones in your image to the foreground color in the Toolbox and highlights in your image to the background color. The result is an image that looks photocopied. To apply the Photocopy filter:

① Follow steps **1** to **4** in this section, but in step **4**, click **Photocopy**.

The Filter Gallery opens with the Photocopy filter selected.

② Adjust the detail and the darkness of the filter effect.

③ Click **OK**.

Photoshop applies the filter.

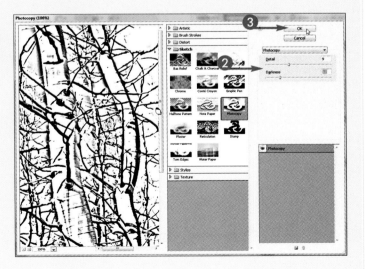

Apply Glowing Edges to an Image

The Glowing Edges filter — one example of a Stylize filter — applies a neon effect to the edges in your image. Areas between the edges turn black. Other Stylize filters produce similarly extreme artistic effects.

The Glowing Edges filter uses the Filter Gallery interface. For more on the Filter Gallery, see the section "Apply Multiple Filters."

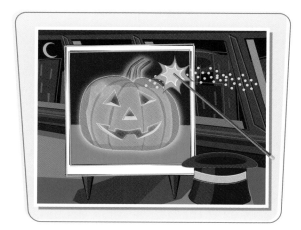

Apply Glowing Edges to an Image

① Select the layer to which you want to apply the filter.

In this example, the image has a single Background layer.

To apply the filter to just part of your image, make a selection with a selection tool.

Note: *For more on layers, see Chapter 8. For more on the selection tools, see Chapter 4.*

② Click **Filter**.

③ Click **Stylize**.

④ Click **Glowing Edges**.

The Filter Gallery dialog box opens with the Glowing Edges filter selected.

The left pane displays a preview of the filter's effect.

The middle pane enables you to select a different filter.

● You can also select a different filter by clicking ⊡ in the right pane.

⑤ Click and drag the sliders (⬜) to control the intensity of the glow you add to the edges in the image.

You can also type values in the slider fields.

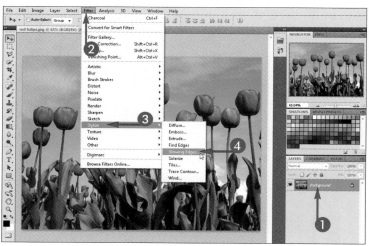

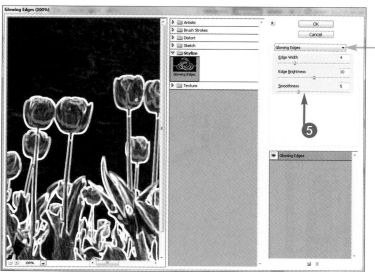

● You can close the middle pane by clicking ⊼.

On a Mac, you can close the middle pane by clicking ▲ (▲ changes to ▼).

In this example, the Edge Width and Edge Brightness values are increased to intensify the neon effect.

⑥ Click **OK**.

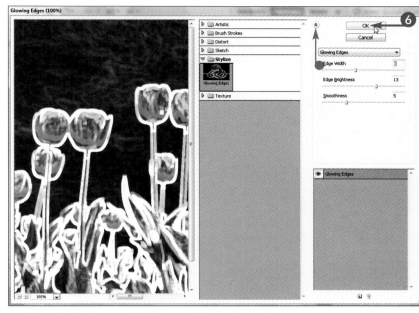

Photoshop applies the filter.

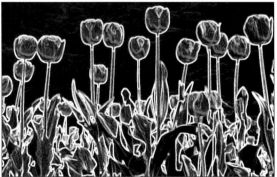

TIP

What is the Find Edges filter?
The Find Edges filter is similar to the Glowing Edges filter, except that it places white pixels between the edges in your image. Find Edges is a one-step filter, which means you cannot fine-tune its effects in a dialog box before you apply it. To apply the filter:

① Click **Filter**.

② Click **Stylize**.

③ Click **Find Edges**.

Photoshop applies the filter.

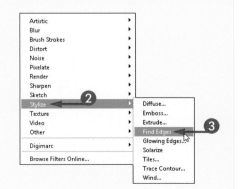

Add Texture to an Image

You can overlay different textures on your image with the Texturizer filter. The other Texture filters enable you to apply other patterns.

The Texturizer filter uses the Filter Gallery interface. For more on the Filter Gallery, see the section "Apply Multiple Filters."

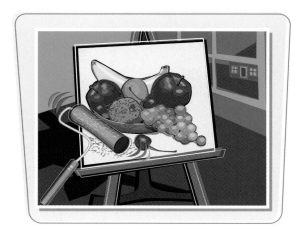

① Select the layer to which you want to apply the filter.

To apply the filter to just part of your image, make a selection with a selection tool.

In this example, the filter is applied to a selection.

Note: *For more on layers, see Chapter 8. For more on the selection tools, see Chapter 4.*

② Click **Filter**.

③ Click **Texture**.

④ Click **Texturizer**.

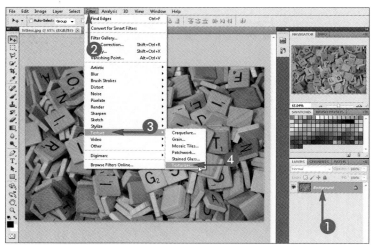

The Filter Gallery dialog box opens with the Texturizer filter selected.

The left pane displays a preview of the filter's effect.

The middle pane enables you to select a different texture or another type of filter.

● You can also select a different filter by clicking ⊡ in the right pane.

⑤ Click here (⊡) to choose a texture to apply.

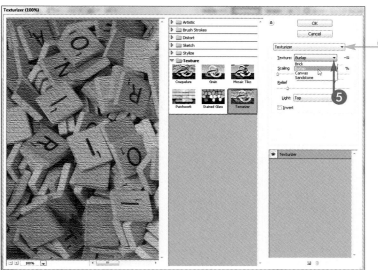

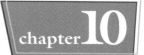

6 Click and drag the sliders (⬚) to control the scaling, or size, and relief, or intensity, of the overlaid texture.

You can also type values in these fields.

7 Click here (⬛) to choose a **Light** direction.

● You can close the middle pane by clicking ⬛.

On a Mac, you can close the middle pane by clicking ▲ (▲ changes to ▼).

8 Click **OK**.

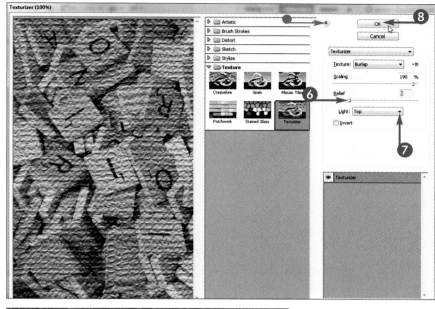

Photoshop applies the filter.

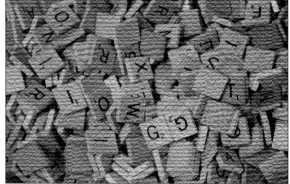

What is a lens flare, and how can I add it to an image?
Lens flare is the extra flash of light that sometimes appears in a photo when too much light enters a camera lens. Photographers try to avoid this effect, but you can add it to make your digital image look more like an old-fashioned photograph.

1 Click **Filter**, **Render**, and then **Lens Flare**.

2 In the Lens Flare dialog box, click and drag ⬚ to control the brightness. You can also type a value for the brightness.

3 Click and drag + to position the lens flare in your image.

4 Click **OK** to apply the filter.

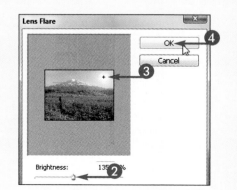

Offset an Image

The filters in the Other submenu produce interesting effects that do not fall under the other menu descriptions. For example, you can shift your image horizontally or vertically in the image window by using the Other submenu's Offset filter.

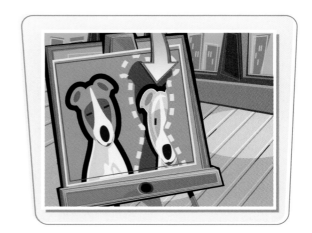

Offset an Image

① Select the layer to which you want to apply the filter.

In this example, the image has a single Background layer.

To apply the filter to just part of your image, make a selection with a selection tool.

Note: For more on layers, see Chapter 8. For more on the selection tools, see Chapter 4.

② Click **Filter**.

③ Click **Other**.

④ Click **Offset**.

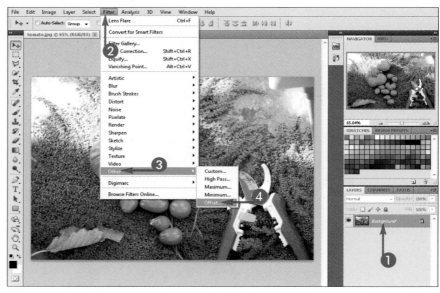

The Offset dialog box opens.

⑤ Type a horizontal offset.

⑥ Type a vertical offset.

You can also drag the sliders (⬚) to set values for the offsets.

⑦ Select how you want Photoshop to treat pixels at the edge (◯ changes to ◉).

⑧ Click **OK**.

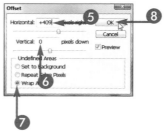

Because a positive value was entered in the horizontal field, the image has been shifted horizontally to the right.

Wrap Around was selected in step **7**, so the pixels cropped from the right edge of the image reappear on the left edge.

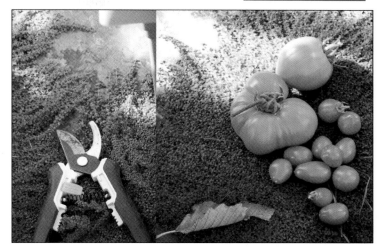

In this example, the same offset is applied but with Repeat Edge Pixels selected in step **7**, which creates a streaked effect at the left edge.

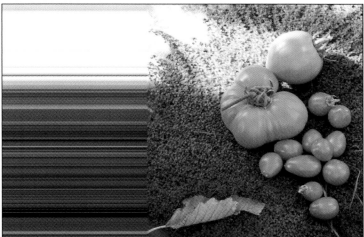

TIP

How do I make a seamless tile?

Seamless tiles are images that when laid side by side leave no noticeable seam where they meet. They are often used as background images for Web pages.

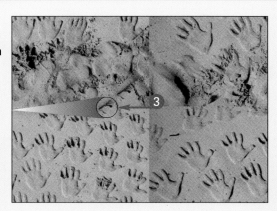

1. Open an image that has even textures and coloring.

2. Perform steps **1** to **8** in this section to offset your image horizontally and vertically.

3. Clean up the resulting seams with the **Clone Stamp** tool ( ). See Chapter 6 for more on the Clone Stamp tool.

   The resulting image tiles seamlessly when you use it as a Web page background.

Using the Liquify Filter

Photoshop's Liquify filter enables you to dramatically warp areas of your image. The filter is useful for making objects in your image look like they are melting. You can also use the filter to make subtle changes to edges of objects by pushing the edges in or out.

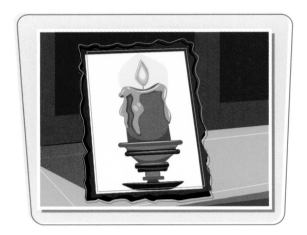

Using the Liquify Filter

① Select the layer to which you want to apply the Liquify filter.

In this example, the image has a single Background layer.

To apply the filter to just part of your image, make a selection with a selection tool.

Note: *For more on layers, see Chapter 8. For more on the selection tools, see Chapter 4.*

② Click **Filter**.

③ Click **Liquify**.

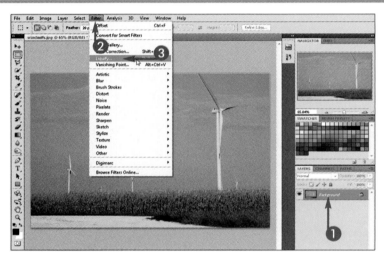

The Liquify dialog box opens.

④ Type a Brush Size from 1 to 600.

⑤ Type a Brush Pressure, or strength, from 1 to 100.

⑥ Click a Liquify tool.

This example uses the Forward Warp tool (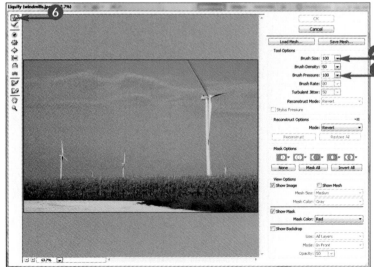).

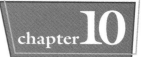

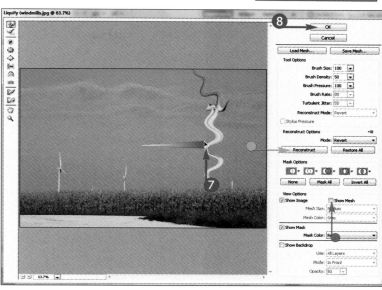

7 Click and drag inside the image preview box.

Photoshop liquifies the image where you drag the brush.

● You can click **Reconstruct** to change the image back to its original state, step by step.

● You can click the **Show Mesh** check box (☐ changes to ☑) to overlay a grid so you can measure your changes.

8 Click **OK**.

Photoshop applies the Liquify effect to your image.

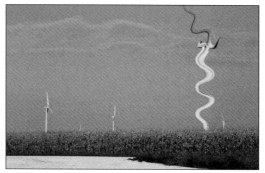

 TIP

What do some of the different Liquify tools do?

🖌	Forward Warp tool	Pushes pixels in the direction you drag	🔶	Bloat tool	Pushes pixels away from the brush center
✎	Reconstruct tool	Restores pixels to their original state	▓	Push Left tool	Pushes pixels to the left of the cursor as you drag
◉	Twirl Clockwise tool	Twirls pixels clockwise; you can press Alt (Option on a Mac) as you apply the tool to twirl pixels counterclockwise.	🔲	Mirror tool	Reflects pixels as you drag
🔳	Pucker tool	Pushes pixels toward the brush center	≈	Turbulence tool	Mimics a roiling liquid

Apply Multiple Filters

You can apply more than one filter to an image by using the Filter Gallery interface. The interface enables you to view a variety of filter effects and apply them in combination.

Many filters open the Filter Gallery interface when you apply them, including Dry Brush, Charcoal Sketch, Glowing Edges, and Texturizer. See previous sections in this chapter for more on these filters. Not all the effects listed under Photoshop's Filter menu appear in the Filter Gallery.

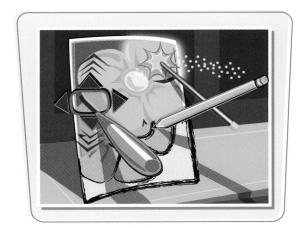

Apply Multiple Filters

① Select the layer to which you want to apply the filters.

In this example, the image has a single Background layer.

To apply the filters to just part of your image, make a selection with a selection tool.

Note: For more on layers, see Chapter 8. For more on the selection tools, see Chapter 4.

② Click **Filter**.

③ Click **Filter Gallery**.

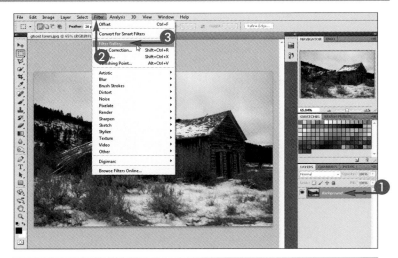

The Filter Gallery dialog box opens with the most recently applied filter selected.

The left pane displays a preview of the filtered image.

④ Click ▷ to display filters from a category (▷ changes to ▽).

⑤ Click a thumbnail to apply a filter.

● The filter appears in the filter list.

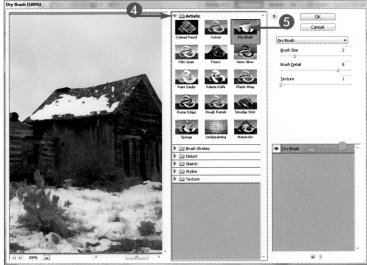

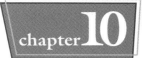

6 Click the **New Effect Layer** button (⬚).

7 Click ▶ to display filters from another category (▶ changes to ⬇).

8 Click a thumbnail to apply another filter.

● The new effect appears in the list.

You can repeat steps **6** to **8** to apply additional filters.

9 Click **OK**.

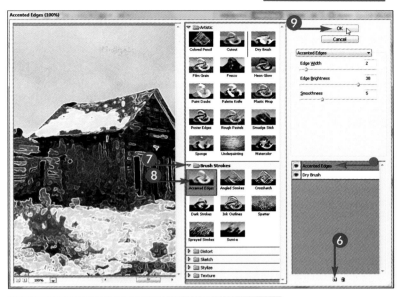

Photoshop applies the filters.

Note: *The order in which multiple filters are applied in the Filter Gallery can result in different overall effects.*

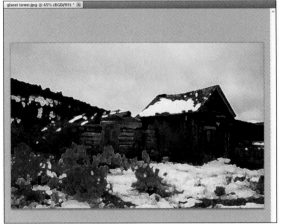

TIP

How can I turn off filters in the Filter Gallery?
Currently applied filters appear in a list in the lower-right corner of the Filter Gallery. You can click 👁 to temporarily hide a filter in the list. A hidden filter's effects are not applied to the preview in the left pane of the Filter Gallery nor are they applied to the image when you click **OK**. You can click 🗑 to delete a filter entirely from the list.

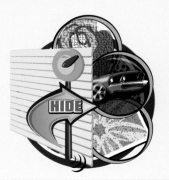

Using Smart Filters

Filters that you apply to Smart Objects in your images are known as Smart Filters. You can edit Smart Filters and turn them on and off as you continue to make changes to your image. You cannot do this with filters applied to normal layers.

For more on Smart Objects, see Chapter 8.

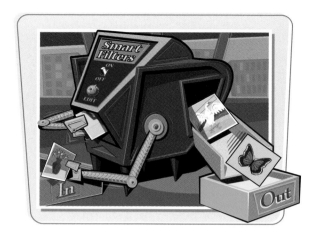

Apply a Smart Filter

1 Select the Smart Object to which you want to apply a filter.

2 Click **Filter**.

3 Click a filter category.

4 Click a filter.

The dialog box for that filter opens.

5 Adjust the filter settings.

6 Click **OK**.

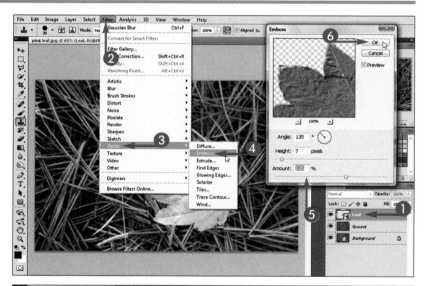

● Photoshop applies the filter to the Smart Object in the image.

● The filter appears in the Layers panel.

You can repeat steps **2** to **6** to apply multiple Smart Filters to the Smart Object.

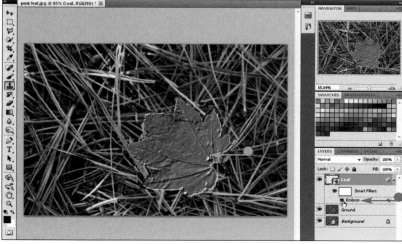

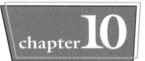
Turn Off a Smart Filter

1 Click next to the Smart Filter.

    changes to ☐, and Photoshop turns off the Smart Filter.

   You can click ☐ to turn the Smart Filter back on.

● You can click next to Smart Filters to turn off all the Smart Filters for a layer.

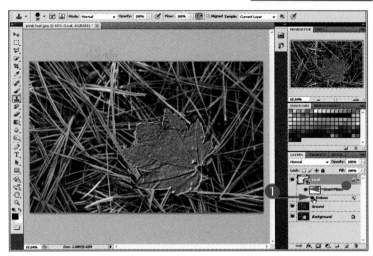

Edit a Smart Filter

1 Double-click a Smart Filter.

   Photoshop opens the dialog box for the Smart Filter.

2 Edit the filter settings.

3 Click **OK**.

   Photoshop applies the edited settings.

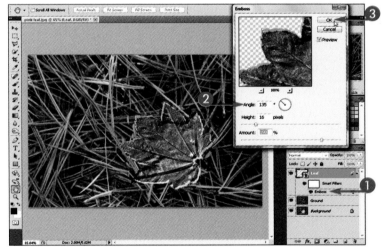

TIP

How can I control how a Smart Filter is blended with the Smart Objects in my image?

1 Double-click **Filter Blending Options** (⧉) next to a Smart Filter.

2 Click here (▾) to choose a blending mode.

● You can click here (⬚) to control the strength of the applied effect.

3 Click **OK**.

   Photoshop applies the Smart Filter with the updated blending.

Note: For more on blending, see Chapter 8.

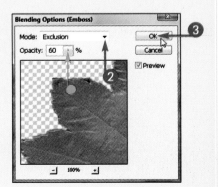

Drawing Shapes

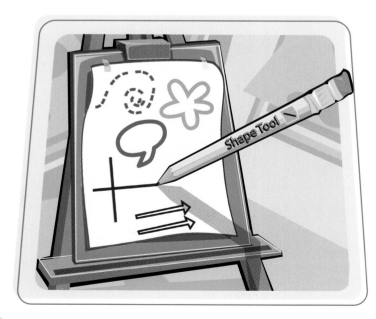

Photoshop offers a variety of tools for drawing geometric and abstract shapes. Other tools let you edit the lines that bound your shapes or change the colors with which the shapes are filled. You can also use the tools to draw lines that have arrowheads at their ends.

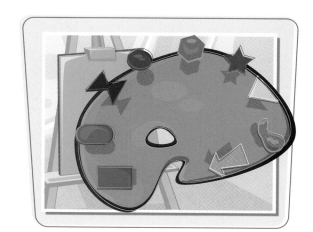

You can add solid shapes to your image by using Photoshop's many shape tools. These tools make it easy to create geometric decorations for your photos or buttons for your Web site.

Photoshop's shapes are *vector-based*, which means you can resize them without loss of quality.

Draw a Shape

Draw a Solid Shape

1 Click the **Shape** tool (▣).

Note: The tool icon may differ, depending on the type of shape you drew last.

2 Click a shape on the Options bar.

3 Click the **Shape Layers** icon (▣) on the Options bar.

4 Click the **Color** box to select a fill color for the shape.

Note: For more on selecting colors, see Chapter 6.

5 Click and drag to draw the shape.

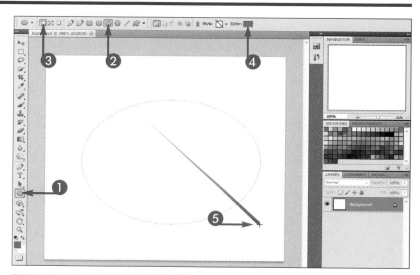

Photoshop draws the shape and fills it with the specified color.

● The shape appears in a new layer in the Layers panel.

Note: For more on layers, see Chapter 8.

This example shows a shape being drawn on a new blank image.

Note: To create a new image, see Chapter 1.

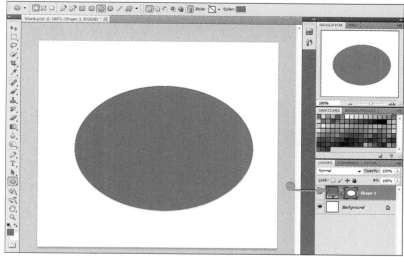

Draw a Stylized Shape

1 Click a shape button.

2 Click here (▾) to open the style menu.

3 Select a style for your shape.

Photoshop offers a variety of colorful 3-D styles.

4 Click and drag to draw the shape.

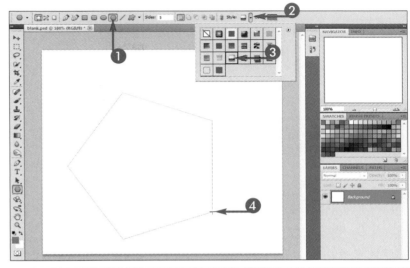

Photoshop draws the shape and applies the specified style.

● The shape appears in a new layer in the Layers panel.

Note: For more on layers, see Chapter 8. For more on styles, see Chapter 9.

● You can move the shape by selecting its layer and then using the **Move** tool (▶+).

Note: For more on the Move tool, see Chapter 5.

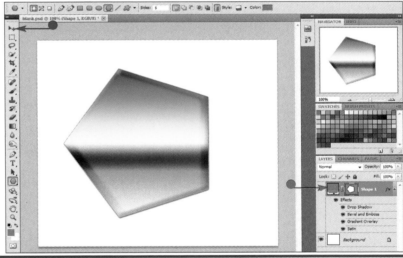

How do I resize a shape after I draw it?

Click the shape's layer and then click the **Shape** tool (▣). Click **Edit, Transform Path**, and then a transform command. You can resize the shape just as you would a selection. See Chapter 5 for more on transforming selections.

How do I overlap shapes in interesting ways?

To determine how overlapping shapes interact, click one of the following options on the Options bar before drawing.

▣	Add to Shape Area	Combines a shape area with another shape area
▣	Subtract from Shape Area	Cuts a shape area out of another shape area
▣	Intersect Shape Areas	Keeps the area where shapes intersect
▣	Exclude Overlapping Shape Areas	Keeps the area where shapes do not overlap

Draw a Custom Shape

You can use the Custom Shape tool to draw a variety of interesting predefined shapes, including animals, frames, and talk bubbles.

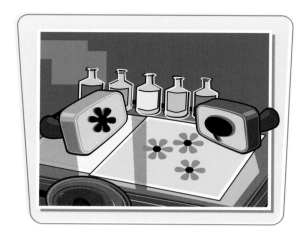

Draw a Custom Shape

① Click the **Shape** tool (▣).

② Click the **Custom Shape** button (▨) on the Options bar.

③ Click here (▾) to open the **Shape** menu.

④ Click the **Option** arrow (▶).

⑤ Click a shape category.

A dialog box opens to ask if you want to replace the current shapes.

● You can click **Append** to append the new shapes to the current shapes.

⑥ Click **OK**.

Photoshop replaces the old shapes with your current shapes.

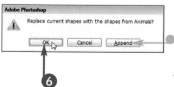

7 Click a shape.

8 Click the **Color** box to select a color for the shape.

Note: *For more on selecting colors, see Chapter 6.*

9 Click and drag to draw the shape.

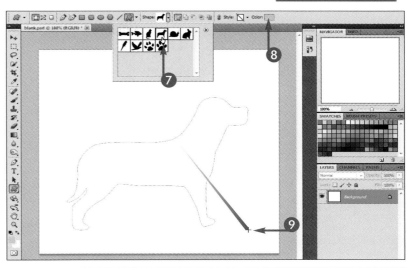

Photoshop draws the shape and fills it with the specified color.

● The shape appears in a new layer in the Layers panel.

Note: *For more on layers, see Chapter 8.*

● You can move the shape by selecting its layer and then using the Move tool ().

Note: *For more on the Move tool, see Chapter 5.*

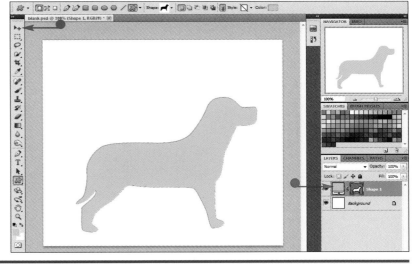

TIPS

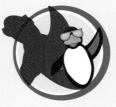

How do I apply a shadow behind a shape?

You can apply a Drop Shadow style to the shape. Select your shape layer in the Layers panel and then click **Layer**, **Layer Style**, and **Drop Shadow**. A dialog box opens that enables you to customize the shadowing. For more on applying styles, see Chapter 9.

How do I overlay text on a shape?

You can click the **Type** tool (T), click your shape, and then type the text you want to overlay. This can be useful when you want to label buttons you create with the Shape tool. You will probably want to select a color for your text that contrasts with the color of your shape. For more on applying type, see Chapter 12.

Draw a Straight Line

You can draw a straight line by using Photoshop's Shape tool. You can point out elements in your image by customizing the line with arrowheads.

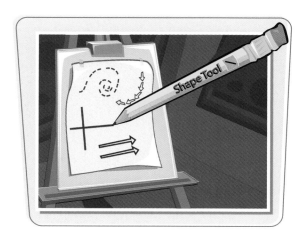

① Click the **Shape** tool (▣).

Note: The tool icon may differ, depending on the type of shape you drew last.

② Make sure the **Shape Layers** icon (▢) is selected on the Options bar.

③ Click the **Line** button (▱).

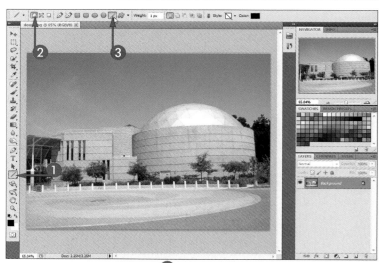

④ Click here (▾) to select the **Start** and/or **End** option (▢ changes to ☑) to add arrowheads to your line.

● You can also specify the size and shape of the arrowheads by typing values here.

⑤ Press Enter (Return on a Mac) to close the menu.

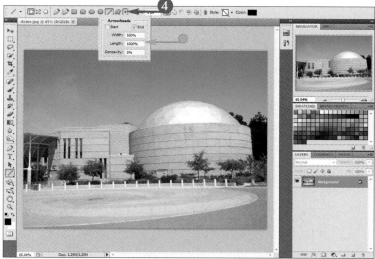

6 Type a line weight.

You can use common units of measure, such as px (pixels), in (inches), or cm (centimeters).

7 Click here (⬇) to choose a style for your line.

● The Default style (◻) creates a plain solid line.

8 Press **Enter** (**Return** on a Mac) to close the menu.

● You can click the **Color** box to select a different line color.

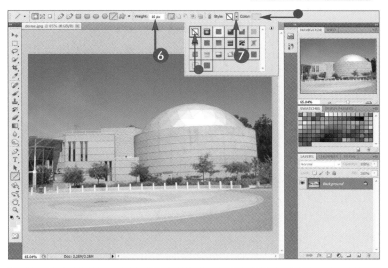

9 Click and drag to draw the line.

● Photoshop places the line on its own layer.

Note: For more on layers, see Chapter 8.

● You can move the shape by selecting its layer and then using the Move tool (⊕).

Note: For more on the Move tool, see Chapter 5.

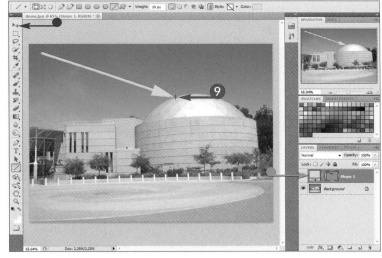

TIPS

How do I draw a horizontal or vertical line?
Press **Shift** as you click and drag to create your line. You can also use this technique to drag lines at 45-degree angles.

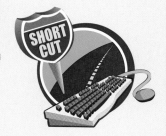

How do I resize a line or another shape?
You can select the layer containing the shape, click **Edit**, and then click **Free Transform**. A bounding box appears around the shape. You can click and drag the handles (◻) on the sides and corners to resize the shape.

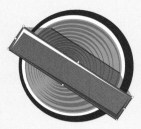

Draw a Shape with the Pen

With the Pen tool, you can create shapes by drawing the lines yourself. This enables you to make shapes that are not included in Photoshop's predefined menus.

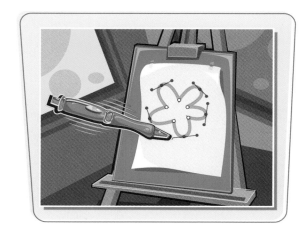

Using the Regular Pen

1 Click the **Pen** tool (✐).

2 Click the **Shape Layers** icon (▣) on the Options bar.

3 Click the **Color** box to select a color for the shape.

Note: *For more on selecting colors, see Chapter 6.*

4 Click inside your image to set an initial anchor point.

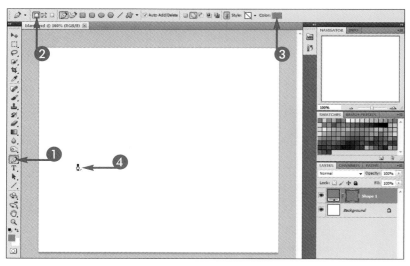

5 Continue clicking to set additional anchor points and define the shape.

6 Click the initial anchor point to close the shape.

Photoshop draws a straight-sided shape.

● Photoshop places the shape on its own layer.

You can create curved paths if you click and drag with the **Pen** tool (✐).

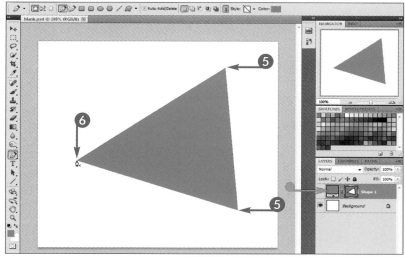

Using the Freeform Pen

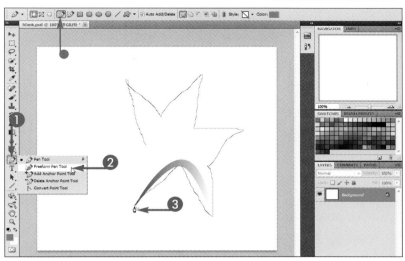

1. Click and hold the **Pen** tool ().
2. Click the **Freeform Pen** tool () in the list that appears.

● You can also select the tool from the Options bar.

3. Click and drag inside your image.

Photoshop draws a free-form line.

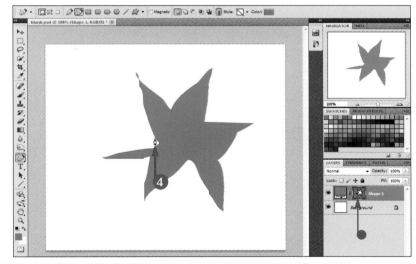

4. Drag to the starting point of the line.

Photoshop completes the shape.

Alternatively, you can release the mouse, and Photoshop completes your shape with a straight line.

● Photoshop places the shape on its own layer.

TIP

How can I trace an object in my image with the Pen tool?
If the object has well-defined edges, you can trace it with the Freeform Pen tool () with the Magnetic option selected on the Options bar (☐ changes to ☑). The tool works similarly to the Magnetic Lasso tool (☐). For more on using the Magnetic Lasso, see Chapter 4.

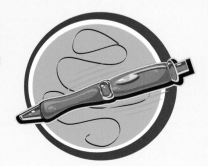

Edit a Shape

You can edit shapes by manipulating their anchor points. This lets you fine-tune the geometries of your shapes. You can edit shapes drawn with the predefined shape tools or the Pen tool. For more shape-editing techniques, see Photoshop's Help documentation.

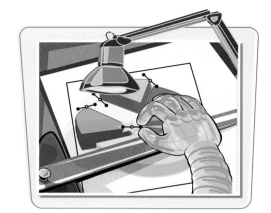

Edit a Shape

Move an Anchor Point

1 Click and hold the **Path Selection** tool ().

2 Click the **Direct Selection** tool () in the list that appears.

3 Click the edge of a shape.

Photoshop shows the anchor points that make up the shape.

4 Click and drag an anchor point.

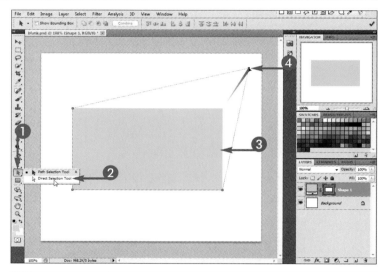

Photoshop moves the anchor point, changing the geometry of the shape.

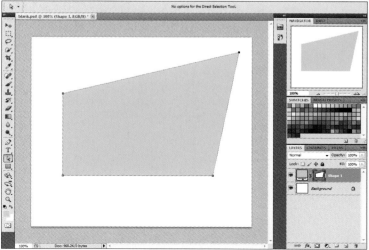

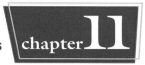

Bend a Straight Segment

1 Click and hold the **Pen** tool (⊿).

2 Click the **Add Anchor Point** tool (⊿) in the list that appears.

3 Click a straight line between two anchor points.

Photoshop adds an anchor point to the line.

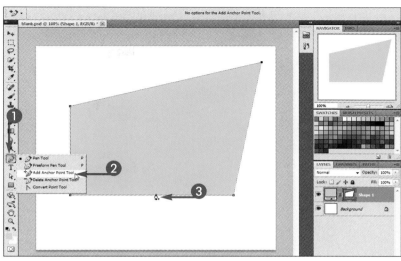

4 Click the anchor point and then drag.

5 Release the mouse.

Photoshop turns the straight line into a curved line.

You can use this technique to create a concave or convex curve.

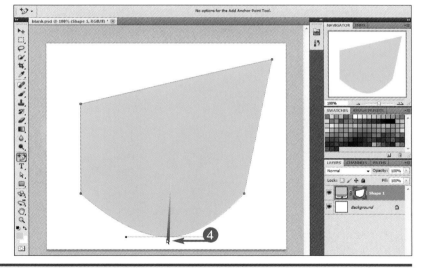

TIPS

How do I edit curved lines?

If you click an anchor point on a curved line with the Direct Selection tool (▷), direction lines appear to the sides of the anchor point. You can click and drag the ends of the direction lines to edit the curve on each side of the anchor point. You can also click and drag the curves themselves with the Direct Selection tool.

How do I turn a shape layer into a regular layer?

You can turn a shape layer into a regular layer by *rasterizing* it. Click the shape layer and then click **Layer**, **Rasterize**, and **Shape**. After rasterizing, the shape's anchor points are no longer accessible. This means you cannot change the geometry of the shape by editing the anchor points. Most of Photoshop's filter commands require you to rasterize a shape before you can apply the commands to it. For more on filters, see Chapter 10.

Adding and Manipulating Type

You can add letters and words to your photos and illustrations. Photoshop lets you add type to your images and precisely control the type's appearance and layout. You can also modify your type by using Photoshop's various styles.

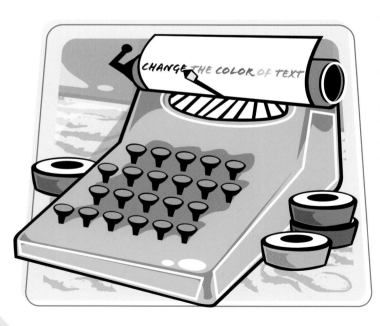

CHANGE THE COLOR OF TEXT

Add Type to an Image

Adding type enables you to label elements in your image or use letters and words in artistic ways. You can customize your type by using the different fonts installed on your computer.

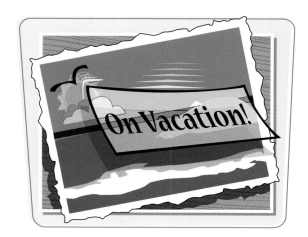

① Click the **Type** tool (T).

② Click where you want the new type to appear.

Note: *You can also create a bounding box by drawing a shape. See Chapter 11 for more.*

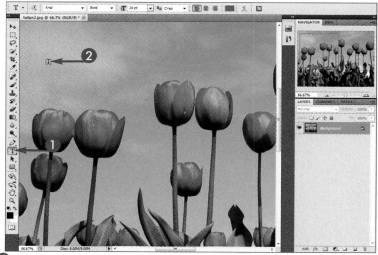

③ Use these menus to choose a font, style, and size for your type.

Note: *To apply a shape by using type, you can choose a shape-oriented font, such as Wingdings.*

④ Click the **Color** box to select a color for your type.

Photoshop applies the foreground color by default.

Note: *See Chapter 6 for more on selecting colors.*

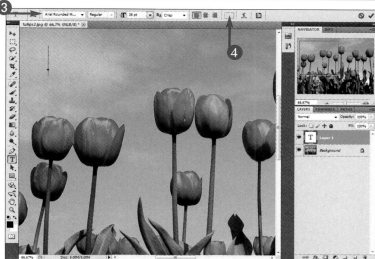

⑤ Type your text.

To create a line break, press Enter (Return on a Mac).

⑥ When you finish typing your text, click here (✓) or press Ctrl + Enter (⌘ + Return on a Mac). You can also click another tool in the Toolbox to complete your text entry.

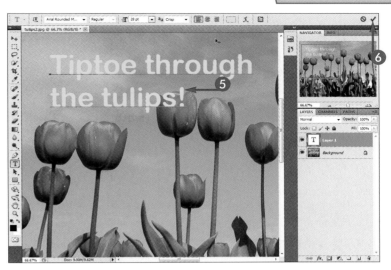

● Photoshop places the type on its own layer.

● You can click the alignment buttons to left-align (▤), center (▤), or right-align (▤) your type.

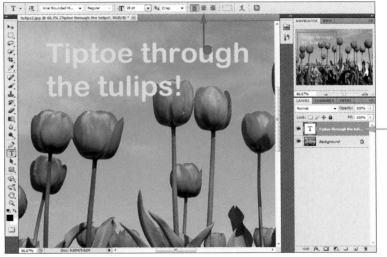

TIPS

How do I create vertical type?
If you click and hold the **Type** tool (T), a list that contains the Vertical Type tool (IT) appears. You can then use the tool to create up-and-down type. When using the regular Type tool, you can click the **Change Orientation** button (▣) on the Options bar to change horizontal type to vertical — and vice versa. Note that with vertical type, lines go from right to left.

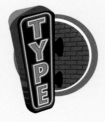

How do I reposition my type?
You can use the Move tool (▶) to move the layer that contains the type. Click the layer of type, click the Move tool, and then click and drag to reposition your type. For more on moving a layer, see Chapter 8.

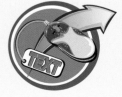

Add Type in a Bounding Box

You can add type inside a *bounding box*, which is a rectangular container for text, to constrain where the type appears and how it wraps.

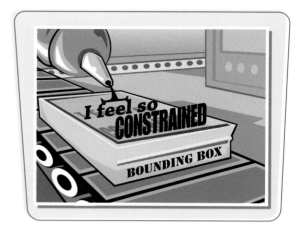

Add Type in a Bounding Box

1 Click the **Type** tool (T).

2 Click and drag inside the image to define the bounding box.

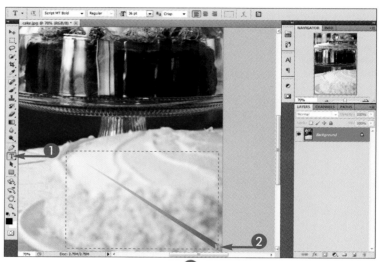

3 Click and drag the handles (□) of the bounding box to adjust its dimensions.

4 Click and drag the center point (⬦) of the bounding box to move the box.

5 Use these menus to choose the formatting for the type to be added.

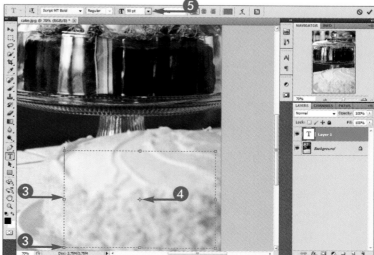

6 Type your text.

Your text appears inside the bounding box.

When a line of text hits the edge of the bounding box, it automatically wraps to the next line.

Photoshop also automatically adds hyphenation.

Note: *You can turn off hyphenation in the Paragraph panel. See the Tip below for more.*

7 When you finish typing your text, click here (✓) or press Enter (⌘ + Return on a Mac).

The bounding box disappears.

● The type is put on its own layer.

● To make the box reappear in order to change its dimensions, click the **Type** tool (T) and then click the text.

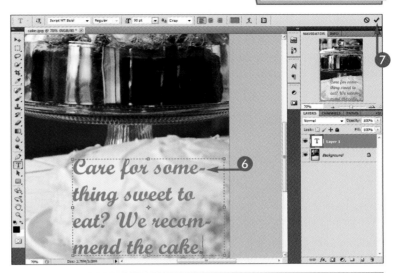

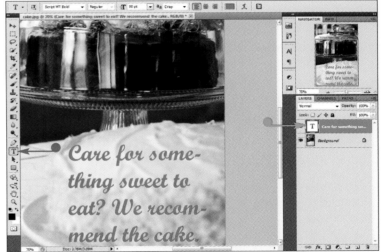

How do I format paragraph text inside a bounding box?
Follow these steps:

1 Click the **Type** tool T.

2 Click the text inside the box.

3 Click **Window** and then **Paragraph**.

The Paragraph panel opens.

4 Type values or click the various tools to control the alignment, indenting, and hyphenation of the text inside the bounding box.

You can also format paragraph text with type styles.

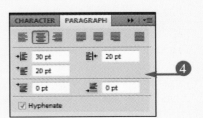

Change the Formatting of Type

You can change the font, boldness, size, and other characteristics of your type. Adding formatting can help text complement the objects in your image.

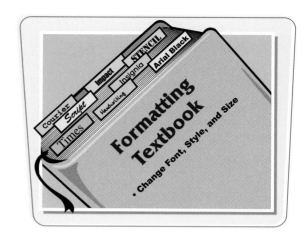

① Click the **Type** tool ([T]).

② Click the type layer that you want to edit.

If the Layers panel is not visible, you can click **Window** and then **Layers** to view it.

③ Click and drag to select some type.

④ Click **Window** and then **Character**.

The Character panel opens.

● You can also make many formatting changes on the Options bar.

⑤ Click here ([▾]) to open the font menu.

Photoshop displays the names of available fonts.

You can turn on font previews in the Type preferences dialog box by clicking **Edit** (**Photoshop** on a Mac), **Preferences**, and then **Type**. Turning on font previews shows examples of each font in the font menu.

⑥ Choose a font.

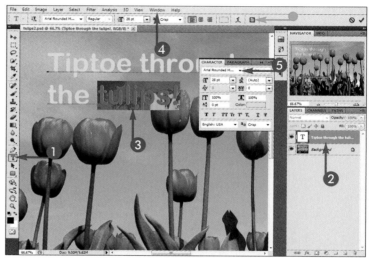

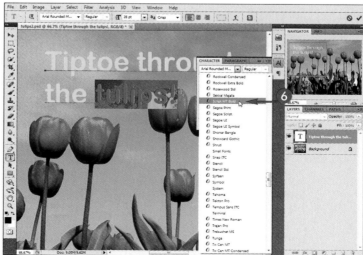

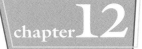
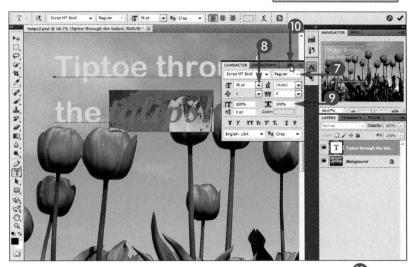
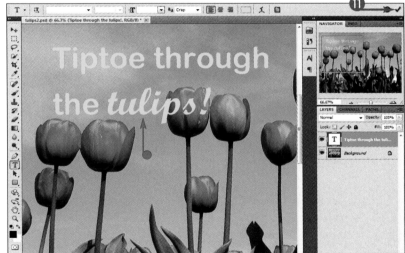

7 Click here (⬇) to choose the type's style.

8 Click here (⬇) to choose the type's size.

9 Type percentage values here to stretch or shrink your type.

You can click other options in the panel to add more formatting.

10 Click here (▶▶) to close the panel.

11 When you finish formatting your text, click here (✓) or press Enter (⌘ + Return on a Mac).

● Photoshop applies the formatting to your type.

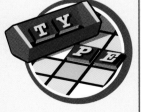

TIPS

How do I edit the content of my type?
With the type's layer selected in the Layers panel, you can click the **Type** tool (T) and then click inside the text. Press Delete to delete letters or you can type new ones. You can press ←, →, ↑, or ↓ to move the cursor inside your type.

How can I check the spelling of my text?
Select your type layer in the Layers panel, click **Edit**, and then click **Check Spelling**. Photoshop compares your text with the text in its dictionary. It flags words it does not recognize and suggests replacements.

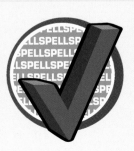

You can change the color of your type to make it blend or contrast with the rest of the image.

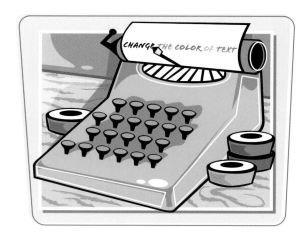

Change the Color of Type

① Click the **Type** tool (T).

② Click the type layer that you want to edit.

If the Layers panel is not visible, you can click **Window** and then **Layers** to view it.

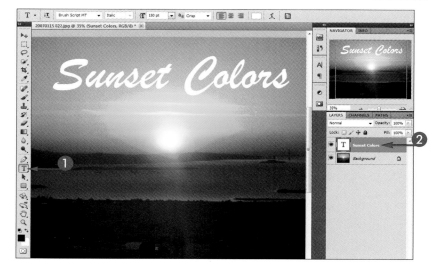

③ Click and drag to select some text.

● You can double-click the layer thumbnail to select all the type.

④ Click the **Color** box on the Options bar.

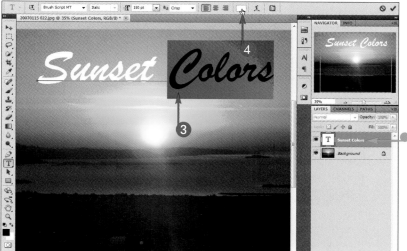

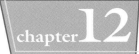

The Select text color dialog box opens.

5 Click a color.

● You can click and drag the slider () to change the colors that Photoshop displays in the selection box.

You can also type values for the color you want.

6 Click **OK**.

7 Click here (✓) or press Enter (⌘ + Return on a Mac).

● Photoshop changes the text to the new color.

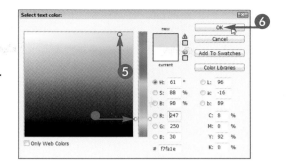

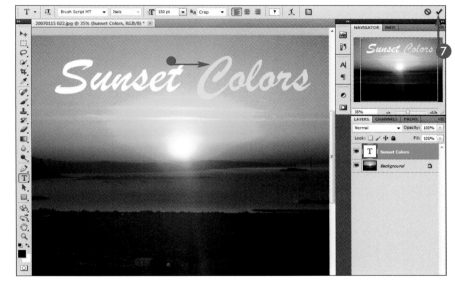

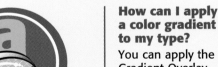

TIPS

What is anti-aliasing?
Anti-aliasing is the process of adding semitransparent pixels to curved edges in digital images to make the edges appear smoother. You can apply anti-aliasing to type to improve its appearance. Text that you do not anti-alias can sometimes look jagged. You can control the presence and style of your type's anti-aliasing with the Anti-Aliasing Method (T) menu on the Options bar.

How can I apply a color gradient to my type?
You can apply the Gradient Overlay style to your type. Click the type layer and then click **Layer**, **Layer Style**, and **Gradient Overlay**. A dialog box opens, allowing you to define the gradient settings. For more on styles, see Chapter 9.

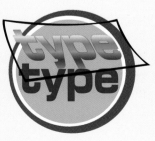

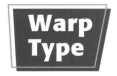

Warp Type

You can easily bend and distort layers of type with Photoshop's Warp feature. This can make words look wrinkled or as if they are blowing in the wind.

You can also warp type by using Photoshop's transformation tools. See Chapter 6 for more.

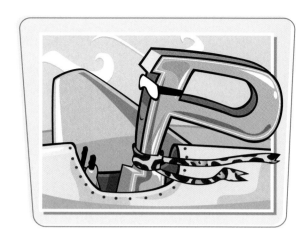

Warp Type

1. Click the **Type** tool (T).

2. Click the type layer that you want to warp.

   If the Layers panel is not visible, you can click **Window** and then **Layers** to view it.

3. Click the **Create Warped Text** button (⌁).

   The Warp Text dialog box opens.

4. Click here (▾) to open the **Style** menu.

5. Click a warp style.

6. Click a radio button to choose an orientation for the warp effect (○ changes to ●).

7. Adjust the Bend and Distortion values by clicking and dragging the sliders (▭).

   The Bend and Distortion values determine the strength of the warp. At 0% for all values, no warp is applied.

8. Click **OK**.

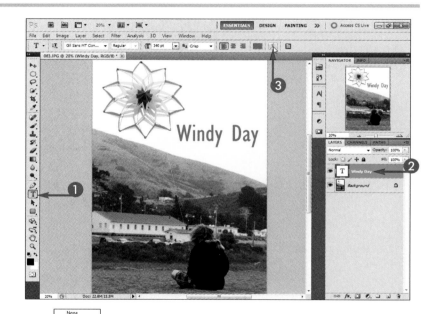

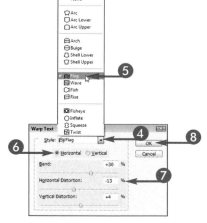

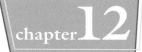

● Photoshop warps the text.

You can edit the format, color, and other characteristics of the type after you apply the warp.

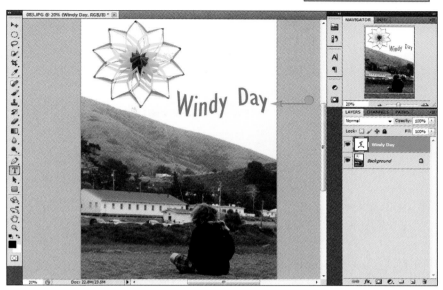

TIP

How do I unwarp text?
Follow these steps:

1 Click the **Type** tool (T).

2 Click the type layer that you want to unwarp.

3 Click the **Create Warp Text** button (🔲).

4 In the Warp Text dialog box, click here (⊡) to open the **Style** menu and then click **None**.

5 Click **OK**.

Photoshop unwarps your type.

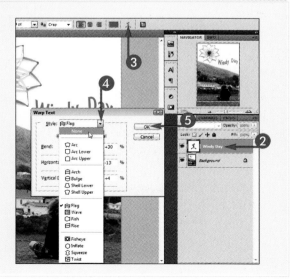

CHAPTER 13

Automating Your Work

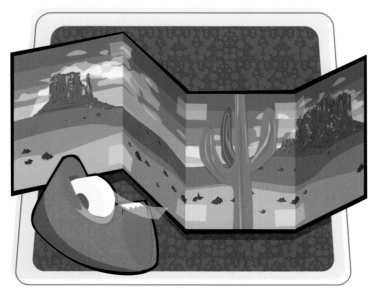

Sometimes, you want to perform the same simple sequence of commands on many different images. With Photoshop's Action commands, you can automate repetitive imaging tasks by saving sequences of commands and applying them automatically to many image files. Other commands enable you to streamline your work by helping you create Web photo galleries, picture packages, panoramas, and high dynamic range (HDR) images.

Record an Action

You can record a sequence of commands as an action and then replay it on other image files. This can save you time when you have a task in Photoshop that you need to repeat.

After you record an action, you can play it. See the section "Play an Action" for more.

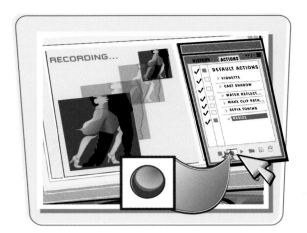

Record an Action

1 Click **Window**.

2 Click **Actions**.

The Actions panel opens.

3 Click a set in which to create your action.

Photoshop starts with a single set called Default Actions.

● You can click the New Action button (□) to create a new actions set.

4 Click the **Create New Action** button (□) to open the New Action dialog box.

5 Type a name for your action.

6 Click **Record**.

7 Perform the sequence of commands that you want to automate on your images.

● In this example, the first command, Auto Contrast, is performed by clicking **Image** and then **Auto Contrast**.

When automatically optimizing contrast, Photoshop performs a Levels adjustment.

Note: See Chapter 7 for more on adjusting colors and contrast.

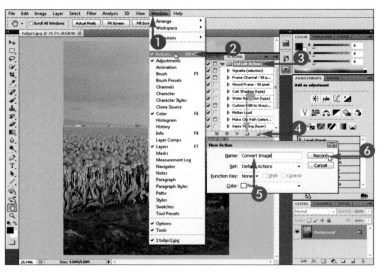

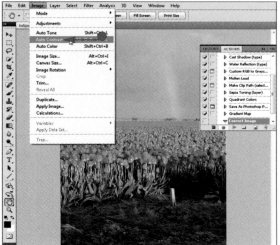

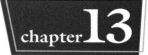

● In this example, the second command is performed by clicking **Image**, **Adjustments**, and then **Desaturate**. This converts the image to black and white.

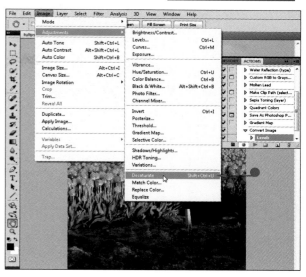

8 Click the **Stop** button (■) to stop recording.

● The Actions panel lists the commands performed under the name of the action.

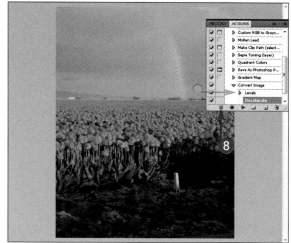

TIPS

What if I make a mistake when recording my action?

You can try recording the action again by clicking 📰 in the Actions panel and then clicking **Record Again**. This runs through the same actions, and you can apply different settings in the command dialog boxes. Alternatively, you can select the action, click the **Trash** icon (🗑) to delete the action, and then try rerecording it.

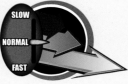

How can I control how fast the steps of an action are performed?

In the Actions panel, click 📰 and then **Playback Options**. A dialog box opens, enabling you to insert a pause after each step of an action. This can help you review the changes Photoshop makes to an image as it performs an action. The default behavior in Photoshop is to complete the actions as quickly as possible.

Play an Action

You can play an action from the Actions panel on an image. This saves time because you can execute multiple Photoshop commands with a single click. You can also play a specific command that is part of an action by itself.

Actions that you record by using one image can be played on other images. See the section "Record an Action" for more.

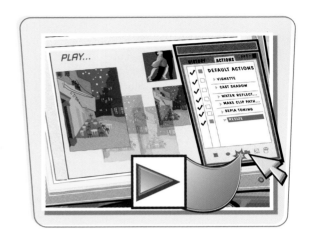

Play an Action

Play a Full Action

1. Click **Window**.

2. Click **Actions**.

   The Actions panel opens.

3. Click ▶ (▶ changes to ▽) to open an actions folder.

   Photoshop comes with several predefined actions in the Default Actions folder.

Note: *To create your own action, see the section "Record an Action."*

4. Click the action that you want to play.

5. Click the **Play Selection** button (▶).

   Photoshop applies the action's commands to the image.

   In this example, a sepia tone is applied to the image.

   You can undo the multiple commands in an action by using the History panel.

Note: *See Chapter 2 for more on the History panel.*

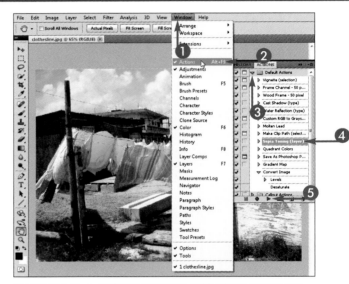

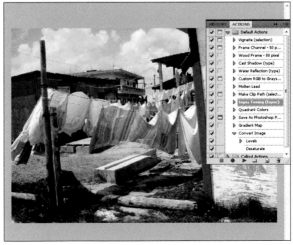

Play a Command in an Action

① In the Actions panel, click ▷ to reveal the commands that make up an action (▷ changes to ▽).

② Click the command that you want to execute.

You can Shift + click to select multiple sequential commands.

③ Ctrl + click ▶ (⌘ + click ▶ on a Mac).

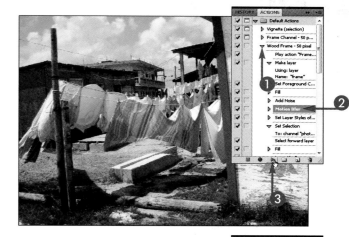

Photoshop executes the selected command but not the commands before or after it.

In this example, the selected command adds motion blur to the image.

Note: *To execute a specific command and all those after it in an action, select the command and then click ▶ without pressing* Ctrl *(*⌘ *on a Mac).*

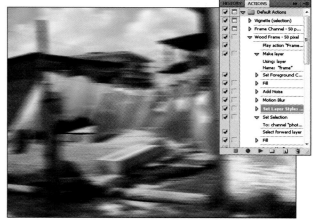

How do I assign a special key command to an action?

① Click ▤ to open the Actions panel menu.

② Click **Action Options**.

③ In the Action Options dialog box, click here (▾) to choose a key command.

④ Click **OK**.

To perform an action on an image, press the key selected in step **3**.

Note: *You may want to avoid assigning function keys that are already associated with a command. To view assigned key commands, click* **Edit** *and then* **Keyboard Shortcuts**.

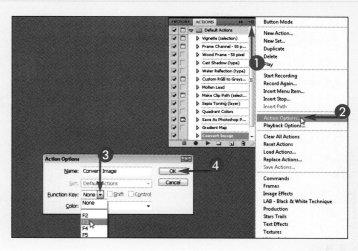

Batch Process by Using an Action

You can apply an action to multiple images automatically with Photoshop's Batch command. The command is a great timesaver for tasks such as optimizing large numbers of digital photos.

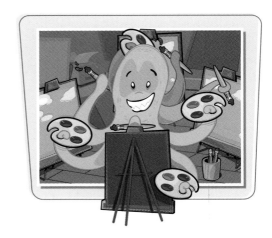

Batch Process by Using an Action

① Place all the images you want to apply an action to in a source folder.

② Create a destination folder in which to save your batch-processed files.

Note: To work with folders, see your operating system's documentation.

③ In Photoshop, click **File**.

④ Click **Automate**.

⑤ Click **Batch**.

The Batch dialog box opens.

⑥ Click here (⊡) to choose an action to apply.

⑦ Click **Choose**.

The Browse for Folder (Choose a batch folder on a Mac) dialog box opens.

⑧ In Windows, click ▷ to open folders on your computer (▷ changes to ◢).

On a Mac, navigate to your source folder.

⑨ Click the folder containing your images.

⑩ Click **OK** (**Choose** on a Mac).

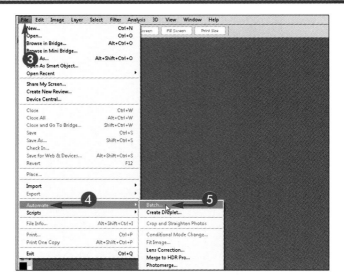

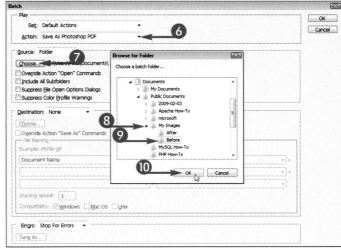

⑪ Click here (▢) to choose **Folder**.

⑫ Click **Choose** and then repeat steps **8** to **10** to select the folder where you want your batch-processed files to be saved.

● You can specify a naming scheme for saving the batch-processed files.

⑬ Click **OK** (**Choose** on a Mac).

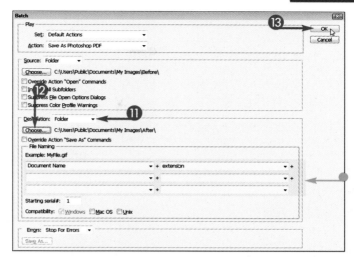

● Photoshop opens each image in the specified folder one at a time and applies the action.

If the action includes a save step, Photoshop automatically saves each image in the destination directory.

● If the action does not include a save step, Photoshop prompts you with a Save As dialog box for each image.

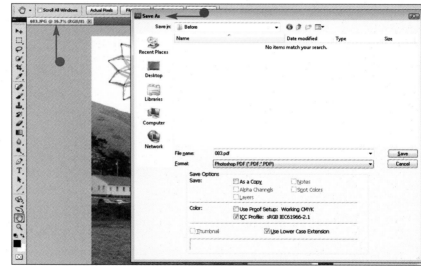

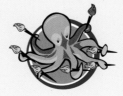
TIPS

How can I change the mode — such as RGB Color or Grayscale — of an image during a batch process, depending on its current mode?
When you record the original action, click **File**, **Automate**, and then **Conditional Mode Change**. A dialog box opens, asking you to specify the source modes that you want to switch as well as a target mode. When the action is run as a batch process, images that are of a selected source mode are converted.

How do I batch-process by using an action in Mac OS X?
You do this very much like a Windows user does but with the Open dialog box instead of the Browse for Folder dialog box. When you click **Choose** in step **7**, the Open-style dialog box opens. Using the file browser in the center of the dialog box, locate the source and destination folders for your batch-processed images.

Create a PDF of Images

Photoshop can automatically create a PDF (Portable Document Format) file that shows one or more of your photos. You can choose from a number of PDF templates, including ones for contact sheets and greeting cards.

You can view PDF files on your computer by using the free Adobe Reader. Download it here: http://get.adobe.com/reader. On a Mac, you can also use the Preview application.

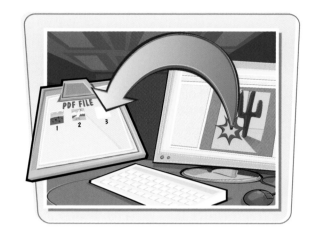

Create a PDF of Images

① Open Adobe Bridge by clicking **Launch Bridge** (Br) in Photoshop.

Note: For more on accessing Bridge, see Chapter 1.

② Click **Window**.

③ Click **Workspace**.

④ Click **Output**.

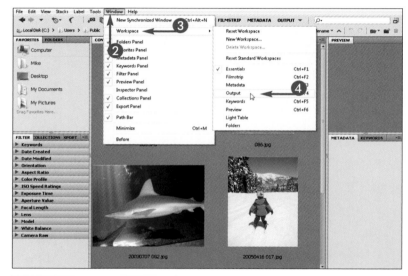

Bridge displays panes for outputting images.

⑤ Make sure the PDF button is selected.

⑥ Click the **Folders** tab.

⑦ Click ▶ to open folders on your computer (▶ changes to ▼).

⑧ Click the folder containing your images.

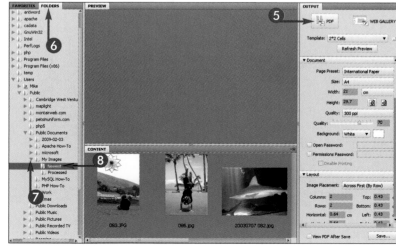

The folder images appear in the bottom pane.

⑨ **Ctrl** + click (⌘ + click on a Mac) to select the images you want to save in your PDF.

You can press **Ctrl** + **A** (⌘ + **A** on a Mac) to select all the images in the folder.

⑩ Click here (▢) to choose a PDF template.

⑪ Click **Refresh Preview**.

● Bridge displays a preview of the PDF.

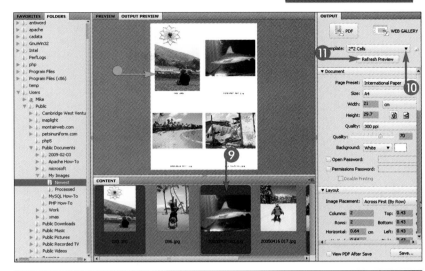

⑫ Click **Save**.

The Save dialog box opens.

⑬ Click here (▢) to choose where to save your PDF file.

⑭ Type a name for your PDF file.

⑮ Click **Save**.

Bridge saves your PDF and displays a confirmation dialog box.

⑯ Click **OK**.

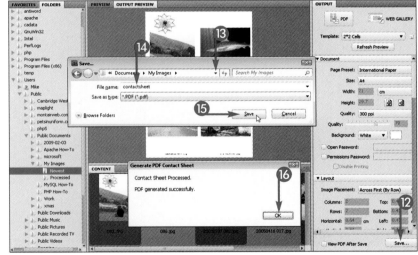

TIP

What are some of the different customization options for PDF files in the Output pane?

● **Document**: These allow you to choose the paper size and orientation. You can also password-protect your file.

● **Layout:** These allow you to change the organization and spacing of the images on the page.

● **Overlays:** These allow you to display file name information over your images.

● **Playback:** These allow you to control how your PDF appears when viewed as a slide show.

● **Watermark:** These allow you to place transparent text over your images to indicate ownership or other information.

Create a Web Photo Gallery

You can have Photoshop create a photo gallery Web site that showcases your images. Photoshop not only sizes and optimizes your image files for the gallery but also creates the Web pages that display the images and builds the links and buttons that let you navigate the pages.

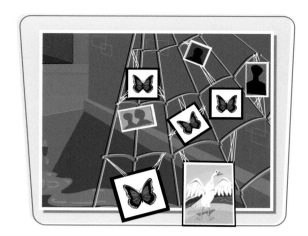

Create a Web Photo Gallery

Build and Preview a Gallery

1. Place the images that you want to put into a gallery into a folder.

2. Open Adobe Bridge by clicking **Launch Bridge** (📷) in Photoshop.

Note: For more on accessing Bridge, see Chapter 1.

3. Click **Window**.

4. Click **Workspace**.

5. Click **Output**.

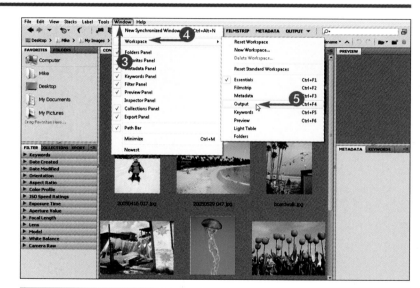

Bridge displays panes for outputting images.

6. Click **Web Gallery**.

7. Click the **Folders** tab.

8. Click ▶ to open folders on your computer (▶ changes to ▼).

9. Click the folder containing your images.

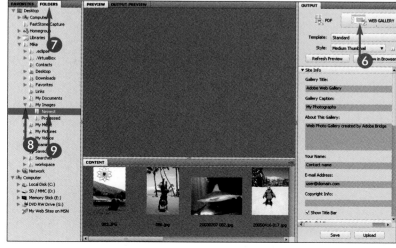

The folder images appear in the bottom pane.

🔟 **Ctrl** + click (⌘ + click on a Mac) to select the images you want to display in your gallery.

You can press **Ctrl** + **A** (⌘ + **A** on a Mac) to select all the images in the folder.

⓫ Click here (▣) to choose a gallery template.

⓬ Click here (▣) to choose a gallery style for your template.

The styles may vary depending on the template chosen.

⓭ Type a gallery title.

In most templates, this appears at the top of your gallery pages.

⓮ Type a caption and other descriptive information for your gallery.

⓯ You can type your name and e-mail address if you want people to be able to contact you through your gallery.

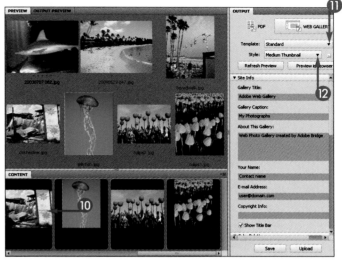

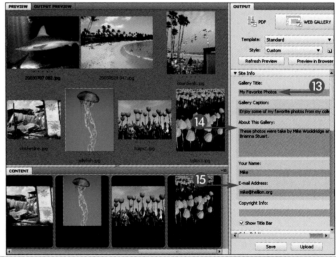

 TIPS

How can I customize the colors or layout of my photo gallery?

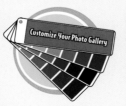

Under the Color Palette section of the Output pane, you can click color swatches to customize the colors of text, background, and other elements in your gallery. In the Appearance section, you can select the number of columns and rows as well as choose the preview size of the gallery images.

Do all the photo galleries require Adobe Flash?

Most of the Photoshop gallery templates make use of Adobe Flash to add interactive features, such as animated buttons and transitions between images. Viewers must have Flash installed in their Web browsers to view your photos. You can choose the HTML Gallery template in step **11** to create a gallery based only on HTML, which means users do not need to have Flash installed to view it.

continued ▶

287

Create a Web Photo Gallery *(continued)*

After you create your gallery, you can preview it in Bridge or a Web browser. Then, you can save it to your computer or upload it to a Web server by using Photoshop's integrated FTP client.

To upload your files to a Web server, you will need an Internet connection.

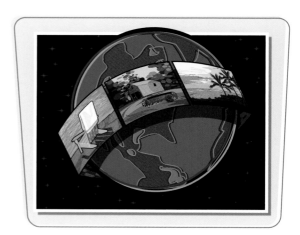

⑯ Click **Refresh Preview**.

● Photoshop displays a preview of the gallery.

● You can click links or thumbnail images in the preview to view larger-sized images.

● You can click **Preview in Browser** to view the gallery in your computer's default Web browser.

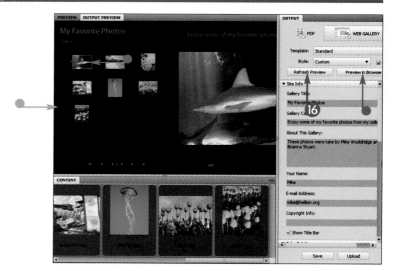

Save to Your Computer

① Click here (⊟) to scroll to the bottom of the Output pane.

② Type a gallery name.

   Photoshop stores the files in a folder with that name.

③ Click **Browse**.

   The Choose a Folder dialog box opens.

④ Select a location in which to save your gallery.

⑤ Click **OK** (**Choose** on a Mac).

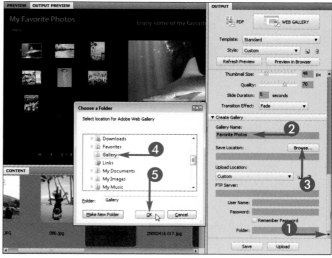

6 Click **Save**.

● Photoshop saves the gallery in the specified location and displays a confirmation dialog box.

7 Click **OK**.

You can view the saved gallery on your computer by opening the gallery folder and then opening the index.html file in a Web browser.

Upload to the Web

1 Type a Gallery name.

Photoshop uploads the files to a folder with that name.

2 Type the login information for the FTP server.

You can check with your Internet service provider (ISP) for this information.

3 To upload your gallery to a specific folder, type the folder name here.

4 Click **Upload**.

Photoshop uploads the gallery files.

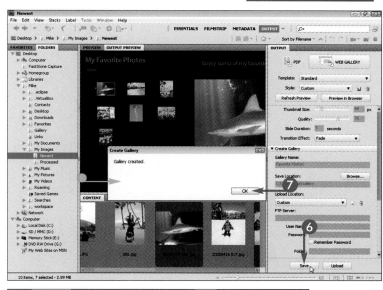

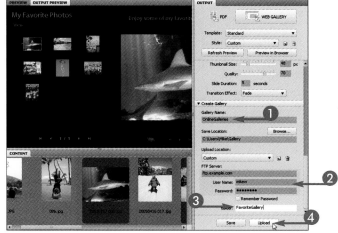

How can I save my FTP settings?

After you type your username, password, and other settings in the Upload section, you can save the settings as a preset by clicking ▣. The New Preset dialog box opens, and you can name your preset. Your saved presets can be selected from the menu in the Upload section. To delete a saved preset, select it from the menu and then click 🗑.

How can I change the behavior of the panels in the Output pane?

You can click **Edit** (**Adobe Bridge CS5** on a Mac) and then **Preferences** to open the preferences dialog box. Then, you can click **Output** to choose your options. If you click the **Use Solo Mode for Output Panel Behavior** check box (▢ changes to ☑), only one of the secondary panels in the Output pane will be active at a time. This is convenient if you would rather click headings to access the output options instead of scrolling.

Create a Panoramic Image

You can use the Photomerge feature in Photoshop to stitch several images together into a single panoramic image. This enables you to capture more scenery than is usually possible in a regular photograph.

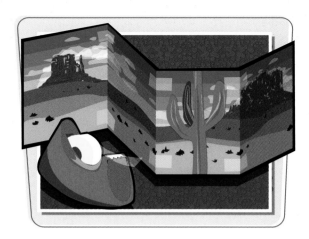

Create a Panoramic Image

1. Click **File**.

2. Click **Automate**.

3. Click **Photomerge**.

   The Photomerge dialog box opens.

4. Click the **Auto** radio button (⊙ changes to ◉).

   With the Auto setting, Photoshop automatically chooses the best method for stitching your photos together.

5. Click **Browse**.

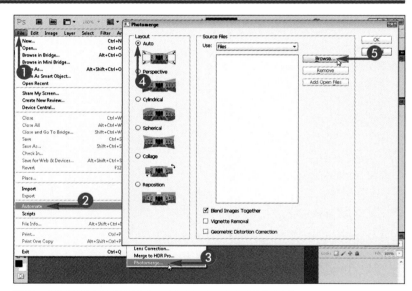

   The Open dialog box opens.

6. Click here (⊡) to choose the folder that contains the images you want to merge.

7. **Ctrl** + click (⌘ + click on a Mac) the images you want to merge into a panoramic image.

8. Click **OK**.

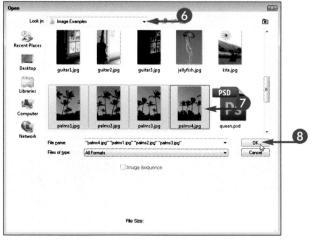

● The file names of the images appear in the Source Files list.

⑨ Click **OK** to build the panoramic image.

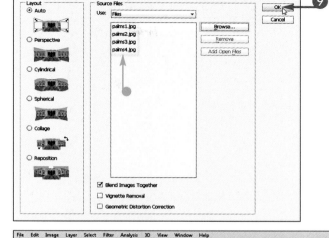

Photoshop merges the images into a single panoramic image.

● Parts of each image appear in separate layers in the Layers panel.

Note: For more on layers, see Chapter 8.

● You can use the Crop tool () to remove extra space around the panorama.

Note: For more on cropping, see Chapter 3.

⑩ Click **File** and then **Save** to save the panorama.

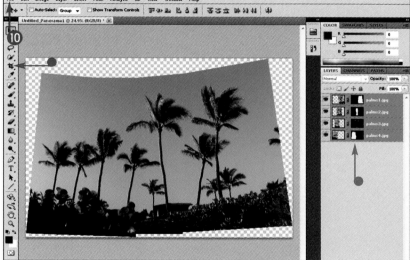

TIP

How can I create photos that merge successfully?
To merge photos successfully, you need to align and overlap the photos as you shoot them. Here are a few hints. For more tips, see the Photoshop Help documentation.

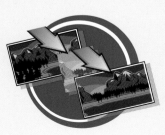

● Use a tripod to keep your photos level with one another.
● Experiment with the different layout modes in the Photomerge dialog box.
● Refrain from using lenses that distort your photos, such as fisheye lenses.
● Shoot your photos so they overlap at least 30%.

Create an HDR Image

An HDR image is a composite image created from several photographs of the same scene, with each photograph having a different exposure. Photoshop combines the best lighting from each image to produce a single optimized image.

HDR images are good for scenes that have both light areas and dark areas. HDR stands for *high dynamic range*.

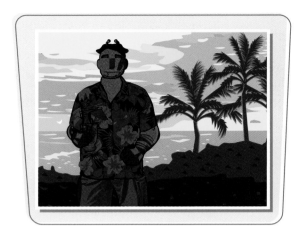

Create an HDR Image

① Click **File**.

② Click **Automate**.

③ Click **Merge to HDR Pro**.

The Merge to HDR Pro dialog box opens.

④ Click **Browse**.

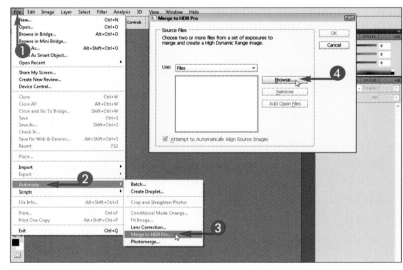

The Open dialog box opens.

⑤ Click here (⊡) to choose the folder that contains the images you want to merge.

⑥ Ctrl + click (⌘ + click on a Mac) the images you want to merge into an HDR image.

⑦ Click **OK**.

⑧ Click **OK** in the Merge to HDR Pro dialog box.

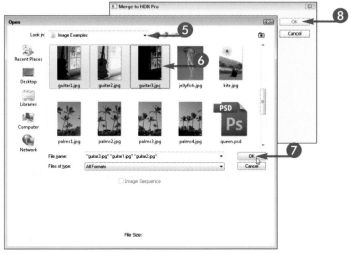

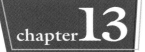

- Photoshop processes the images, merging their exposures and creating a single image.

⑨ You can click here (⊟) to choose the method by which Photoshop adjusts exposures.

⑩ For the Local Adaptation and Exposure and Gamma methods, you can click and drag the sliders (▣) to fine-tune the lighting and colors.

⑪ Click **OK**.

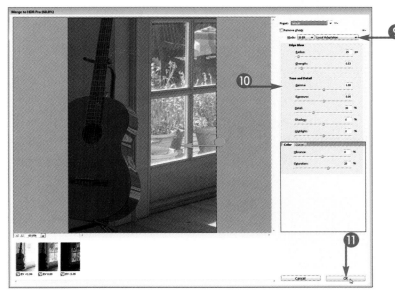

Photoshop displays the HDR image.

- In this example, tones for the lighter part of the image are taken from the source image with the shorter exposure.

- The tones for the darker part of the image are taken from the source image with the longer exposure.

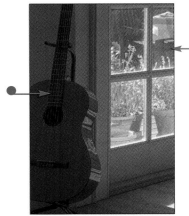

How can I create source photos to use for my HDR image?
To create a good HDR image, you need several photos of the same scene, with each photo shot at a different exposure. Here are a few tips:

- Use a tripod to help ensure the content in your photos is aligned. A cable release can also help keep your camera steady between shots.

- When adjusting your camera settings, change the shutter speed instead of the aperture. This will result in different exposures without changing the depth of field.

- If your camera offers it, you can use Auto Exposure Bracketing. This feature makes it easy to automatically shoot photos at several evenly spaced exposures.

- The more exposures you merge for your HDR, the more control you will have over the tones in the resulting image.

Convert File Types

You can quickly and easily convert images from one file type to another in Photoshop by using the Image Processor script. This makes it easy to convert a collection of TIFF files to the JPEG format for posting on the Web.

The Image Processor script allows you to convert to the JPEG, PSD, and TIFF file formats only.

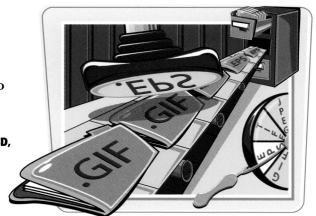

Convert File Types

1. Place the images that you want to convert into a folder.

Note: To work with folders, see your operating system's documentation.

2. Click **File**.

3. Click **Scripts**.

4. Click **Image Processor**.

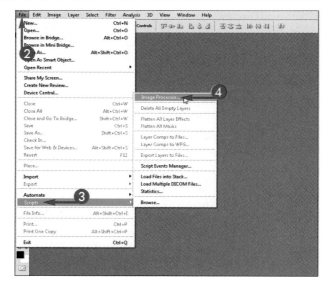

The Image Processor dialog box opens.

5. Click **Select Folder**.

The Choose Folder (Choose a folder on a Mac) dialog box opens.

6. In Windows, click ▷ to open folders on your computer (▷ changes to ◢).

On a Mac, navigate to your source folder.

7. Click the folder containing your images.

8. Click **OK**.

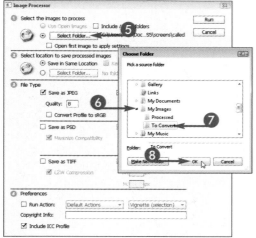

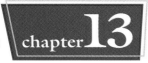
9 Specify where you want your processed images to be saved.

10 Click an image file type check box (☐ changes to ☑).

● If you click **Save as JPEG**, you can also specify a quality setting from 1 to 12; the higher the quality setting, the larger the resulting file size.

You can click multiple format check boxes; Photoshop saves a separate image file for each format selected.

● You can optionally click the **Resize to Fit** check box (☐ changes to ☑), type a new width and height, and then Photoshop resizes the images before saving.

Note: *Photoshop leaves the proportions of any resized images unchanged.*

● You can optionally click the **Run Action** check box (☐ changes to ☑) to have an action executed on each image before saving.

Note: *For more on actions, see the other tasks in this chapter.*

11 Click **Run**.

Photoshop processes the images.

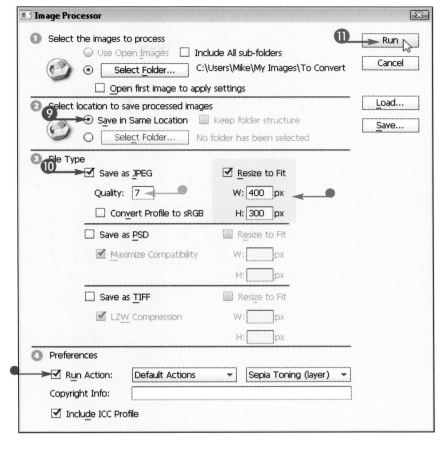

How can I quickly add the same copyright information to multiple images?

In the Image Processor dialog box, type the copyright information into the Copyright Info field. Photoshop adds the information to the processed images. To view the copyright information of an image in Photoshop, open the image, click **File**, and then click **File Info**.

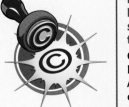

How can I save my Image Processor settings so I can use them again later?

Click **Save** in the Image Processor dialog box. Another dialog box opens, enabling you to save the settings as an XML file. To load previously saved settings, click **Load** in the Image Processor dialog box.

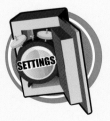

Batch Rename Images

You can change the file names of multiple images automatically with Bridge's renaming feature. You can customize the new name by using custom text, the date, sequential numbers, and more.

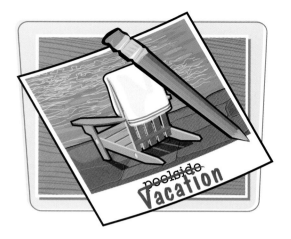

Batch Rename Images

① Place the images that you want to rename into a folder.

② Open Adobe Bridge by clicking **Launch Bridge** (🖼) in Photoshop.

Note: For more on accessing Bridge, see Chapter 1.

③ Click the **Folders** tab.

④ Click the folder containing the images to rename.

⑤ Ctrl + click (⌘ + click on a Mac) to select the images you want to rename.

You can press Ctrl + A (⌘ + A on a Mac) to select all the images in the folder.

⑥ Click **Tools**.

⑦ Click **Batch Rename**.

The Batch Rename dialog box opens.

● By default, the renamed images are saved in the same folder.

● You can click the **Move** or **Copy** radio buttons (○ changes to ◉) to save the images elsewhere. After you click Move or Copy, you can click **Browse** to select a destination folder.

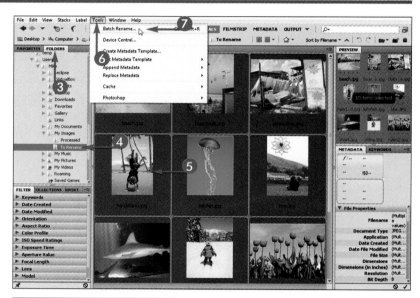

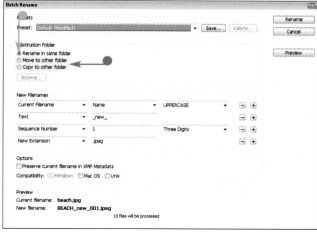

⑧ Click here (⊟) to choose a file-naming option.

⑨ Type in the text fields or choose from menus to customize the file name.

In this example, the images are renamed with an all-caps version of their file names.

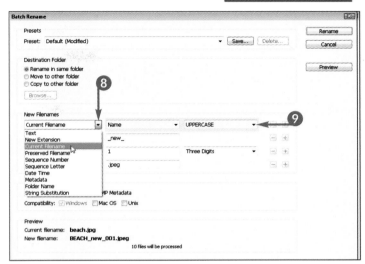

⑩ Repeat steps **8** and **9** for other parts of the naming scheme.

● You can add or remove naming scheme options by clicking ⊞ or ⊟, respectively.

● An example of the new file name appears here.

⑪ Click **Rename**.

Photoshop renames the images in the folder.

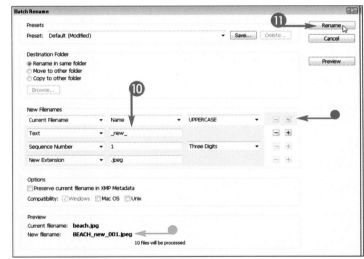

 TIPS

How can I rename images based on the camera settings they were taken with?

Choose **Metadata** for a file name option in step **8** and then select a camera setting in the menu that appears. You can use aperture value, exposure setting, focal length, and other camera settings in your new file names.

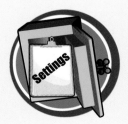
How can I save my renaming settings for use later?

Click **Save** in the Batch Rename dialog box. A Save As dialog box opens, enabling you to save the settings. To load previously saved settings, click **Load** in the Batch Rename dialog box.

Using Tool Presets

You can specify commonly used options for a tool and then save that set of options for loading and using later. For example, it can be helpful to define presets for brush styles and opacities you use often.

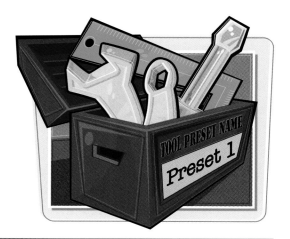

Define a Tool Preset

1. Click a tool.

2. On the Options bar, specify the settings you want to save for that tool.

3. Click here (□).

● Previously defined and default presets are listed.

4. Click the **Create New Tool Preset** button (□).

5. In the New Tool Preset dialog box, type a name for the tool preset.

6. Click **OK**.

Photoshop saves the tool preset.

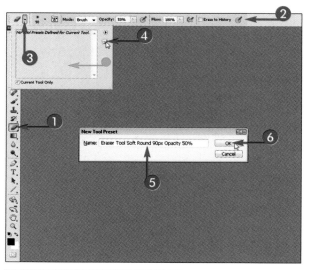

Load a Tool Preset

1. Click **Window**.

2. Click **Tool Presets**.

The Tool Presets panel opens, listing the presets available for that tool.

● You can deselect the **Current Tool Only** check box (☑ changes to ☐) to display the presets for all the tools.

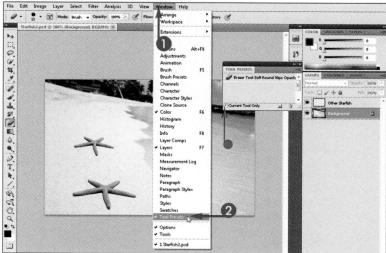

③ Click a preset.

● The tool settings on the Options bar change to reflect those defined in the preset.

④ You can apply the tool to see the effects of the preset.

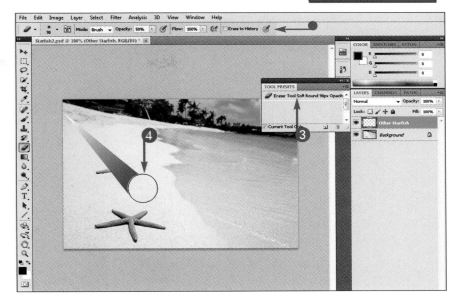

How can I easily manage a large number of tool presets?
The Tool Presets panel menu features a variety of commands for managing your presets.

① Click 📧 to open the Tool Presets panel menu.

② Click a command.

● You can open the Preset Manager to view and organize your presets in a dialog box. You can also access it by clicking **Edit** and then **Preset Manager**.

● You can save groups of presets as separate files on your computer and then reload them later.

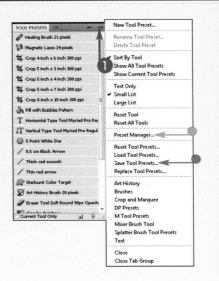

CHAPTER

14

Saving and Printing Images

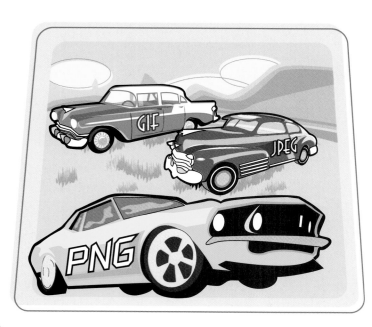

You can save your images for use later or so you can use them in another application or on the Web. You can also print your images to have a hard copy of your work. This chapter shows you how.

Save in the Photoshop Format

You can save your image in Photoshop's native image format. This format enables you to retain multiple layers in your image, if it has them. This is the best format in which to save your images if you still need to edit them.

Photoshop PDF and TIFF files also support multiple layers.

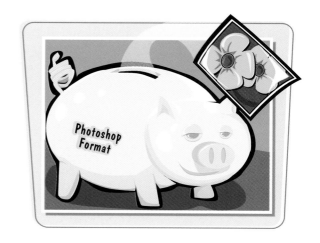

① Click **File**.

② Click **Save As**.

● If you have named and saved your image previously and just want to save changes, you can click **File** and then **Save**.

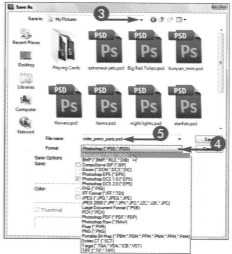

The Save As dialog box opens.

③ Click here (⊡) to choose a folder into which to save the image file.

④ Click here (⊡) to choose the Photoshop file format.

⑤ Type a name for the image file.

Photoshop automatically assigns a .psd extension if you do not specify an extension.

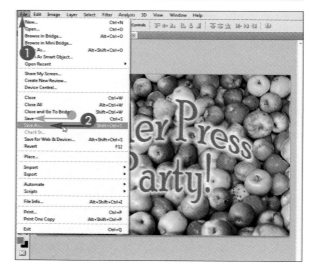

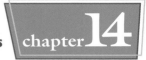

- To save a copy of the file and keep the existing file open, you can click the **As a Copy** check box (☐ changes to ☑).

- To merge the multiple layers of your image into one layer, you can deselect the **Layers** check box (☑ changes to ☐).

6 Click **Save**.

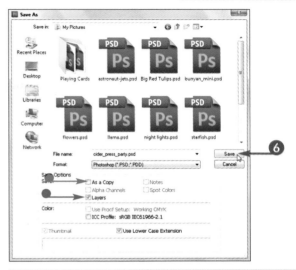

The Photoshop Format Options dialog box opens.

7 Click **OK** to make sure your image is compatible with other applications.

Photoshop saves the image file.

- The name of the file appears in the image's title bar.

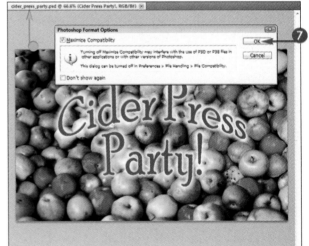

 TIP

What are the shortcuts for saving an image in Photoshop?
You can use several keyboard commands to save your image.

Command	Windows Shortcut	Mac Shortcut
Save	Ctrl + S	⌘ + S
Save As	Shift + Ctrl + S	Shift + ⌘ + S
Save for Web & Devices	Alt + Shift + Ctrl + S	Option + Shift + ⌘ + S

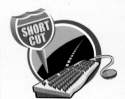

Save an Image for Use in Another Application

You can save your image in a format that can be opened and used in other imaging or page layout applications. TIFF (Tagged Image File Format) and EPS (Encapsulated PostScript) are standard printing formats that many applications on both Windows and Mac platforms support.

BMP — bitmap — is a popular Windows image format. Most image formats — with the exception of Photoshop PSD, Photoshop PDF, Large Document, and TIFF — do not support layers.

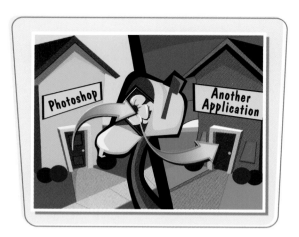

Save an Image for Use in Another Application

1 Click **File**.

2 Click **Save As**.

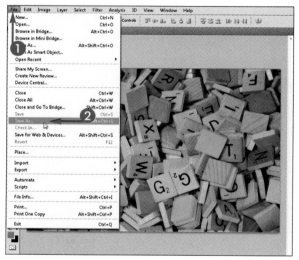

The Save As dialog box opens.

3 In Windows, click here (⬒) to choose a folder into which to save the image file.

4 In Windows, click here (⬒) to choose a file format.

If you are saving a multilayer image and you select a file format that does not support layers, an alert icon appears. Photoshop saves a flattened copy of the image.

Note: See the section "Save in the Photoshop Format" to save a multilayer image. For more on flattening, see Chapter 8.

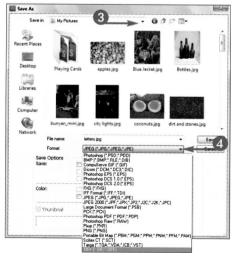

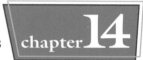

5 Type a file name.

Photoshop automatically assigns an appropriate extension for the file format, such as .tif for TIFF or .eps for EPS, if you do not specify an extension.

6 Click **Save**.

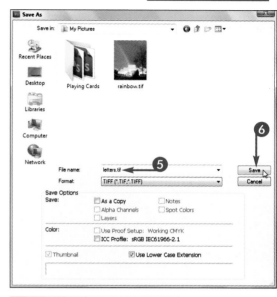

A dialog box opens with options specific to the format in which you are saving — the TIFF format, in this example.

7 Click **OK**.

Photoshop saves the image.

If a flattened copy is saved, the original multilayer version remains in the image window.

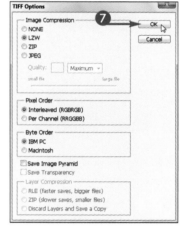

 TIPS

How do I choose a file format for my image?

You should choose the format based on how you want to use the image. If it is a multilayered image and you want to preserve the layers, save it as a Photoshop file or TIFF. If you want to use the image in word-processing or page layout applications, save it as a TIFF or EPS file. If you want to use the image on the Web, save it as a JPEG, PNG, or GIF file. For more on file formats, see the rest of this chapter as well as Photoshop's documentation.

How can I save several images as a slide show presentation?

To create a slide show, you can save a selection of Photoshop images as a PDF in the Bridge application. See Chapter 13 for more. In the PDF Playback settings, you can adjust how the images are displayed when shown as a slide show.

Save a JPEG for the Web

You can save a file in the JPEG — Joint Photographic Experts Group — format and then publish it on the Web. JPEG is the most common file format for saving photographic images. Photoshop saves JPEG images for the Web at 72 dpi (dots per inch).

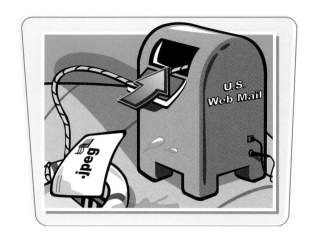

Save a JPEG for the Web

1 Click **File**.

2 Click **Save for Web & Devices**.

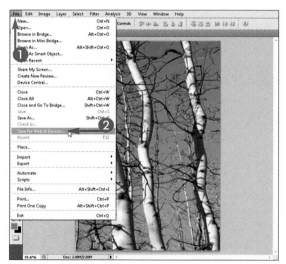

The Save for Web & Devices dialog box opens.

3 Click the **2-Up** tab.

4 Click here to select the optimized version of your image.

5 Click here (🔽) to choose **JPEG**.

6 Click here (🔽) to choose a quality setting.

● Alternatively, you can select a numeric quality setting from 0 (low quality) to 100 (high quality).

The higher the quality, the larger the resulting file size.

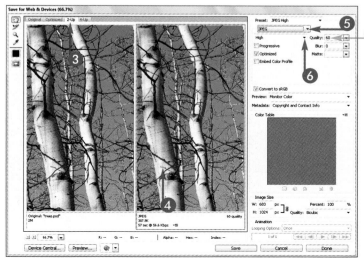

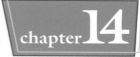

7 Check that the file quality and file size are acceptable in the preview pane.

● You can use the Hand tool (🖑) to move the image in the preview window.

● You can use the Zoom tool (🔍) to magnify the image in the preview window.

8 Click **Save**.

The Save Optimized As dialog box opens.

9 In Windows, click here (🔽) to choose a folder into which to save the file.

On a Mac, use the Where pop-up menu or the File Browser to choose a folder.

10 Type a file name.

Photoshop automatically assigns a .jpg extension if you do not add an extension.

11 Click **Save**.

The original image file remains open in Photoshop.

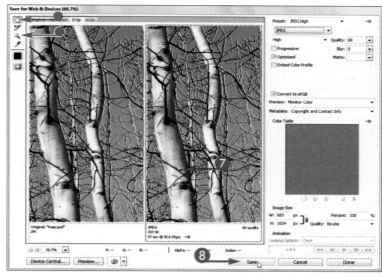

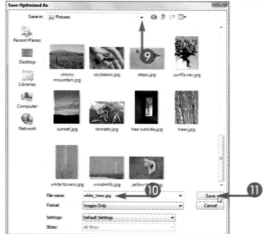

TIPS

What is image compression?

Image compression involves using mathematical techniques to reduce the amount of information required to describe an image. This results in smaller file sizes, which is important when transmitting information on the Web. Some compression schemes, such as JPEG, reduce image quality somewhat, but the loss is usually negligible compared to the savings in file size.

How can I optimize my Web images to a specific file size?

In the Save for Web & Devices dialog box, click 🔳 in the upper-right corner and then choose **Optimize to File Size**. A dialog box opens, allowing you to specify a target file size and other settings. Click **OK** to have Photoshop automatically select optimization settings to meet your requirements. The tool works with regular images and sliced images. For more on saving sliced images, see the section "Save a Sliced Image."

Save a GIF for the Web

You can save an image as a GIF — Graphics Interchange Format — file and then publish it on the Web. The GIF format is good for saving illustrations that have a limited number of colors. The GIF format supports a maximum of 256 colors. Photoshop saves GIF images at 72 dpi (dots per inch). Unlike JPEG images, GIF images can include transparency.

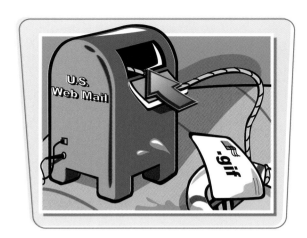

① Click **File**.

② Click **Save for Web & Devices**.

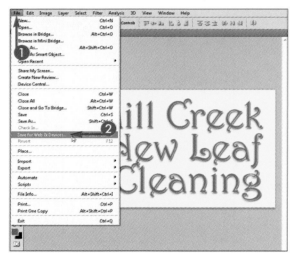

The Save for Web & Devices dialog box opens.

③ Click the **2-Up** tab.

④ Click here to select the optimized version of your image.

⑤ Click here (⬜) to choose GIF.

⑥ Click here (⬜) to choose the number of colors to include in the image.

● The Color Table displays the included colors.

GIF allows a maximum of 256 colors.

● You can click here (⬜) to choose the algorithm Photoshop uses to select the GIF colors.

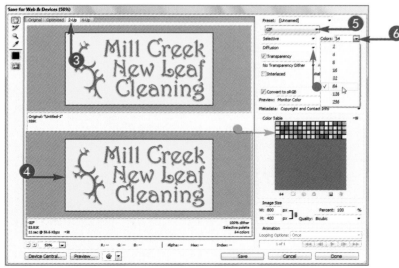

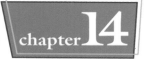

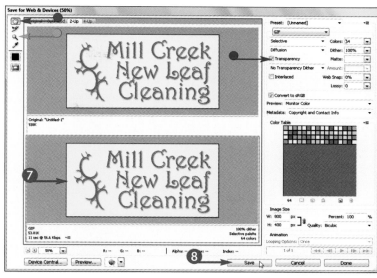

7 Check that the file quality and file size are acceptable in the preview window.

● You can use the Hand tool () to move the image in the preview pane.

● You can use the Zoom tool (🔍) to magnify the image in the preview pane.

● Clicking the **Transparency** check box (☐ changes to ☑) ensures that any transparent areas of your image remain that way in your final GIF image.

8 Click **Save**.

The Save Optimized As dialog box opens.

9 In Windows, click here (▾) to choose a folder into which to save the file.

On a Mac, use the Where pop-up menu or the File Browser to choose a folder.

10 Type a file name.

Photoshop automatically assigns a .gif extension if you do not add one.

11 Click **Save**.

The original image file remains open in Photoshop.

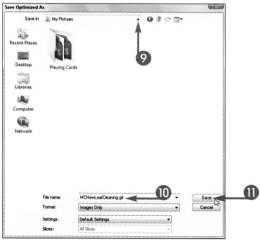

TIPS

How do I minimize the file sizes of my GIF images?

The most important factor in creating small GIFs is limiting the number of colors in the final image. GIF files are limited to 256 colors or fewer. In images that have just a few solid colors, you can often reduce the total number of colors to 16 or even 8 without any noticeable reduction in quality. See step **6** in this section to set the number of colors in your GIF images.

How can I use GIF transparency in my Web images?

GIF images that include transparency allow the background of a Web page to show through. Transparent GIFs enable you to add nonrectangular elements to your Web projects. Because Background layers cannot contain transparent pixels, you need to work with layers other than the Background layer to create transparent GIFs. See Chapter 8 for more.

Save a PNG for the Web

You can save an image as a PNG — Portable Network Graphics — file and then publish it on the Web. PNG was devised as a higher-quality alternative to GIF. Unlike GIF, PNG can support more than 256 colors. However, it is not as universally supported as GIF and JPEG are by older Web browsers.

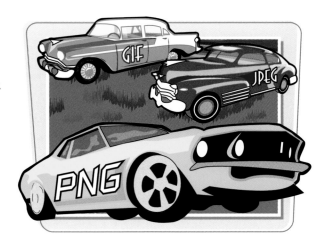

Save a PNG for the Web

① Click **File**.

② Click **Save for Web & Devices**.

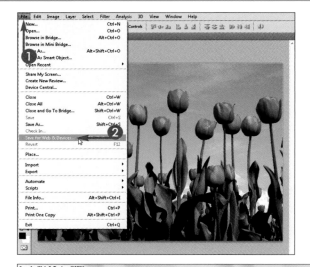

The Save for Web & Devices dialog box opens.

③ Click the **2-Up** tab.

④ Click here to select the optimized version of your image.

⑤ Click here (⊡) to choose **PNG-8** or **PNG-24**.

Note: See the tip on the opposite page for more on the different PNG settings.

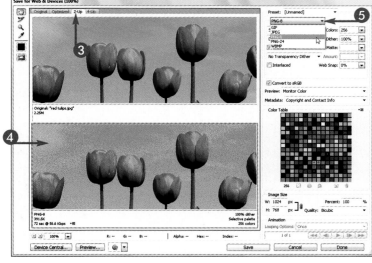

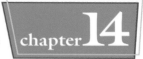

6 Check the file quality and file size in the preview pane.

● You can use the Hand tool (🖑) to move the image.

● You can use the Zoom tool (🔍) to magnify the image.

● Clicking the **Transparency** check box (☐ changes to ☑) ensures that any transparent areas of your image remain that way in your final PNG image.

7 Click **Save**.

The Save Optimized As dialog box opens.

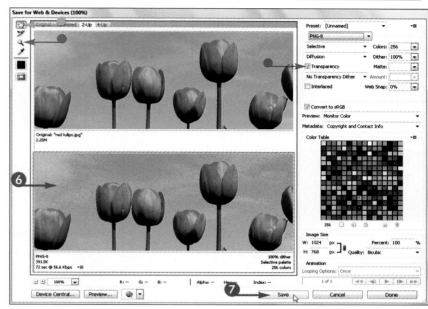

8 In Windows, click here (⯆) to choose a folder into which to save the file.

On a Mac, use the Where pop-up menu or the File Browser to choose a folder.

9 Type a file name.

Photoshop automatically assigns a .png extension if you do not add one.

10 Click **Save**.

The original image file remains open in Photoshop.

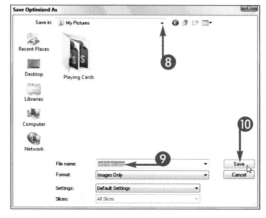

TIPS

What is the difference between the PNG-8 and PNG-24 settings?

PNG-8 stands for PNG 8-bit. With it, you can limit the number of colors in the final PNG image and thereby decrease the resulting file size. PNG-24 stands for PNG 24-bit. This format includes a wider range of colors than 8-bit and leads to better image quality but generally results in much larger file sizes.

How does the PNG format support transparency?

Like GIF files, PNG files can include transparency. But unlike GIFs, the PNG format supports a more advanced feature called alpha-channel transparency, which allows a background behind an image to show through partially. You can add partial transparency to your image by decreasing the opacity of a layer. For more on layers and opacity, see Chapter 8.

Add Descriptive and Copyright Information

You can store title, author, description, and copyright information with your saved image. You may find this useful if you plan on publishing the images online and want them to retain information about their source.

Some image-editing applications — such as Photoshop — can detect copyright information in an image and display it when the image is opened. Copyright laws give the creators of images certain rights to exclusively publish and distribute their works.

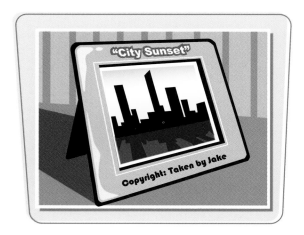

Add Descriptive and Copyright Information

① Click **File**.

② Click **File Info**.

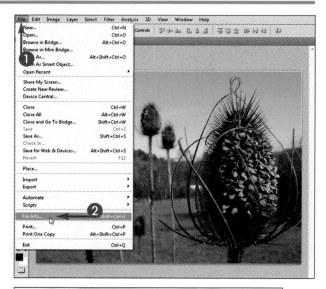

The File Info dialog box opens.

③ Type title and author information for the image.

④ Type a description for the image.

⑤ Type keywords for the image.

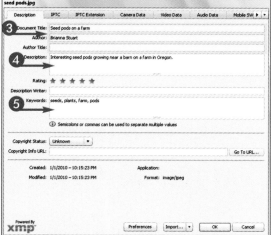

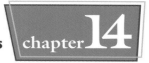

6 Click here (⊡) to choose a copyright status.

7 Type a reference Web address for the image.

8 Click **OK**.

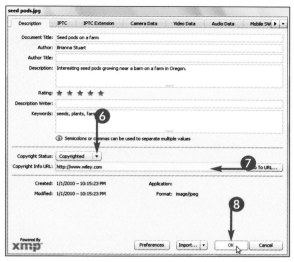

● If you mark the image as copyrighted, Photoshop places a copyright symbol in the title bar.

To save the image, see the other tasks in this chapter.

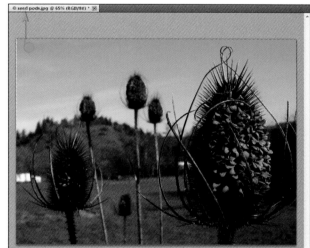

TIPS

How do I view information about a photo taken with a digital camera?

You can access information about photos taken with a digital camera in the File Info dialog box. You can view the information by clicking the **Camera Data** tab in the dialog box. The information includes the model of the camera, date and time the photo was shot, shutter speed, aperture value, and more.

What does Public Domain mean?

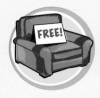

You can choose Public Domain from the Copyright Status menu to specify that your image is not owned or controlled by anyone and that the public is free to use it for any purpose. Marking something as public domain is in contrast to marking it as under copyright control.

Save a Sliced Image

You can save an image that has been partitioned with the Slice tool. Photoshop saves the slices as separate images and also saves an HTML file that organizes the slices into a Web page. Slices enable you to save different parts of an image as JPEGs, GIFs, or PNGs. This can result in a smaller overall file size for the image.

For more on using the Slice tool, see Chapter 4.

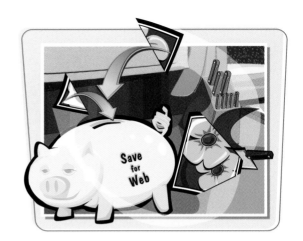

1 Open your sliced image.

2 Click **File**.

3 Click **Save for Web & Devices**.

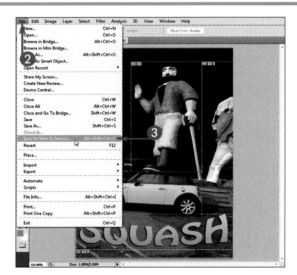

The Save for Web & Devices dialog box opens.

4 Click the **Optimized** tab.

5 Click the **Slice Select** tool ( ).

6 Click one of the image slices.

7 Specify the optimization settings for the slice.

8 Repeat steps **6** and **7** for each of the slices.

9 Click **Save**.

The Save Optimized As dialog box opens.

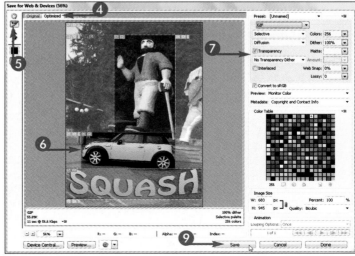

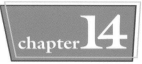

⑩ In Windows, click here (⊡) to choose a folder into which to save the file.

On a Mac, use the Where pop-up menu or the File Browser to choose a folder.

⑪ In Windows, click here (⊡) to choose **HTML and Images** as the file type.

On a Mac, click the **Format** drop-down arrow (⬦) and then choose **HTML and Images**.

⑫ Type the name of the HTML file that will organize the slices.

Photoshop saves the images by appending slice numbers to the original image name.

● To change the naming scheme, you can click here (⊡) to choose **Other**.

⑬ Click **Save**.

You can access the HTML and image files in the folder that you specified in step **10**.

● The image files are saved in a separate images subfolder.

● To view the Web page, you can double-click the HTML file. The file opens in a Web browser.

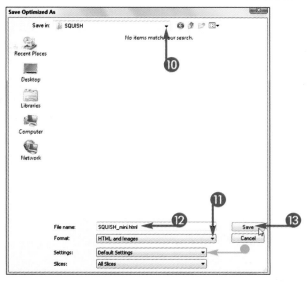

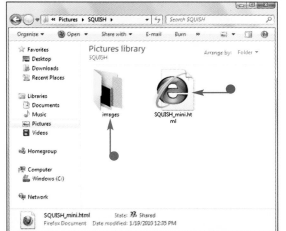

TIPS

How do I publish my Web page online?

After you create a Web page by saving your sliced Photoshop image, you can make the page available online by transferring the HTML and image files to a Web server by using an FTP program. Most people arrange for Web server access through an Internet service provider (ISP).

How do I preview my optimized image in a Web browser from inside Photoshop?

You can click **Preview** at the bottom of the Save for Web & Devices dialog box to open your optimized image in your computer's default Web browser. Photoshop also lists statistics for the image, including the format, dimensions, and file size, in the browser window. After you preview the image in the browser, you can switch back to Photoshop to change the optimization settings or save the image.

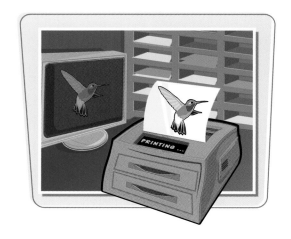

You can print your Photoshop image on a PC by
using an inkjet, laser, or another type of printer.

You can preview your printout — as well as adjust the size and
positioning of your printed image — before printing.

Print by Using a PC

① Make sure the layers you want to
print are visible.

*Note: The visibility icon (👁) means that a layer
is visible. For more on layers, see Chapter 8.*

② Click **File**.

③ Click **Print**.

● To quickly print a single copy
without previewing, you can click
Print One Copy.

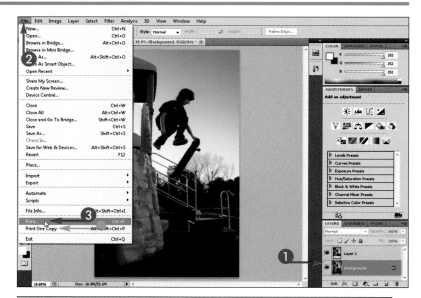

The Print dialog box opens.

④ Type a percentage in the Scale
box to shrink or enlarge the
image.

⑤ To resize the image by dragging
the corners, click the **Bounding
Box** check box (☐ changes
to ☑).

⑥ Deselect the **Center Image** check
box to allow repositioning of the
image (☑ changes to ☐).

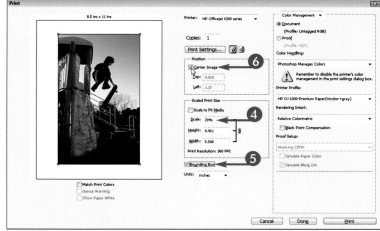

⑦ Click and drag in the image window to reposition the image on the page.

● You can position your image precisely by typing values in the Top and Left fields.

● You can click and drag the handles (☐) on the image corners to scale the image by hand.

⑧ Click here (☐) to choose a printer.

⑨ Type the number of copies to print.

⑩ Click **Print**.

Photoshop prints the image.

● You can click **Cancel** while printing is in progress to cancel the printing.

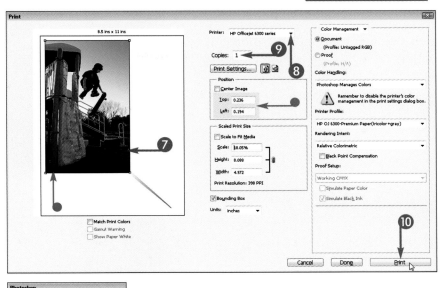

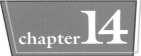

TIPS

How can I maximize the size of my image on the printed page?

In the Print dialog box, you can click the **Scale to Fit Media** check box (☐ changes to ☑) to scale the image to the maximum size given the current print settings.

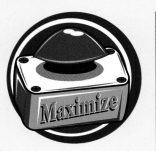

How can I print my image on a page in landscape orientation?

Landscape orientation is when a rectangular piece of paper has its longer edge oriented horizontally. In the Print dialog box, you can click ☐ to print in landscape orientation instead of the usual portrait orientation, which is with the longer side vertical.

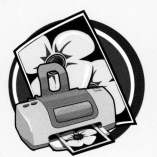

Print by Using a Mac

You can print your Photoshop image in color or
black and white on a Mac by using an inkjet, laser,
or another type of printer.

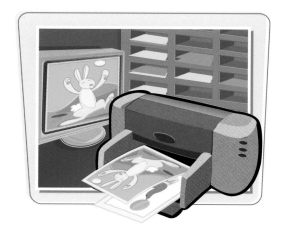

Print by Using a Mac

1 Make sure the layers you want to
print are visible.

*Note: The visibility icon (👁) means that a layer
is visible. For more on layers, see Chapter 8.*

In this example, there is a single
Background layer.

2 Click **File**.

3 Click **Print**.

● To quickly print a single copy
without previewing, you can click
Print One Copy.

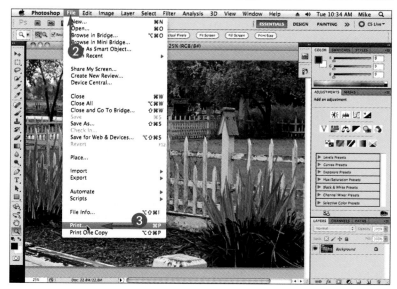

The Print dialog box opens.

4 Type a percentage in the Scale
box to shrink or enlarge the
image.

5 To resize the image, click the
Bounding Box check box
(☐ changes to ☑).

6 Deselect the **Center Image** check
box to allow repositioning of the
image (☑ changes to ☐).

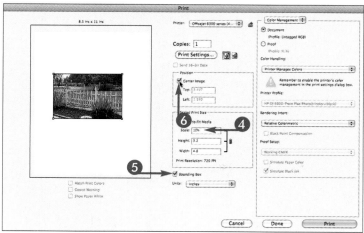

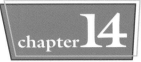

7 Click and drag in the image window to reposition the image on the page.

● You can position your image precisely by typing values in the Top and Left fields.

● You can click and drag the handles (□) on the image corners to scale the image by hand.

8 Click 🔽 to choose a printer.

9 Type the number of copies to print.

10 Click **Print**.

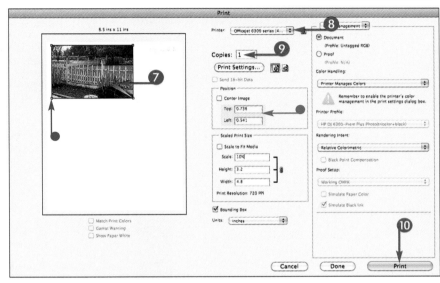

A smaller Print dialog box opens.

● You can set printer-specific options from the pop-up menus that appear.

Note: See the tip on this page on re-creating a group of printer settings to make future print session setups fast and easy.

● You can optionally print to a PDF file by clicking here and selecting an option.

11 Click **Print** to print the image.

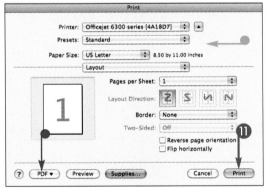

 TIPS

What is halftoning?

In grayscale printing, *halftoning* is the process by which a printer creates the appearance of different shades of gray by using only black ink. If you look closely at a grayscale image printed on most black-and-white laser printers, you see that the image consists of tiny, differently sized dots. Larger dots produce the darker gray areas of the image, and smaller dots produce the lighter gray areas.

How do I save a group of printer settings on a Mac?

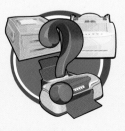

After specifying the settings for a print job, click the **Presets** pop-up menu, choose **Save As**, and then give the settings a name. You can access your saved printer settings in the Presets pop-up menu in the Print dialog box.

Index

Index

Index

Index

finding for projects, 11
flattening, 189
flipping, 93
grouping in Bridge, 23
growing selections, 79
increasing area, 59
inserting as Smart Objects, 207
inverting
    color in, 149
    selections, 78
managing with Mini Bridge, 24–25
matching color between, 164–165
maximizing size of, 317
moving
    selection borders, 75
    selections, 84–85
offsetting, 244–245
opening, 16–17, 25
optimizing Web, 307
organizing, 5
overexposed, 173
painting, 4
performing content-aware scaling, 94–95
previewing
    optimized, 315
    print size, 51
    Web Photo Gallery, 286–288
printing
    using Macs, 318–319
    using PCs, 316–317
purchasing online, 11
refining selection edges, 96–97
reverting, 43
rotating selections, 89
saving
    adding descriptive/copyright information, 312–313
    as GIF for Web, 308–309
    as JPEG for Web, 306–307
    Photoshop format, 302–303
    as PNG for Web, 310–311
    sliced, 314–315
    for use in other applications, 304–305
scaling selections, 90–91
scanned, 11
selecting areas
    Color Range command, 72–73
    Lasso tool, 64–65
    Magic Wand tool, 70–71
    Magnetic Lasso tool, 66–67
    Marquee tools, 62–63
    Quick Selection tool, 68–69
selecting pixels, 74
sharpening, 230–231
skewing selections, 92
"snap to" feature, 41

sorting in Bridge, 20
straightening, 56
subtracting from selections, 77
tinting, 171
trimming, 57
underexposed, 173
uses for, 5
viewing with Mini Bridge, 24
views, 45
increasing
    image area, 59
    magnification, 34
    saturation, 158
inserting images as Smart Objects, 207
Internet resources, 11
inverting
    colors in images, 149
    image selections, 78
iStockPhoto Web site, 11

J

J (Spot Healing Brush tool), 30
JPEG (Joint Photographic Experts Group), 125, 133, 306–307

K

keyboard, copying and pasting selections, 86

L

L (Lasso tool)
    overview, 30
    selecting image areas, 64–65
labels, adding to images, 19
landscape orientation, 317
Lasso tool (L)
    overview, 30
    selecting image areas, 64–65
layer groups, 208–209
Layer Properties dialog box, 190
Layer Style dialog box
    applying
        beveling and embossing, 216–217
        multiple styles to layers, 218–219
    editing layer styles, 220–221
layer styles
    accessing, 223
    applying
        beveling, 216–217
        drop shadows, 212–213
        embossing, 216–217
        multiple styles to layers, 218–219
        Outer Glow effects, 214–215
        overview, 222–223
    deleting, 219
    editing, 220–221
    Styles panel, 222–223

Index

Index

Index

Index

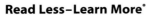

Read Less–Learn More®

Visual®

There's a Visual book for every learning level...

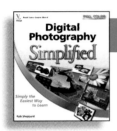

Simplified®

The place to start if you're new to computers. Full color.

- Computers
- Creating Web Pages
- Digital Photography
- Internet
- Mac OS
- Office
- Windows

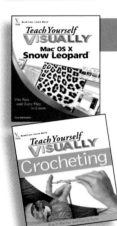

Teach Yourself VISUALLY™

Get beginning to intermediate-level training in a variety of topics. Full color.

- Access
- Bridge
- Chess
- Computers
- Crocheting
- Digital Photography
- Dog training
- Dreamweaver
- Excel
- Flash
- Golf
- Guitar
- Handspinning
- HTML
- iLife
- iPhoto
- Jewelry Making & Beading
- Knitting
- Mac OS
- Office
- Photoshop
- Photoshop Elements
- Piano
- Poker
- PowerPoint
- Quilting
- Scrapbooking
- Sewing
- Windows
- Wireless Networking
- Word

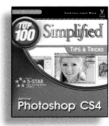

Top 100 Simplified® Tips & Tricks

Tips and techniques to take your skills beyond the basics. Full color.

- Digital Photography
- eBay
- Excel
- Google
- Internet
- Mac OS
- Office
- Photoshop
- Photoshop Elements
- PowerPoint
- Windows

...all designed for visual learners—just like you!

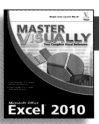

Master VISUALLY®

Your complete visual reference. Two-color interior.

- 3ds Max
- Creating Web Pages
- Dreamweaver and Flash
- Excel
- Excel VBA Programming
- iPod and iTunes
- Mac OS
- Office
- Optimizing PC Performance
- Photoshop Elements
- QuickBooks
- Quicken
- Windows
- Windows Mobile
- Windows Server

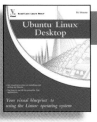

Visual Blueprint™

Where to go for professional-level programming instruction. Two-color interior.

- Ajax
- ASP.NET 2.0
- Excel Data Analysis
- Excel Pivot Tables
- Excel Programming
- HTML
- JavaScript
- Mambo
- PHP & MySQL
- SEO
- Ubuntu Linux
- Vista Sidebar
- Visual Basic
- XML

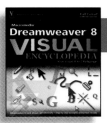

Visual Encyclopedia™

Your A to Z reference of tools and techniques. Full color.

- Dreamweaver
- Excel
- Mac OS
- Photoshop
- Windows

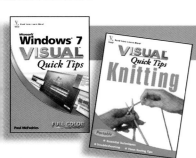

Visual Quick Tips

Shortcuts, tricks, and techniques for getting more done in less time. Full color.

- Crochet
- Digital Photography
- Excel
- Internet
- iPod & iTunes
- Knitting
- Mac OS
- MySpace
- Office
- PowerPoint
- Windows
- Wireless Networking

Visual
An Imprint of ⊕WILEY
Now you know.

For a complete listing of Visual books, go to wiley.com/go/visual